FROM EQUALITY TO DIVERSITY

A BUSINESS CASE FOR EQUAL OPPORTUNITIES

Rachael Ross &
Robin Schneider

D0310258

Pitman Publishing
128 Long Acre, London WC2E 9AN

A Division of Longman Group UK Limited

First published in 1992

© Rachael Ross and Robin Schneider 1992

British Library Cataloguing in Publication Data

A CIP catalogue record for this book can be obtained
from the British Library

ISBN 0 273 03370 0

Typeset, printed and bound in Great Britain.

Contents

PART 3   DIVERSITY AT WORK

Foreword

As its title suggests, this book argues powerfully that Equal Opportunities requires a rethink. The authors say in their preface:

> Employers should not be looking to change because they are being forced into it by the law, the Government, Local Authorities or campaigning groups. They should choose to embrace change in order to realise particular business benefits.

No doubt this is why they asked a businessman such as myself to write this Foreword!

For Esso, the concept of Equal Opportunities being business led is not new. Back in the early 1980s it became clear that our key recruitment pool – Chemical and Mechanical Engineers – was dwindling. We had a skills shortage on our hands. Obviously a priority had to be to expand the pool of potential recruits to include people whom traditionally we had not attracted.

That is not to suggest however that the business benefits of Equal Opportunities are just associated with a wider recruitment pool. The task of recruiting the best is dwarfed by the subsequent tasks of ensuring that the best are promoted and that all employees are able to develop to their full potential. It is those organisations that have quality employees that are the ones that meet their customers' requirements.

Equal Opportunities should be part of good management practice and not left for the Human Resources function to deliver. It is only when line managers see the need for change and the positive benefits it brings that change really occurs. At Esso, I can review progress, but real change depends upon managers – indeed, all employees – applying the principles of good Equal Opportunities practice.

The process of gaining this support is not easy and I would not suggest that we have got it totally right within Esso. However, what we do believe is that this process is absolutely vital. Indeed, this is one of the strengths of this book. The authors, building on their practical experience within organisations, recognise that there are no short cuts and they offer convincing arguments for their strategic approach. They are not prescriptive, and their arguments ensure that we do not leap to policy solutions as the simple answer to complex issues.

This book presents an optimistic outlook for Equal Opportunities – an outlook I share. We all have some way to go before any of us can really say we are 'Equal Opportunities Employers', but this book helps us to see the extent of our journey and offers us some valuable insights along the way. It must be a journey well worth travelling.

Sir Archibald Forster, Chairman, Esso UK

Preface

In the two years that it took to write this book, there has been one particularly long-running debate between ourselves and the publishers: what should the title be? The reason for the difficulty was straightforward and leads us directly to the heart of the book: its topic to most people is known as 'Equal Opportunities' and yet, as far as we are concerned, that term is itself misleading and can cause needless hostility.

We argue that the time is right for a comprehensive re-evaluation of this whole field and that one of the concepts we have to stand on its head is that of Equal Opportunities itself. Its emphasis upon equality (ensuring parity of treatment between groups), and association with the legal process, is a recipe for confrontation, resistance to change and lack of progress.

In our view there is a simple solution to this impasse. It is time for employers to claim this subject as their own. They should not be looking to change because they are being forced into it by the law, the Government, Local Authorities or campaigning groups. They should choose to embrace change in order to realise particular business benefits; the stimulus for change must be internal not external. The aim of this book, therefore, is to make the business case for change and to give employers a framework for achieving change.

As early as the 16th century, Machiavelli recognised that change is a risky business. 'The innovator makes enemies of all those who prospered under the old order, and only lukewarm support is forthcoming from those who prosper under the new.' We should not be surprised that campaigners for 'Equal Opportunities' encounter resistance: after all, implementation is in the hands of the very people (white males) who might fear they have the most to lose. This book, however, deliberately sets out to explore how organisations can develop widespread support for change. This means moving 'From Equality To Diversity'.

In this thinking we recognise that we have been shaped by our personal experiences and this preface is an opportunity to acknowledge our key influences – both in order to record our thanks and also in order to make clear to readers 'where we are coming from'.

We first began to address Equal Opportunities issues when we worked for Esso UK. The company's pragmatic, rational approach to issues and the sheer quality of the people we were able to work with there have certainly influenced us. Our emphasis on using statistics to get to the facts is undoubtedly the result of our years at Esso. Also it was there that we seriously began to tackle the subject, in the round, as a cultural change programme.

It is to The Coverdale Organisation, however, that we owe much of the conceptual framework for our approach. Since leaving Esso, we have divided our time between developing our Equal Opportunities consultancy and working for Coverdale on more general 'process consultancy' assignments. Throughout this period, our Coverdale colleagues have been a source of much encouragement and help. Moreover, as we acknowledge in the text, we have applied in our specific field some of Coverdale's general thinking – in particular about how to gain commitment to change. To them we owe much of our understanding of cultural change.

We owe a debt of a different kind to Rank Xerox (UK). It would have been all very well to have a fine conceptual model but unless we had some clients on which to try it out, it would simply have remained an untested theory. Rank Xerox was our first client and our thanks go to them for deciding to choose us. There is no doubt that the challenge of implementing a programme across Rank Xerox acted as a considerable spur to our thinking.

In addition, our personal lives as well as our work lives have left their mark on this book. As a relatively young 'dual-career couple' we share the emerging concern of our generation for quality of life and achieving a balance between our home and work responsibilities. Indeed, it was our desire to be more in control of this balance that led us to develop our own consultancy business in the first place. Moreover, this is in all senses a joint book – it is a better book than either of us could have written on our own – and we have developed the ideas together.

All of which perhaps goes some way to explaining the way in which we address our topic and we hope that this book can make a contribution to the debate about how to achieve what is still known as 'Equal Opportunities'.

Moreover, we look forward to working with our clients in order to demonstrate the benefits that are available to all of us – individuals, employers and society at large – if we embrace 'Diversity At Work'.

Throughout our careers, we have received a great deal of support and encouragement from people along the way. We would particularly like to thank the following for the time they have given during the preparation of this book: Mike Bamforth, Gerry Cronan, Viki Ford, Sir Archibald Forster, Jenny Ivy, David Robinson, Susan Scott-Parker and Vern Zelmer.

Micheldever, Hampshire, March 1992

Introduction

In 1919, W. A. Appleton (Secretary General of the Federation of Trade Unions) argued:

'The imposition of equality by Act of Parliament is inconceivable. It is impossible to escape the conclusion that while men and women may and should be equal in the sight of God and the law, they are not generally equal in intellectuality, in personal activity or physique or in that indefinable "knack" that enables some to accomplish so much more than others.'

Well, we have come some way since 1919. We not only have legislation which seeks to achieve equality between the sexes, but also between people of different races. Even the TUC (successor to Appleton's Federation) set up an Equal Rights Department, although admittedly not until 1988.

All sorts of people seem to have been able to acquire that 'indefinable knack' of achievement. Indeed, it is vital for our country that they have done so. As Norman Fowler, the Employment Minister at the time, put it in 1989 when he was introducing legislation to repeal some restrictions on the employment of women:

'A nation that fails to use fully the skills and talents of more than half of its population will be competing with one hand tied behind its back.'

In the Europe of the 1990s, competition is getting tougher not easier.

The question is therefore: how are we doing? Over 20 years since equal opportunities was first on the legal agenda, what progress has been made? In the course of the next few pages we intend to give our answer to this question. Of course, it is not a simple issue and we will argue that progress has been made at different rates in different areas. In overall terms, however, we will be suggesting that the legislation has not been particularly effective and that one of the problems is, in fact, the way the law encourages us to think about the topic in the first place.

Of course, we need to safeguard the progress that has been made, but the aim of this book is to argue that the time is now ripe for a fundamentally different approach. In our view this spells an end to what we commonly conceive as equal opportunities.

We will begin therefore by reviewing the progress that has been made in the various areas that Parliament has decided constitute illegal discrimination.

Sex discrimination

The 1975 Sex Discrimination Act set out to eliminate discrimination on the basis of sex or marital status. Obviously, it exists equally to protect men or women from unfair discrimination. The majority of discrimination that was taking place, however, was directed against women.

At first sight there has been some impressive progress. In the 1950s, women made up about a third of the UK labour force, today that figure has risen to almost half. More women are economically active in the United Kingdom than any other country in the EC, with the exception of Denmark. Discriminatory restrictions have been swept away. Women can work down the mines, fight fires, train as fighter pilots and even go to sea with the Royal Navy.

There are impressive role models in all walks of life. Jaguar cars appointed their first woman welder in 1987. In 1990, John Major appointed Sarah Hogg to head his economic think-tank. The first Briton into Space was a woman: Helen Sharman in 1991. Anita Roddick's Body Shop seems to have achieved that rare retailing feat of being as successful in the early 1990s as it was in the 1980s. In 1991 BTR appointed Kathleen O'Donovan as their Finance Director.

In fact, women's participation in the labour market is no longer at issue. It is inconceivable that they will be 'sent home' as they were after the Second World War. What is at issue, though, is the sorts of jobs they are doing and the rewards they are getting for them.

Exceptional women are clearly starting to break through into the traditional male preserves. A better test of equal opportunity is to compare the progress of the average man and the average woman. Here, the picture is not so rosy. Women's average pay has remained stubbornly at about 75 per cent of men's despite the Equal Pay Act which came into force in 1975. Women still seem to have jobs rather than careers.

That is not to say that there has been no progress. Estimates of women's participation in management vary according to how broadly 'management' is defined. At its broadest definition, women now make up 27 per cent of an estimated three million managers in the United Kingdom. More conventional estimates put the figure at about 9 per cent. What we are sure about, however, is that the higher one looks the fewer the women there are. This extends to areas where women are well represented. Forty-five per cent of all employees in the Civil Service are women, but they only represent 6 per cent of those in the top grades. Ninety-two per cent of nurses are women, but they hold only 63 per cent of chief nursing posts. Women are not exactly unheard of as directors, but they are very few and far between.

The argument, no doubt, is that increasing the representation of women among management is simply a question of time. After all, there has been an undeniable increase in the proportion of women among university graduates – 45 per cent in 1989 – and, in time, this is expected to feed through into the number of women appointed to management positions.

Whether this is inevitable, is debatable. At the moment, women seem to have succeeded by making personal sacrifices. A survey by the BIM (British Institute of Management) showed that female managers were both less likely to be married (58 per cent to 93 per cent) or to have children (52 per cent to 89 per cent) than their male colleagues. Whether women (and also men) will continue to be prepared to put their careers before their family life in such a dramatic way, we very much doubt. Whether the country can afford to let them, we also doubt.

Not only employers, but also the Government have continued to behave as if people's work and family lives are totally unrelated. In the United Kingdom, we have one of the highest participation rates of women in the labour market, but the lowest provision of childcare. Ninety-five per cent of French and German and 85 per cent of Italian children between the ages of three to five years are in nurseries. The figure in the United Kingdom is 35 per cent – only Portugal, at 30 per cent, has a lower percentage.

If the State continues to remain indifferent to the provision of childcare, and organisations continue to structure work on the assumption that they have exclusive call on employees' time, then there is unlikely to be such a transformation in the prospects for women. Some, the best, will succeed. Women's participation in the labour market, through sheer economic necessity will probably remain high, but they will still be limited to the lower-skilled, lower-paid jobs.

Race discrimination

The aim of the 1975 Race Relations Act was to eliminate discrimination on the basis of race, colour, ethnic or national origin, and nationality. The majority of employment race discrimination, but not all, occurs on the basis of colour and this is the issue we will explore here.

Ethnic minorities, as defined in the 1991 National Census, are estimated to form about 5 per cent of the UK population (2.6m). We have yet to receive the necessary information from this Census to have an accurate, up-to-date picture of the size of the ethnic minority population. What we do know, however, is that it is increasing as a proportion of the UK population as a whole. While 1 in 5 of the total population is aged under 16, the figure is 1 in 3 for the ethnic minority population.

There is a European dimension to this issue too. We tend to forget that the largest Muslim population in Europe is actually in France (3m). Turkish workers and Afro-Germans are, in the wake of unification, seen to be taking jobs and flats away from the real 'Germans'. Le Pen, who gained four-and-a-half million votes in the last Presidential election in France, argued that the only good European is a white European. The demise of Communism is everywhere confusing nationalism and racism.

In the United Kingdom, we tend to be rather smug about all this. After all, we have laws against race discrimination, but there is no protection under EC law. The Commission for Racial Equality is the only body of its kind in Europe. The National Front seems to have had its heyday. Yet, the police in 1989 reported six racist incidents in London per day.

There is no doubt, however, that in society as a whole overt race discrimination has decreased over the last two decades. A recent survey by the Runnymede Trust showed that 48 per cent of Afro-Caribbeans, 40 per cent whites and 36 per cent Asians felt that Britain had become less racist over the last 10 years. Moreover, the same survey showed that younger people were less likely to be prejudiced than their elders. When Bill Galbraith in 1990 directed racist insults at John Taylor, the prospective parliamentary candidate for Cheltenham, he was expelled from the Conservative Association and the Prime Minister made a statement in the House of Commons.

Nevertheless, while this might be the public attitude, there still seems to be discrimination in private. Unemployment is disproportionately high among ethnic minorities – 60 per cent higher than for white people. It may no longer be possible to admit to racial prejudice oneself, but people can still blame someone else – usually the customer. In November 1990, a survey by Thames TV found that 17 out of 20 London employment agencies were at least initially willing to comply with discriminatory instructions.

This seems to tally with the findings in the survey by the Runnymede Trust. The majority of people from all ethnic groups felt that they were fair minded, but 67 per cent of Afro-Caribbean, 42 per cent Asians and 38 per cent of the white interviewees thought that employers treated non-whites less favourably.

Unfortunately, this seems to be borne out by the facts. Although more teenagers from ethnic minority backgrounds stay on in full-time education than their white counterparts, they have more difficulty in finding a job. Surveys have found that prospective solicitors and accountants with ethnic minority backgrounds had half the success rate of their white colleagues in gaining training contracts.

That is not to deny that there has been some progress. There are now some very prominent people in public life with ethnic minority backgrounds. There are currently four sitting MPs, and there are a number of prospective candidates, across the political spectrum, who have ethnic minority backgrounds. High profile newscasters like Moira Stuart and Trevor McDonald have inspired others to follow suit. Mahesh Kumar founded the flourishing Asian City Club in 1987. In 1989, Nazumu Virani hosted a dinner to raise money for assisting young Asians who wanted to start their own businesses and raised £3.2m.

Above all, young ethnic minorities have succeeded (and perhaps, because it fits the stereotypes, have been allowed to succeed) in sport. Black athletes have long been amongst the most successful. Over the 1991 summer five black and Asian Britons figured in the English cricket team playing against the West Indies (so much for Norman Tebbit's cricket test). Most teams in the Football League have black players. The test, of course, will come when some of these players decide that they want to become managers.

Thus, while women have at least begun to break out of the stereotypes and be recruited, ethnic minorities still have a long way to go. They have succeeded in specialist areas – like sport and entertainment – or by setting up on their own. They have not, in the main, succeeded by joining the larger 'blue chip' employers. Moreover,

70 per cent of companies do not have ethnic monitoring procedures, so we do not know whether the recruitment situation is getting better or worse, and we certainly do not know the proportion of ethnic minorities who are making it through to management positions.

Discrimination against people with disabilities

There has been legislation in the United Kingdom covering disability since 1944 – evidently, however, it had its origins in accommodating men returning from war and was not framed as part of the 1970s movement to eliminate discrimination at work. It provides for a quota system – which in any case is widely ignored – and beyond this quota it is perfectly legal to discriminate against people with disabilities.

There are a wide variety of disabilities – we tend to think immediately of wheelchair users, but forget less obvious disabilities – and, in total, people with disabilities are estimated as representing about 10 per cent of the working age population.

Successive Labour Force Surveys have shown, however, that people with disabilities suffer from disproportionate unemployment. In 1988, this was at 19 per cent compared to 8.6 per cent for the population as a whole. Moreover, of the 360,000 people with disabilities unemployed in spring 1988, over 22 per cent had academic or vocational qualifications at 'A' Level or above.

The Government's Employment Service commissioned an SCPR (Social and Community Planning Research) survey which recently estimated that there were 1,272,000 people categorised as 'economically active and occupationally handicapped' (representing therefore about 5 per cent of those in work). Of this group 70 per cent were in work when they began to experience problems from their disability, and 65 per cent of this group had had to leave their jobs. Eleven per cent had been dismissed or felt they had been pressured into leaving.

Clearly, we seem to be blinded by someone's disability and therefore fail to see his or her ability. Perhaps, the various charities have not helped by portraying the person with a disability as the 'victim'. Employers often see 'disability' as an issue for the Community Affairs Department, and they lose sight of the fact that they represent a very large group of potential employees.

While this is the group who have been protected the longest by legislation, and where the law (theoretically) has the most draconian powers, they are the group for whom least has changed. If anything, less employers comply with the legislation now than did 10 years ago. Not surprisingly there have been calls for fresh legislation – in line with the USA's Americans with Disabilities Act, which is being implemented in 1992.

Religious discrimination in Northern Ireland

There is one final area of discrimination defined by the law which we have yet to mention. In 1976 the Fair Employment (Northern Ireland) Act made it unlawful to discriminate on the grounds of religious or political belief in employment and it established the Fair Employment Agency

This legislation has already been recognized as ineffective. In 1988, the Fair Employment Agency reported unemployment among male Roman Catholics at two-and-a-half times higher than the figure for Protestants. Catholics were also under-represented in skilled jobs. More than 10 years of legislation had clearly failed to deal with the problem of religious discrimination.

In this area, however, the Government could not simply ignore the problem. Under the pressure of the Anglo-Irish Agreement, and the potential for wide-scale disinvestment by US companies (under the campaign for the MacBride principles) the Government decided to introduce new legislation. The 1989 Fair Employment Act replaced the Agency by a Commission and gave it much tougher powers. It is too early to see whether this new legislation has had any greater success at combating discrimination.

Other areas of discrimination

These, then, are the areas of discrimination that equality opportunity legislation has sought to address. There are, of course, many other areas where discrimination occurs. Here, however, discrimination may be misguided, but it is not illegal.

The most obvious area is discrimination against older people. After all, we have an ageing population. By the year 2000, 26 per cent of the total UK population will be aged over 55. Yet we know that the participation rate of older people in economic life is declining. In 1970 81 per cent of men aged 60–64 were working, by 1986 this had dropped to 53 per cent.

For some, this is a dream come true – early retirement is something they welcomed and maybe actively sought. For others, however, this is not the case. In 1988, the Labour Force Survey showed that there were 673,000 economically inactive men and women aged 50 and over who wanted regular paid work.

A survey of 250 personnel directors conducted by Gallop in 1990 sheds some light on this situation. Eighty-six per cent said that they would prefer not to recruit those over 55. Older people were perceived to be set in their ways and slower to learn. Yet a survey by the Industrial Society of people over 55 found that 77 per cent still rated the challenge of a job as highly important to them, and 59 per cent used a computer terminal at work and 36 per cent used a terminal at home. B & Q found that the over 50s picked up systems technology as quickly as their younger colleagues.

If organisations continue to put 35 as a cut-off age in their recruitment advertisements, they will be ruling out the vast majority of qualified candidates. By the turn of the century 46 per cent of the population will be aged 35–54.

While we see discrimination against older people regularly in the job pages of our national papers, the same is certainly true for homosexual men and lesbian women. The spread of the AIDS epidemic has probably heightened prejudice that already existed and the introduction of Clause 28 into the local Government Bill exemplifies this.

Discussing the furore concerning Sir Ian McKellen's knighthood, Bernard Levin, writing in *The Times* on 11 February 1991, put it rather well when he asked: when would the British regard homosexuals as

'a number of ordinary people who have only one thing in common, just as heterosexuals are a number of ordinary people who have only one thing in common?'

There is a general point here that bears consideration. One of the drawbacks of any discussion about equal opportunities is that it concentrates, by its very nature, on discrimination against groups. It forces us to think of women primarily as women, of minorities primarily as minorities, of people with disabilities as disabled, of Catholics as Catholics, of people over 55 as old and of homosexuals as homosexuals. We see people as representatives of particular groups, we summon up a set of characteristics in our minds, and we are blind to the individuals concerned.

The fact is, of course, that the individuals within each of these groups have very many more differences than they have things in common. Who wants to be totally defined by just one of their characteristics? Down this route lies the American system of 'quotas' and the inevitable 'tokenism'. Women will be appointed because they are women, or minorities because they are minorities, not because they are the best candidates.

We should not do away with the law, which has played a valuable role. It has had to define and outlaw discrimination against particular groups. Both the Commission For Racial Equality and the Equal Opportunities Commission have played, and can continue to play, important law enforcement and campaigning roles.

After two decades of limited equal opportunities, it is time for what Edward De Bono calls 'provolution': more radical than evolution, but more gradual than revolution.

The cause of equal opportunities has been argued on moral and ethical grounds – both of course, very strong arguments – and the law has been centre stage. It is time, however, for the argument to shift. Launching the Equality Agenda in November 1991, Joanna Foster, the Chair of the Equal Opportunities Commission recognised the importance of the economic case: 'Equal opportunities in the 1990s is about economic efficiency and social justice'.

The ethical case stands up, but it is the economic case that will win the argument. So long as equal opportunities is pursued as an end in itself, progress will be limited. The real issue is not whether any particular group achieves parity, but whether this country can compete internationally. As the 1990s unfold, and work becomes increasingly 'knowledge-based', requiring higher levels of skill, it is essential that we allow each individual to realise his or her full potential.

In the tight labour market for skills, employers have a strong incentive to ensure that they make their selection decisions based on merit and create an environment in which all individuals can develop. Vern Zelmer, managing director of Rank Xerox (UK) Ltd, makes this point: 'Equality of opportunity is vitally important in the face of a changing labour market, skills shortages, and the necessity of attracting the brightest and best. . . It is not only the right thing to do, it is a business necessity.' It is time for employers to claim this issue as their own and it is the aim of this book to help them do so.

This is not an equal opportunities guide for equal opportunities managers. There are plenty of books that detail case law, best practice, and offer advice about how to make things happen in practice. Worthy as they are, we believe they miss a vital dimension.

By exploring equal opportunities in isolation from its business context, such books both underestimate its importance and the complexity of the challenge that it represents. For an organisation to embrace equal opportunities is no less of an effort than for it to become a Total Quality organisation. Short-term results are achievable, but the full transition will take years rather than months.

It is our hope that by writing this book we can help senior managers to appreciate what equal opportunities can do for their organisations. In addition, we believe that our strategic approach provides them with some confidence that the transition is not only worthwhile, but is also possible. Perhaps not quite a safe passage, but at least a way of ensuring that all possibilities are covered.

We have separated the book into three parts.

In **Part 1** we look at the external context. First of all, we examine the law, look at how it defines discrimination and consider its effectiveness in encouraging good practice. We then turn to the labour market and explore, in more detail, some of the assertions that we have made in this Introduction. In our view, it is the increasing requirements for skills that will drive progress and cause employers to turn to traditionally under-utilised groups. This tightening of the labour market, regardless of the current recession, also tips the power balance in favour of employees rather than employers. We argue that employees – both men and women – are less happy to sacrifice either their home life or their work life. They want the best of both worlds. We conclude Part 1 by offering our redefinition of equal opportunities.

In **Part 2**, which forms the main body of the book, we develop our five-stage strategic approach. After an overall summary we cover each stage in turn: conducting a diagnosis, setting aims, spreading ownership, policy development and training. We conclude Part 2 by exploring how these various elements of an equal opportunities programme can be managed effectively in order to sustain momentum.

In **Part 3** we explain what this has all been in aid of: 'Diversity At Work'. We describe a real life case study: Rank Xerox (UK)'s Customer Response Centre in Milton Keynes.

WINDS OF CHANGE

THE LAW – SETTING MINIMUM STANDARDS

It was with some reluctance that we decided to devote a whole chapter in this book to legislation. In general, we feel that equal opportunities has been burdened with an over-legalistic approach. As we outlined in the Introduction, our view of the law is that it can establish principles and set standards but is mostly ineffective as a change agent. The real debates lie elsewhere.

This does not mean that we do not need legislation, but it does suggest that we should not have exaggerated expectations of what it can actually achieve in practice.

In this chapter, therefore, we will describe the role legislation has to play in equal opportunities and the way it seeks to exercise its influence. By contrast, what we are *not* seeking to do here is to give a blow-by-blow detailed account of the content of each Act of Parliament and the latest case law. In the chapters that follow in Part 2 of this book, we have sought to incorporate the impact of the latest legislation into our considerations of personnel policy and practice. In our view, this is a more digestible way of dealing with some of the practical implications of the law.

In this chapter, therefore, we will:

- Describe the role of legislation and the statutory bodies
- Look at how the law defines discrimination
- Consider how the law seeks to encourage good practice
- Draw some conclusions about the influence of legislation

The aim of legislation in this field is to *eliminate unfair discrimination* (and ensure equal treatment). In order to do this it needs to:

(1) define what it means by unfair discrimination; and
(2) encourage good employment practice.

These are separate and complementary issues and we will discuss each in turn in this chapter. Before we do so, however, we will describe the relevant European and UK legislative framework.

■ THE RELEVANT LEGISLATION AND STATUTORY BODIES

There are two sources of legislation which seek to define what is meant by unfair discrimination:

(1) through Treaty obligations and Regulations and Directives in European Community law and their interpretation in the European Court of Justice; and
(2) through Acts of Parliament in the United Kingdom and their interpretation in UK courts.

There are also parallel ways of encouraging good employment practice. In Europe, the European Commission can issue Recommendations and, from time to time, it draws up action programmes. In the United Kingdom, the Acts have set up two separate Commissions dealing with race and sex discrimination respectively and these can issue Codes of Practice.

We will describe both the European and UK approaches. We will tackle them in this order because where there is a combination of the two, it is European law which takes precedence over UK law.

Treaty of Rome

Equality is a fundamental objective of the Treaty of Rome (1957) and it could be considered a basic right to which each citizen is entitled. Article 119 establishes the principle of equal pay between men and women. It is directly enforceable in the United Kingdom and an individual can apply to the courts if they believe this Article has been infringed.

European law clearly defines and takes account of sex discrimination. In contrast, there is no explicit reference to race discrimination. The argument would be that respect for fundamental personal human rights is one of the general principles of Community law, and therefore an individual complainant could argue that she/he had suffered 'degrading treatment'.

Regulations and Directives

Both Regulations and Directives are binding; they are the mechanisms through which Community law evolves. A Regulation is general in its application, a Directive leaves open the form and method by which a member state translates the intention of the Directive into practice. Directives are binding on states, not individuals, and have to be implemented by national legislation.

The Treaty obligation to equal treatment between men and women has been translated into three relevant Directives: the Directive on Equal Pay (1975), the Directive on Equal Treatment (1976) and the Directive on Equal Treatment in Occupational Social Security Schemes (1986).

The Equal Pay Directive has had a direct impact on UK legislation and illustrates how this procedure works. The Commission decided that the UK's Equal Pay Act did not completely fulfil the obligations of the 1975 Directive so in 1982 they took the UK Government to court. The European Court found in favour of the Commission and this led directly to the amendment of the Equal Pay Act in 1983 which incorporated, among other changes, a procedure for pursuing equal value claims.

Currently, each Directive proposed by the Commission must (in this field) receive unanimous support at the Council of Ministers (the responsible Ministers from each of the countries). This allows some countries to exercise, in effect, a power of veto. The United Kingdom and the Republic of Ireland have twice used their vetos in order to block draft Directives on Parental Leave. It is for this reason that the 11 member states (excluding the UK) who wanted to make more rapid progress on the 'social dimension' of European harmonisation ended up negotiating a separate Protocol as part of the Maastricht Treaty, which comes into effect on 1st January 1993.

Recommendations

As well as issuing Directives, the Commission can choose to issue Recommendations. These are not binding on member states. For example, in 1986 a Recommendation sought to encourage measures to: 'provide fair opportunities for disabled people in the field of employment and vocational training'. The United Kingdom chose not to take any new initiatives.

In 1990, the area of sexual harassment was tackled in a Resolution concerning: 'Protection Of The Dignity Of Men And Women At Work' and this subsequently led to a Code being issued.

Action programmes

From time to time, the Commission will commit to particular Action Programmes. These are designed to highlight particular areas where progress is deemed to be required and where Recommendations and

5

Directives may well be appropriate. The first social action programme was adopted in 1974. This led to the Directives on Equal Pay and Equal Treatment in 1975 and 1976 respectively.

The 1989 Social Charter (see below) also has an accompanying action programme. Article 19 of the Charter, for instance, states that action to implement the principle of equal treatment will be intensified. Directives associated with rights of Part-Time Workers have already been adopted and there are proposed Directives on Parental and Family Leave, Burden of Proof in Equal Treatment cases, and Protection at Work of Pregnant Women.

There have been two previous action programmes covering people with disabilities, and the Helios Programme 1992–1996 is incorporated into the Social Charter action programme.

An action programme by no means guarantees that there will be any subsequent Directives or (even) Recommendations.

■ THE SOCIAL DIMENSION OF EUROPEAN HARMONISATION

There has long been an argument that the increasing economic integration of Europe needed to be balanced by a social dimension – so that there is a common framework of workers' rights across Europe thus preventing so-called 'social dumping'. This 'social' aspect to the process of European harmonisation has been resisted by the UK.

The 1989 Social Charter was designed as an expression of the 'social dimension'. It enshrines a number of fundamental rights and does include equal treatment for men and women and integration of people with disabilities. Many of the provisions within the Charter, however, were watered down as part of the protracted discussions that preceded its adoption and the Charter itself is not binding upon member states.

Not surprisingly, therefore, the issue of the 'social dimension' resurfaced at the Maastricht negotiations in December 1991 and proved to be a difficult stumbling block. It was only resolved by allowing the UK to opt out of the so-called 'Social Chapter'. A Protocol was agreed, which will come into effect with the rest of the treaty on 1st January 1993, which enables the other 11 states to agree measures that may speed up the implementation of the principles outlined in the Social Charter. Equal opportunities measures can be agreed on the basis of qualified majority voting. The UK, of course, does not have to adopt these measures and will not play a part in developing them.

Should there be a change of mind in the UK, for instance due to a change in Government, then the UK would be obliged, of course, to implement whatever measures had been agreed by the other 11 members.

Acts of Parliament

In the United Kingdom, our current 'discrimination' legislation is covered by the following Acts: The Disabled Persons (Employment) Act 1944 (amended 1958 and 1981), Equal Pay Act 1970 (amended 1983), Sex Discrimination Act 1975 (amended and extended 1986) and Race Relations Act 1976, Fair Employment (Northern Ireland) Acts 1976 and 1989.

As their titles indicate, these various Acts set out an approach to discrimination in each of these distinct areas. While it would be fair to say that the Acts passed in the mid-1970s propose parallel approaches for sex and race discrimination, it would also be fair to say that some of the approaches outlined in the other Acts are at odds with these. For example, there is a quota system in the disability legislation that would be illegal in the fields of sex or race discrimination. Similarly, the Fair Employment Act makes monitoring compulsory, but it is only recommended in the areas of sex or race discrimination.

The Commissions

There are two Commissions in the United Kingdom concerned with discrimination: the Equal Opportunities Commission promoting equality between the sexes and the Commission For Racial Equality (CRE). They are, in effect, law enforcement agencies and, unlike in the United States, Canada and Australia, we have two 'single purpose' agencies rather than one 'general purpose' agency dealing with all forms of discrimination. (This has its advantages and disadvantages.)

These Commissions, like the legislation itself, are charged with a two-fold task:

(1) to assist the implementation of the law in order to eliminate specific discrimination; and
(2) to promote equality of opportunity in employment.

In addition, they are also charged with reviewing the relevant Acts and making recommendations for change. To date, however, the Governments have not really taken account of this advice.

7

In the main, the Commissions seek to meet these needs by: assisting individual complainants in court cases, instituting formal investigations and issuing Codes of Practice.

Tribunals

Acts of Parliament are interpreted through the courts. This can be a lengthy process – starting at industrial tribunal level, through Employment Appeal Tribunals, eventually (in the UK) to the House of Lords and only then to the final appeal to the European Court of Justice. The courts have the ability to award compensation to complainants (with a current maximum of £8,925, although this figure is being questioned in the light of the £30,000 limit in Northern Ireland) and other individual remedies. They can make general recommendations about how to avoid discrimination in the future, but these are not binding.

The Commissions are able to support individual complainants in individual cases. Given that the legal costs can be very high, because the legal processes are so inordinately lengthy, this support can be critical. By the time the case of *Surinder Singh* v. *the Chief Constable of the Nottinghamshire Constabulary* was won in October 1990, the CRE had incurred over £150,000 legal costs.

This support is vital not only so that individuals have a chance of justice, but also for the progress of the legislation itself. If the Acts establish some overall principles, then there is still an essential role to be played by the courts in interpreting this legislation. As in the rest of the British legal system, precedent is critical, and it is decisions in individual cases that have brought progress. For example, it was the decision in the *Porcelli* case in 1985 (10 years after the Sex Discrimination Act) which conclusively established that sexual harassment represented sexual discrimination.

To this end, the Commissions have very sensibly channelled their limited resources into the cases which are breaking new legal ground. Typically, the CRE have over 1,200 requests for assistance in a year, in 1990 they granted representation in 188 cases.

Formal investigations

The Commissions are also able to carry out investigations. There are two sorts of investigations:

(1) a named person investigation, where a breach of one of the Acts is suspected; and
(2) a general investigation.

The difference is that in the former, non-discriminatory notices can be issued which are binding. In the latter, it is only possible to make recommendations.

Between them, the Commissions have published over 60 investigations since the mid-1970s.

There is no doubt that these investigations can be effective. A number of those organisations that would now be considered to be at the forefront of equal opportunities practice (Barclays Bank, for instance) were either formally investigated or threatened with investigation. A difficulty, however, is that there can only be a named investigation where a breach of an Act is suspected, and this inevitably starts an investigation off down a track of confrontation between the Commission and the organisation involved. For that reason, formal investigations are not the best vehicle for bringing about change.

Codes of Practice

In the mid-1980s, about 10 years after the Acts of Parliament, the Commissions issued their Codes of Practice. This was followed by the Code of Practice affecting employment of people with disabilities issued by the Manpower Services Commission (as it was then) with the support of the CBI and the TUC. In these Codes, they sought to clarify what is meant by discrimination and to advise organisations on the sorts of steps they could take in order to promote equality of opportunity.

The most important point about the Codes is that, like the European Recommendations, they are voluntary. A tribunal may take into account the fact that an organisation did not adopt a practice recommended in one of the Codes, but failure to do so does not in itself make an organisation liable to proceedings. As we shall see, this has some fairly inevitable consequences.

■ DEFINING UNFAIR DISCRIMINATION

The legislation defines two sorts of discrimination: direct and indirect.

Direct discrimination

This is the most overt form of discrimination. This occurs when a person is treated less favourably because, for instance, they are black.

It can be deliberate: 'I'm not going to recruit a black.' It can be disguised as someone else's prejudice: 'My customers wouldn't like it.' It can be caused by a concern for the applicant: 'I couldn't put him in with that team, they'd give him an awful time.' The motive does not matter, in each case there has been direct discrimination – someone has suffered detrimental treatment, in this case, due to his colour.

Such 'detriment' can occur at any stage of the employment process: from before recruitment (an applicant can take legal action) through to retirement, redundancy or dismissal. It does not have to be associated with a selection decision: denying access to training opportunities would be considered 'detriment', as (of course) would sexual or racial harassment. It should be pointed out here that any adverse treatment based on the fact of a woman's pregnancy is inevitably direct discrimination (men can't get pregnant, so the detrimental treatment must be based on sex).

Indirect discrimination

This occurs where a job requirement:

(1) although applied equally causes a disproportionately adverse impact on a particular group; and
(2) the job requirement is not justifiable.

The concept comes to us from the United States and is neatly captured in the decision of the US Supreme Court in *Griggs* v. *Duke Power Company* as: 'practices that are fair in form, but discriminatory in operation.'

This is best illustrated with an example. Quite frequently, organisations will have a service requirement that applicants for promotion need to meet in order to be considered for a vacancy. It is also quite common for women and ethnic minorities to have fewer years of service and therefore for a service bar to have a disproportionate effect on them. If it is also the case that the service requirement is not justifiable (i.e. people could still have the skills to do the job) then this would constitute indirect discrimination.

For indirect discrimination to have taken place, therefore, there needs to be evidence that:

(1) there is disproportionate impact; and
(2) that the requirement is not justified.

Types of discrimination

There are generic forms of discrimination, there is then a separate question about which 'groups' the law provides protection for. Discrimination has its roots in stereotypical assumptions, which become prejudices, and there are many people whom we 'lump' together in this way.

Against whom is discrimination illegal, and against whom is it simply unfair? In the main, our answers to these questions are dictated by UK law. As we have discussed, there are general principles in Community law, and in the Social Charter, but the precise current position is indicated by the UK Acts of Parliament.

As discussed in the Introduction, it is illegal to discriminate on the basis of: sex, marital status, race (including colour, ethnic or national origin, nationality) disability and religion (in Northern Ireland). There is no specific legislation affecting: religion (outside Northern Ireland) or age (although this might constitute indirect discrimination). There is also no legislation to prevent discrimination against homosexual men or lesbian women, short or fat people, or people who simply wear the wrong sorts of clothes: all of which have been shown to influence the way some selection decisions have been made.

We will discuss each of these areas in turn.

Sex and marital status

The Sex Discrimination Act tends to be seen to be about securing equal opportunities for women but, of course, it is there to eliminate discrimination against either sex. The Equal Opportunities Commission is currently taking the UK Government to court, seeking to achieve equal retirement ages in the state pension scheme. They contest that the scheme discriminates unfairly against men who have to wait until 65 before they can draw a pension – five years after women.

Another aspect of the Act that tends to be forgotten is that it outlaws discrimination on the basis of marital status. In the past, some women – teachers and airline cabin crew for example – were dismissed when they married. The equation was simple: marriage

11

equals children and children are not compatible with the job. While this sort of automatic discrimination is a thing of the past, it lives on in many recruitment practices. Those recruiters who still want to know about domestic plans are working on exactly the same assumptions as their predecessors 20 years ago.

Another area that is covered by sex discrimination is discrimination against part-timers. Insisting on appointing a full-timer may in itself constitute indirect discrimination (if the requirement cannot be justified) because the vast majority of part-timers are women. In addition, organisations may well have contractual arrangements that discriminate against part-timers – they often used to be excluded from pension plans, for example – and this has been ruled as discriminatory by the European Court.

Race, colour, ethnic or national origin, nationality

These are all covered by the Race Relations Act. In the context of equal opportunities, the focus here is on ethnic minorities. These minorities are most closely associated with colour because it is on the grounds of colour that much discriminatory behaviour takes place and we would use the same categories as in the 1991 National Census: Black African, Black Caribbean, Black Other, Bangladeshi, Indian, Pakistani, Chinese.

The Act itself, of course, is wider than this in its application. Irish people, for instance, have taken and won cases under this legislation. The Act aims to eliminate any racial discrimination, including discrimination against white people.

Disability

There is legislation in this field, but it is not very effective. There is a quota system that means that there should be at least 3 per cent registered disabled in all organisations that employ over 20 people. If organisations have not filled their quota then they need to apply for an exemption certificate in order to carry on recruiting. It sounds like tough legislation but it is not very effective. Registration is voluntary, and perhaps because there is no perceived benefit, by 1986 the number of people with disabilities who registered had fallen to less than 1 per cent of the labour force. Not surprisingly, therefore, the quota system has fallen into disrepute. Applying for an exemption certificate either becomes a routine six-monthly task, or it simply gets ignored. This legislation is not, as such anti-discrimination legislation – if a company has filled its quota it can legally discriminate against people with disabilities. At present, the Government is resisting calls for fresh legislation.

Religion

There is widespread assumption that we have legislation that seeks to eliminate discrimination on the basis of religion.

In Northern Ireland this is the case. The Fair Employment Act of 1989 requires employers to monitor 'perceived religious affiliation' among their employees and to make returns to the Fair Employment Commission. Employers with more than 250 staff also have to submit returns on applicants for employment. The point that this is 'perceived' religious affiliation is important. It does not matter whether someone does or does not actually believe and go to church, it is whether they are likely to suffer discrimination because they are perceived to belong to one or other section of the community, that is important.

Religion is also dealt with in the Race Relations Act. Both Jews and Sikhs, for instance, are included as distinct ethnic groups.

Beyond this, however, there is no specific legislation to eliminate religious discrimination.

Age

Outside specific laws to exclude exploitation of children, there is no legislation against age discrimination. Indeed, age ranges are very common in job advertisements, and most seem to have a cut-off age at about 40. In May 1991, David Winnick sponsored a Backbench Bill aimed at stopping employers specifying upper age limits in recruitment advertisements, but it did not have Government sponsorship and hence failed.

Age restrictions, however, have been shown to discriminate indirectly against women. Because the number of women in the labour force drops in the typical child-bearing years, job adverts which exclude older candidates therefore have a requirement which disproportionately affects women. Unless the requirement is justifiable, this can constitute indirect discrimination.

Other forms of discrimination

The categories above deal with some of the more obvious groups who can suffer discrimination. There are plenty of other forms of discrimination which are not covered by legislation. For example, the arrival of AIDS has probably increased the discrimination felt by homosexual men. Yet the legislation that does exist in this area tends to support rather than eliminate discrimination – for instance, the exclusion of homosexuals from the Army.

Moreover, every recruiter will have his or her own prejudices based, particularly, on appearance. Those recruiters, probably the majority, who pride themselves on being able to make up their minds about candidates rapidly are fooling themselves if they think they are doing a good job. In the first few minutes of an interview, the recruiter will have been able to ascertain some facts about the applicant. The overriding impression, however, will be based not on the facts but on physical attributes. Stereotypical assumptions abound. Someone who is fat is either jovial or lazy. Someone who wears white socks is sharp, but lacks taste.

Defining discrimination: conclusion

In the main, the law has done its job of defining discrimination relatively effectively. It has:

(1) established the principles of direct and indirect discrimination; and
(2) specified groups against whom discrimination is illegal.

While, in our view, the legislation might be too exclusively focused on particular causes of discrimination, it does set some minimum standards and principles which can be applied more generally.

■ ENCOURAGING GOOD PRACTICE

As well as defining discrimination, the law also seeks to encourage good practice.

There are five specific ways of encouraging good practice that have been the subject of legal definition:

(1) Codes of Practice;
(2) monitoring;
(3) positive action;
(4) setting equality targets; and
(5) contract compliance.

The law deals with each of these and, as we shall see, there is not necessarily a consistent approach across the various Acts. This reflects that, in the United Kingdom, we do not have a comprehensive approach to discrimination per se, but rather specific measures to address particular forms of discrimination.

Codes of Practice

We have already described the Codes of Practice that currently exist. They were each designed to encourage organisations to embrace a positive (rather than a merely legalistic) approach to equal opportunities.

The point about the Codes, however, is that they are voluntary and as indicated earlier this has had inevitable consequences. In a survey carried out for the CRE in late 1985 and early 1986 (almost two years after the Code had become effective) only 25 per cent of employers had even glanced at the Code and only 4 per cent had comprehensive equal opportunities policies with effective monitoring systems. Moreover, this survey was skewed towards larger employers.

The Codes may well have been helpful in the 1980s to large employers who wanted to be seen to be socially responsible. They provided a framework for approaching equal opportunity issues. Beyond that, however, they have been of limited use.

Monitoring

Put at its simplest, monitoring is counting. As we shall argue in Chapter 6, we believe that having factual information about the profile of both applicants and employees is essential for an effective equal opportunities programme. The law seems to believe this too, but there are degrees of enthusiasm across the various Acts.

Monitoring is compulsory with regard to disability and religious affiliation in Northern Ireland. It is merely encouraged in the areas of sex and race discrimination.

In effect, most organisations know the gender of their applicants and employees so the real issue becomes whether to monitor ethnic origin. This is very much encouraged by the CRE (specifically in the Code of Practice) and, as we shall see, was an explicit aim associated with contract compliance. It is estimated, however, that 70 per cent of large private firms still do not monitor ethnic origin.

In 1988, following the CRE's investigation into chartered accountancy, all 14 firms indicated that they would introduce ethnic origin monitoring. By 1990, only three had done so.

Positive action

Positive action is explicitly encouraged by both European and UK legislation. It is designed to help those in a minority compete on equal terms when it comes to selection. In this situation, a minority is defined as where there have been no or few members of one sex or race in a particular type of work over the last 12 months.

This might involve, for example, takings steps to increase the number of applications from minorities or providing targeted training courses to minorities. It does not mean that, when it comes to making a selection decision, any criterion other than merit can be taken into account. This would constitute 'positive discrimination' and (with the exception of Oxbridge colleges for women) is illegal in the United Kingdom. By contrast, it is legal in the United States and this is a vehicle they may use to achieve particular quotas of minorities.

Setting equality targets

In general in the United Kingdom, setting targets is legal, having quotas is not. A target is an aspiration, it represents a realistic appraisal of what is possible in the future. A quota reserves a certain number of jobs regardless of the merit of the applicants. The distinction might be fine but it, and the principle of merit upon which it relies, is very important.

Quotas are legal in the United States. This is essentially the point at issue between the British Government and those in the United States who advocate the MacBride principles for Northern Ireland. The latter advocate quotas, while the Fair Employment Act still insists on the merit principle at the point of selection and therefore proposes targets but not quotas.

There is only one area where quotas are legal in the United Kingdom and that is for people with disabilities. However, as we have seen, this system is highly ineffective and many people are keen to review the legislation and to do away with the quotas.

The reason why quotas are resisted is that they undermine the very principles that the Acts are trying to sustain. Quotas mean that a woman can receive different treatment precisely because of her sex. This is not only inconsistent and likely to alienate the men in the organisation, it also undermines the validity of the selection decision. Was she appointed because she was the best person for the job, or because she was a woman? This leads to what people call 'tokenism' – which is disastrous both for those appointed and the organisation itself.

Equality targets, therefore, are legal providing they do not compromise the merit principle. Such targets are explicitly part of the legislation in Northern Ireland, and are advocated by the two Commissions. Obviously, setting realistic targets depends upon organisations having accurate information about their profile. It goes hand-in-hand with monitoring.

It is this consideration that has led to a slight shift on this issue by the CRE. When they were reviewing the Race Relations Act in 1985, the Commission proposed that where candidates were deemed to be of equal merit, the candidate from the under-represented group should be appointed. This is always somewhat problematic: are there ever really equal candidates? It makes a target much more like a quota. Moreover, by advocating the use of ethnic origin as the determining factor this again undermines one of the basic principles of the Act. In their 1991 review of the Act, the CRE have withdrawn this proposal, commenting: 'It does have the drawback that it would stop the use of ethnic monitoring data being neutral in its impact on individuals'.

As we shall explore in future chapters, this is a particular tightrope that organisations have to walk. In our view, too exclusive a focus on equality targets can become a problem. These targets should be a measure of progress, not an end in themselves.

Contract compliance

Contract compliance has had a key role to play in bringing about change in the United States. Its scope here has been limited by legislation. It is legal, but only within certain constraints.

Contract compliance is a way of making a direct link between equal opportunities and business performance. It is a way of putting pressure on companies to take the topic seriously. What it means is that the Government, and its various agencies, use their commercial power as potential customers to put pressure on their suppliers.

It has, surprisingly to some, a long pedigree in the United Kingdom. From 1969, there was a clause in all Government contracts requiring contractors to conform to employment provisions of the Race Relations Act. Local authorities were placed under

a statutory duty by the 1976 Act

> *'to make appropriate arrangements with a view to securing that their various functions are carried out with due regard to the need – (a) to eliminate unlawful racial discrimination; and (b) to promote equality of opportunity, and good relations between persons of different groups.'*

It was the vigour with which these obligations were pursued in the mid-1980s, particularly by the Greater London Council (GLC), that led to clauses in the 1988 Local Government Act which limited contract compliance activities. The legislation established approved questions which were designed to ease the administrative burden on companies and limit the requests for information that authorities could make. They can no longer request ethnic origin data from companies and because the Sex Discrimination Act did not put local authorities under any specific obligation, all questions on sex equality were banned.

Contract compliance therefore exists but in a very muted form in the United Kingdom. As we will argue in later chapters, there are many more effective ways of linking equal opportunities and business performance.

Encouraging good practice: conclusion

There are a number of ways that the law seeks to encourage good practice. It has to be said, however, that their effectiveness has been limited. Moreover, the various Acts are themselves inconsistent in the manner in which they seek to encourage good practice. It is only where particular practices have become mandatory – such as monitoring of religious affiliation in Northern Ireland – that the law is likely to have a significant impact. All the evidence suggests that where recommendations have remained voluntary – such as with the Codes – then adoption has remained very patchy.

■ CONCLUSION

If the overall aim of legislation is to eliminate discrimination, then clearly there is still much to do. The law has done something to establish principles specifying what sorts of actions constitute discrimination and specifying what sorts of actions might be legitimately taken in order to counter discrimination. All this was done by the mid-1970s.

The little progress that has been made since is coming about through the influence of European law. The concept of 'equal pay for work of equal value' we owe to Europe. The current challenges to pension schemes – both the inclusion of part-timers and the equal-isation of retirement ages – have come from European Court judgements.

Moreover, there is potential for the scope of European influence to be significantly increased. We shall have to wait and see what impact the UK opt-out on the 'Social Chapter', negotiated at Maastricht, has on developments in this field. It may free up policy development whilst still enabling the UK to choose to 'opt in' at a later stage.

In time, therefore, new thinking may well emerge from Brussels that will bring equal opportunities another step forward in the United Kingdom. This may force, for example, the UK Government to take a more positive approach to the issue of childcare. This would be change at the 'macro' (State) level and, as such, would be warmly welcome.

It would not, however, make the difference at the 'micro' (organisational) level. Here the emphasis would not be so much on the enabling, as the constraining factors. As we have seen, the law has been more able to define unfair discrimination than it has been to encourage good practice. The law is not a very effective vehicle for bringing about change because:

(1) by its very nature, the law is more preoccupied with what not to do, rather than with what to do;
(2) it therefore encourages a minimalist approach: organisations doing the minimum in order to ensure that they do not break the law.

Quite simply, organisations, as with people, do not like being told what to do. This was well illustrated by a 1988 survey commissioned by the Equal Opportunities Commission and the Economic and Social Research Council. It investigated 40 employers who had been found guilty of sex discrimination in tribunals and found that losing a case was unlikely to have any positive effect on equal opportunities. Only one in five employers had either introduced an equal opportu-nities policy or reviewed an existing policy.

Most employers seem prepared to do the minimum to ensure that they are not at risk of being punished, but they will not go any further. The law, therefore, has some deterrent effect. However, because the law defines discrimination in terms of the groups who are most likely to suffer it, over-concentration on the law turns equal opportunities into a confrontational issue. There is a 'them' and an 'us'.

The law had to set some minimum standards. There is a case, however, to suggest that this is all that we should look to the law to do. Now that we know what those minimum standards are, we have to look elsewhere for the arguments to raise those standards. It is our belief that there are compelling business reasons for embracing equal opportunities. The law marks a starting point, not the finishing point.

Chapter 2

THE LABOUR MARKET – SKILL SHORTAGES

We have argued that the law is not a particularly effective change agent. In our view, it is the labour market that has the power to shake organisations out of their traditional thinking. In essence, it will leave them little choice.

This argument is not based so much on the anticipated reduction of people coming in to the labour market. That is obviously influential, but the real issue is not the sheer numbers of people available for work, it is the skills that they are able to offer. As we view the future, it is only too likely that high levels of unemployment will co-exist with skill shortages. This is a measure of the extent to which, as a nation, we have failed to help people develop the skills that are, and will be, in demand.

In spite of short-term fluctuations, we would see the labour market of the future, therefore, remaining tight. This will have two effects:

(1) it will force employers to look at traditionally under-utilised groups; and
(2) it will be a 'sellers' market, with the applicant doing as much of the decision making as the employer. Both of these factors provide a powerful stimulus to equal opportunities.

Currently, however, the UK economy is in recession and thoughts about skill shortages are probably a distant memory.

During this chapter, therefore, we will:

- Discuss the impact of economic cycles on the labour market
- Look specifically at the changing demand for labour in the United Kingdom
- Identify changes in the supply of labour
- Consider the implications for equal opportunities of these changes.

■ IMPACT OF ECONOMIC CYCLES ON THE LABOUR MARKET

In order to explore how the economic cycle affects the labour market, we will:

(1) consider the factors that influence supply and demand;
(2) look at recent discussions about the labour market;
(3) examine the historical context; and
(4) draw some conclusions.

Supply
The absolute number of people coming into the labour market is a 'known' – there is at least a 16-year time lag between birth and full-time employment. It is relatively easy therefore to predict the numbers of people available for work. The post-war baby boom has meant that we have been seeing an increase in the number of people coming through to the labour market. Among other things, this meant that we could retire earlier. The minimum pensionable age of 65 rapidly became the maximum.

It is essential, however, to overlay on top of these overall numbers the skill profile of those available for work. This is the other, and crucial, aspect to the supply side of the labour market.

Demand
The economic cycle obviously has a considerable impact on the demand for labour: high in periods of boom and low in periods of recession. In essence, the higher the output, the more people are required in order to create this output. There is another factor at work, however, and this is increasing productivity (output per head) which makes it feasible to increase output while actually decreasing the amount of labour required.

Again, the skill dimension is critical to the demand side of the labour market. Gone are the days when the majority of the jobs in the economy were low-skilled and this trend towards the 'professionalisation' of work is accelerating.

Recent discussion about the labour market

Inevitably, there are fluctuations in the demand and supply of labour. In the late 1980s there were concerns about the supply side. CBI manufacturing surveys in 1988 showed that output, in some companies, was being limited by skill shortages. Moreover, there was an underlying problem.

In 1988, NEDO (National Economic Development Office) and The Training Agency issued a report 'Young People And The Labour Market' drawing attention to the 20 per cent decline in the number of 16-24 year olds over the period 1987-1995. They followed this up a year later with 'Defusing The Demographic Time Bomb' to gauge the level of awareness among employers and to propose some ways of tackling the problem.

Subsequently, of course, the UK economy has been in recession, unemployment is again above 2.5 million and looks like it will continue to climb in 1992. Discussion is no longer about the 'demographic time bomb', but about how we can stimulate demand, encourage growth and get people back to work. Moreover, increasing productivity, the argument goes, will mean that we can absorb the projected reduction in school leavers.

The historical context

We would argue that the increase in unemployment is not an argument for becoming complacent about the labour market. The central argument should not be about the overall numbers available for work.

This is not the first time the UK economy has been in recession and unemployment has soared. In 1983, Samuel Brittan wrote an article in *The Financial Times* which explored these issues. He attacked the simplistic view of what he called the 'lump of labour fallacy':

> *'It is the belief that there is a fixed amount of work to be done; so that if there are more people or technological progress enables one man to do the work of two or 10, the result is bound to be unemployment.'*

He argued, instead, for a more complex relationship between supply and demand. There could not be 'too many workers' so long as there were unsatisfied needs or desires. The demand for labour was not fixed; it was itself influenced by the supply. For example, output per head between 1860 and 1960 trebled (due to increasing productivity) but total output increased six-fold. This was sufficient to absorb both productivity gains and the increase (from 12m to 26m) in the working population.

In broad terms, therefore, changes in demand for labour have kept pace with changes in supply. Recessions cause employers to look again at their costs and redouble their efforts to increase productivity. Long-term unemployment, however, is not so much caused by increases in productivity as by the accompanying switch in the skills required to do the jobs. Technology has enabled employers to increase productivity by replacing men (and women) doing low-skilled jobs, by machines. As the pace of technological progress increases, so less and less jobs require low skills.

Some conclusions

We would suggest that the real issue is not so much the number of people available for work, but the skills that they possess. If we could encourage more of the working age population to train and develop new skills we would not need to be so concerned about the fall in school leavers.

Recession in 1990/91 has taken the heat out of some particular skill shortages but, over the long term, they are still there. As Bob Horton, the Chairman of BP, put it:

'Managerial talent is always in demand and perpetually in short supply.'

As we shall see, it is managerial jobs that are likely to grow most in the UK economy.

■ THE INCREASING DEMAND FOR SKILL

Although the 1990/91 recession has been seen as a 'white collar' recession, with redundancies common among this previously exempt group, this does not disturb the underlying trend in the UK economy towards the service sector.

In 1988, the CBI estimated that 68 per cent of employees in the United Kingdom were already in the service sector. It also appears that these are the areas in which the United Kingdom is seen to have a competitive advantage within Europe: media, management consultancy, financial services, advertising, design and the professions. Perhaps it should not be surprising, therefore, that the IMS (Institute of Manpower Studies) was projecting that between 1985 and 1990 there would be a 500,000 increase in those employed in the services sector and a decrease of 600,000 in the manufacturing sector.

This shift towards the service sector is also taking place at a time when organisations are having to respond to unprecedented levels of change. The desire for quality and satisfying customer requirements means that organisations must be fleet of foot. This increase in employment in the service sector, therefore, cannot mean an increase in 'paper shuffling'. Bureaucracies are highly unlikely to provide the service that is being expected in the 1990s. There will need to be less form-filling, and more listening to people's requirements. Employees will need to be able to use their own initiative as well as understand the regulations. Technology will be able to take care of the low-skilled paper work. This is the primary reason for the current redundancies in the retail banking sector.

Not surprisingly, all this is having a considerable impact upon the skills that are in demand. Everyone's work is becoming less 'pro-grammable'. It is for this reason that it is possible to have both rising unemployment and skill shortages. The economy is creating jobs which require increasing levels of skill. The manufacturing sector, and indeed the service sector during this recession, is in particular laying off people with low skills.

Projections by the IER (Institute For Economic Research) suggest that by the year 2000 the three key growth occupations will be:

(1) managers and administrators;
(2) professional occupations; and
(3) associated professional and technical occupations.

We are already seeing these changes reflected in the increase in demand for graduates. The number of graduates entering UK employment has increased by a third since 1981. Admittedly, those students graduating in 1991 are finding it difficult to get the jobs that they want, but the long-term trends remain in their favour.

Looking at the growth occupations in the IER projections, it is worth recalling that many of the professions are becoming almost exclusively graduate entry only. Accountants and lawyers have already become so; in the wake of reports in 1987 by Handy and Constable & McCormick, there are those who believe 'management' should become a graduate profession too. Either way, it is likely that the managers of the future will be more qualified (in the academic sense) than their predecessors. Therefore, there might be particular years when the demand for trainees is reduced, but this will hardly induce the professions to drop their graduate status requirements. The economy's appetite for graduates may fluctuate with the economic cycle, but there is no doubt that it is on an upward trend.

There is another area of demand that we should at least note here. Increasing harmonisation in Europe not only means free movement of goods, but also free movement of labour. Professional qualifications should be recognised across national boundaries. Given the levels of pay available in other Northern European countries, this freedom of movement is more likely to lead to people moving there than others coming here. In particular, of course, the increased demand will be in the areas where supply is already short – leading again to increased competition for graduates.

The one thing that we are sure about, therefore, is that a movement towards the 'knowledge worker' is already taking place and that the trend is accelerating. In December 1988, Professor Charles Handy gave evidence to the Select Committee on Employment on the changing nature of skills which will be needed in the work force in the late 1990s. He estimated that between 70 per cent and 80 per cent of all jobs, by the end of the 1990s, will be 'knowledge' jobs. Half of those (i.e. 35% to 40% of the total jobs) will require brain skills of the order of a higher education degree or professional qualification. The percentages for the new jobs that will be created in this period are, of course, even higher.

This represents a fundamental shift in the demand for labour.

■ CHANGES IN THE SUPPLY OF LABOUR

In looking at the supply side of the labour market, we will examine two aspects:

(1) the changing composition of the working age population; and
(2) the supply of high skills linked to employers' demands identified above.

Composition of the working age population

In the 10 years leading up to 1989, the working age population in the United Kingdom grew by nearly two million (to 34.4m). Such growth, however, is a thing of the past. The working age population will remain stable in the first half of the 1990s and will then rise slowly (to 34.7m) at the end of the century.

Beneath this seeming stability, however, there are significant changes that are taking place within the structure of the available pool of labour.

Age

As we have seen, there will be a reduction in the number of young people and there will be a corresponding increase in the middle age groups – by the turn of the century, 46 per cent will be in the 35-54 age group.

Moreover, by the year 2000, people aged 55 or over will represent 26 per cent of the total population. The participation rate of older people in the economy, however, has been falling. In 1970, 81 per cent of men aged 60-64 were working, by 1986 this had dropped to 53 per cent. According to the 1988 Labour Force Survey 673,000 economically inactive men and women aged 50 and over would like regular paid work.

These trends, therefore, are working in opposite directions. The working population is ageing but people are retiring earlier. It is this sort of analysis that is prompting calls to move to a flexible decade of retirement between the ages of 60 and 70.

Women

Currently, 70 per cent of women are economically active. Non-married women have the highest representation at work, 74 per cent are economically active, and this falls to 68 per cent of married women. Child rearing is obviously the main cause of this reduction. The General Household Survey, however, in 1987 found increasing evidence of women with dependent children working.

It is anticipated that there will be a further increase in the number of 'women returners'. With the increase in single parent families and the high levels of earnings needed to sustain mortgages (particularly in the South) economic need, as much as personal interest, is likely to lead to an increase in the number of women who return to employment. The Labour Force Survey in 1988 suggested that over

Table 2.1

Age of youngest child	Full-time	Part-time	Econ. active
0-2 years	11%	19%	39%
3-4 years	11%	35%	51%
5-9 years	14%	48%	66%
10 years and over	29%	45%	77%
All with dependent children	18%	37%	60%

820,000 people would like to be in regular work, but were prevented by family commitments.

Of course, some (but by no means all) of these 'returners' will come back as part-timers. Indeed, the increase in female employment, the move towards the service sector and the increase in part-time work have all gone hand-in-hand. In 1990, 4.8m women worked part-time.

Ethnic minorities

While 1 in 5 of the total population is aged under 16, this figure is 1 in 3 for the ethnic population. In other words, of the declining population of young people, an increasing proportion will be from ethnic minorities.

The National Census in 1991, which included a question on ethnic origin, will provide us with up-to-date information, but we already know that in some areas ethnic minorities make up a high proportion of those entering the labour market. It is estimated that 40 per cent of school leavers in the old GLC area in the 1990s will be from ethnic minorities.

Yet we know that people from ethnic minorities suffer from unemployment disproportionately. In 1988, 13.5 per cent of those with ethnic minority origins were unemployed versus a figure of 8.6 per cent for the whole population. The figure was highest for those with Pakistani/Bangladeshi origins, whose unemployment rate was 24 per cent. At every qualification level, people from ethnic minorities had higher unemployment rates than white people. The March 1990 *Employment Gazette* reported an ethnic minority unemployment rate 60 per cent above that for white people.

People with disabilities

There is a high level of unemployment among people who are in some way or other occupationally handicapped. In 1988, this stood at 19 per cent (versus 8.6% for the total population). The same survey indicated that of the 360,000 who were unemployed, 22 per cent had academic and vocational qualifications at 'A' Level or above. Moreover, these figures understate the case because they exclude the 'economically inactive' – long-term unemployed. It is estimated that only 31 per cent of all people with some form of disability are in work.

Europe

The future supply of labour from Europe is, at the moment, an unknown. There is a potential for an increase – if only for people 'on assignment' in order to learn English. As we argued above, we do not believe, however, that there will be a significant influx of skilled workers – employment conditions in the United Kingdom would need to be considerably improved to make this likely in the short term.

The break up of Communism in Eastern Europe potentially offers a further supply of labour. Presently, of course, these countries are not members of the EC and would therefore not easily be able to get work permits for their workers. Even if this were to change in the future, it is perhaps unlikely that they will be able to provide the skills that the UK economy is lacking.

The upshot of all this is that the supply of labour is changing and changing out of all recognition. Traditionally, employers used to recruit young, white males. It is quite clear that this is the group that is shrinking most of all. In the United States, by 1995 it is estimated that 85 per cent of new entrants to the American work force will be either women or minorities. While the United Kingdom is not quite at this point, it is certain that the trends are in the same direction. More women than ever are in the work force and an increasing percentage of the youngest employees come from ethnic minorities. This is why we feel that the labour market is not going to give organisations much of a choice about equal opportunities. If they want to carry on recruiting, they will inevitably have to look to under-utilised groups: women, minorities, people with disabilities, and older people.

Supply of high skill labour

In recent years, there has been increasing competition between employers for students but, in general, supply has been roughly in balance with demand. This has been in a period when there has been an increasing number of young people. We can no longer rely, however, on the demographics which in the future will be working against us. The way to stabilise and (then) increase supply will be for an increasing proportion of our young people to stay on in full-time education.

In the 1987 White Paper titled 'Higher Education – Meeting The Challenge' the Government made the following projections for numbers in higher education:

Table 2.2

1985	1990	1996	2000
693,000	726,000	691,000	723,000

At present, 14 per cent participate in higher education; by the year 2000 this is predicted to rise to 20 per cent. Whether this anticipated rise actually takes place, we shall have to see.

We know, however, that we already compare poorly with other countries. In what was West Germany, 28 per cent of the relevant age population go on to higher education (double the UK rate). In Japan, 95 per cent of 18 year olds are in full-time schooling (32% in the UK). Nor does the United Kingdom compare favourably in terms of the investment employers are prepared to make in training their employees in new skills. Off-the-job training occupies an average 1.9 days a year, in West Germany the figure is four times as high. The concept of continuous training and development still has a long way to go in the United Kingdom.

As the changing nature of work demands an increasingly skilled work force, it looks unlikely that we are prepared in the United Kingdom to make the investment in training people to develop the required skills. In 1988, the IMS (Institute Of Manpower Studies) held a conference under the heading of: 'Skills for the 1990s'. Geoffrey Holland, former Director of the MSC and Permanent Secretary of the Department of Employment gave a pre-dinner speech. He summarised the situation:

'The real skills gap is that our country is under-educated, under-trained, and under-skilled. And that is because our approach to education and training is and has been for decades too little, too narrow, for too few, with too few expectations and hardly any follow-through.'

Of course, training and education are now relatively high up the political agenda. Whatever the outcome of these debates, however, it is clear that there are no overnight solutions to problems that have persisted for decades. In short, the supply of skilled workers is unlikely to meet the demand.

■ THE IMBALANCE OF SUPPLY AND DEMAND

The imbalance of supply and demand is not so much a matter of overall numbers in the work force. Providing employers are prepared to recruit from non-traditional sources, there are enough people to meet the likely requirements. What does not exist, however, is a supply of the right sort of people.

If Charles Handy's projections for the increase in knowledge workers are even partly accurate, then we have a significant problem. At best, by the year 2000 20 per cent of our younger population will be going on to higher education, but over 40 per cent of the newly created jobs will require higher education skills.

■ CONCLUSION: IMPLICATIONS FOR EQUAL OPPORTUNITIES

As stated earlier, we believe there are two consequences of this tight labour market which have profound implications for equal opportunities:

(1) it will force employers to look at non-traditional recruitment sources; and
(2) it puts applicants for employment in a powerful bargaining position.

We will look at each of these areas in turn.

We will illustrate our argument by examining changes occurring within 'the professions'. It is our contention that what is happening now amongst 'the professions' (which symbolise the 'knowledge worker') foreshadows changes that will occur much more widely across all industries.

Increasing representation of women and minorities in education

Both women and minorities are increasing their representation among those who stay on in education after the minimum leaving age.

In 1988, 36 per cent of women left school to undertake degree, teacher training, further or higher education courses. The corresponding figure for men was 27 per cent. Between 1985 and 1989 there was an overall 12 per cent increase in applications to university – applications from women during this period increased by 17 per cent. Women now represent 45 per cent of those qualifying with first degrees in the United Kingdom.

The 1985 Labour Force Survey found that 13 per cent of white males and 12 per cent of white females aged 16-24 were students; the figures were noticeably higher for ethnic minorities: 16 per cent of West Indian men, 14 per cent of West Indian women, 36 per cent Indian men, 27 per cent Indian women, 42 per cent Pakistani/ Bangladeshi men and 13 per cent Pakistani/Bangladeshi women. A survey of 28,000 16-19-year-olds in 1990 showed that this trend continues. Forty per cent white, 50 per cent Afro-Caribbean, and 70 per cent Asian teenagers were in full-time education or on training courses.

In the past, universities and polytechnics have not monitored ethnic origin of applicants. What we do know is that the representation of ethnic minorities is likely to increase.

However, Commission for Racial Equality surveys of graduates carried out in 1982 and 1985 showed that 52.6 per cent of white students were offered a job in their final year. 72.2 per cent of ethnic minorities were not. . . despite sending more applications than their white fellow students.

Women in the professions

As the number of women entering higher education is increasing, there is an increasing proportion subsequently entering the professions. As we shall see, they now make up about half of those entering the medical and legal professions. This is noticeably higher than the proportion coming in to, for example, industry to train as managers. No doubt, this is partly because women are still under-represented in scientific and technical degree disciplines. It is also consistent, however, with women choosing careers where there is a clear skill-based assessment of an individual's capability (at least on entry). You either are or are not a chartered accountant. You either are or are not a qualified solicitor. Becoming a recognised 'manager' is an altogether more ad hoc process.

The Law Society reports that in 1988 women were already representing 52 per cent of new articles registered. Interestingly, they were also gaining a disproportionately high share of good honours degrees. In 1987/88 women represented 48 per cent of the honours graduates but 61 per cent of those with good honours degrees.

In 1970, 70 women qualified as chartered accountants, in 1989 there were over 1,000. In 1985, 23 per cent of the new admissions to the Institute of Chartered Accountants in England and Wales were women. By 1989, this had increased to 31 per cent. Women represented 34 per cent of those entering training contracts in 1988/89.

There has been a noticeable change, therefore, in the proportion of women who are entering the professions. As we have seen, an increasing proportion of ethnic minorities are also staying on in education and becoming qualified. This change, however, has yet to be reflected in an increase in the proportion of ethnic minorities in the professions.

Ethnic minorities in the professions

In 1987, 1.5 per cent of the UK's practising solicitors came from ethnic minorities. In 1990, a study by Brunel University, commissioned by the Law Society and the CRE, found entrenched racial discrimination. White finalists wrote an average of four letters for every interview, ethnic minorities wrote an average of 7.5. The Bar has a higher representation of ethnic minorities, estimated at 6 per cent, but the Bar Council in June 1991 caused a storm of protest by suggesting that all barristers' chambers should recruit at least 5 per cent of their members from ethnic minorities.

The situation appears to be no better in the accountancy profession. An investigation by the CRE into chartered accountancy training contracts, published in 1988, showed that, across the profession, the success rate for whites (after controlling for qualifications) was much higher than for ethnic minorities. Despite this report, two years later in 1990, white applicants still had twice as much chance of getting a training contract.

Increase in non-traditional recruits: conclusion

In our view, what has already started to happen for women, will happen for ethnic minorities, and (perhaps more slowly) for people with disabilities. What the professions need is skilled people and, as we have seen, they will be in short supply in the future. This will mean, in time, that the professions will have to change their recruiting habits. The Bar Council's suggestion of a 5 per cent ethnic minorities target was inevitably interpreted in some quarters as a 'quota'. In the future, resistance will give way to common sense. In the meantime, a target such as 5 per cent represents a reasonable aspiration.

We have chosen to look at progress in the professions because these are the most clearly skill-based jobs and, to that extent, represent the way that the rest of the economy is going.

It is, nevertheless, true that other employers will feel – and in some cases are feeling – the same pressures. As all jobs are requiring higher levels of skill, employers have less room to take account of non-skill criteria in their selection decisions. In the future, how can employers continue to ask for applicants under the age of 35, when the vast majority of qualified candidates will be older than this?

In the rush to recruit young white able-bodied men, a lot of excellent candidates have been overlooked. As the labour market for skilled candidates becomes increasingly tight, the hour for equal opportunities has come. The law has taken 15 years to make very little progress. A few years of skill shortages will do an awful lot more to lift the blinkers from the eyes of the recruiters.

Employee power

The competitive labour market for skills also has the effect of putting the applicant and subsequently the employee in a stronger bargaining position. This then combines with the fact that more applicants come from non-traditional groups (as we have seen, in particular women) which will provide another powerful stimulus for equal opportunities. This starts at the recruitment stage and continues thereafter.

In order to attract the best, organisations have to offer what applicants want. This does not mean just offering competitive salaries. In 1987, a large multinational company surveyed recent graduates to see whether offering childcare facilities would be an influential factor in choosing an employer. One hundred per cent of the women and 68 per cent of the men said that it would. American Express in Brighton were experiencing difficulty in recruiting, so they introduced a whole series of flexible working measures.

Indeed, the increase in part-time working among professionals is almost entirely due to the pressure exerted by women with scarce skills. Instead of returning full-time after maternity leave, they have insisted on returning on a part-time basis. For example, a survey by the City of London Law Society found that 40 per cent of firms provided part-time work for assistants (qualified solicitors). Although this figure dropped to 13 per cent for partners, it is still significantly ahead of most of industry where managing is still presumed to be an exclusively full-time occupation.

Change in the way we work is on the way. This is not because senior managers have suddenly become converted to the benefits of flexible working (although, as we will argue later on in this book, there are significant advantages to the organisation), it is because employees with scarce skills are demanding it. In the words of Sir John Harvey-Jones:

> *'Companies look for a degree of unswerving and unhesitating loyalty above family commitments, but with future labour shortages, companies are going to have to adapt to the individual.'*

It is these changing attitudes to work that form the subject of our next chapter.

Chapter 3

CHANGING ATTITUDES TO WORK AND THE FAMILY – THE BEST OF BOTH WORLDS

In the previous chapter, we explored the changes in the labour market and concluded that employers would need to respond to the changing needs of employees. In this chapter we will explore what these changing attitudes to work are and illustrate how they affect employers. In essence, we will argue that employees want the best of both worlds: they want a challenging career at work, but they also want a fulfilling home life. If organisations want to remain competitive then, somehow or other, they need to be able to help employees meet both their work and home expectations.

In this chapter, therefore, we will explore the following themes:

- Historical influences on home and work
- Social trends – the statistical evidence for change
- New attitudes to work and home
- Implications for employers

What we are not seeking to do in this chapter is to suggest that any particular view about work and the family is 'right'. What we are pointing out is that there has been a shift in attitudes and that employers need to take account of this.

■ HISTORICAL INFLUENCES ON HOME AND WORK

It is worth looking at some of the historical influences on society, which partly account for the clash in expectations which may now arise as the new generation begins to challenge accepted 'norms'. The first legacy we have been left with is the separation of public and private life.

■ SEPARATION OF PUBLIC AND PRIVATE

At the end of the last century, women – within accepted society – were very much part of the private world of the home. Their role was defined as wife and mother. The public world of work and politics was seen as something completely separate and one in which women played little or no part. As we know, 'behind every great man lies a woman'. Only in 1918 did women in the United Kingdom have full voting rights.

In her book, *Sex and Suffrage In Britain*, 1987, Princeton University Press, (UK paperback 1990, Routledge, London) Susan Kingsley-Kent argues that part of the difficulty in gaining full citizenship for women at the end of the last century and the beginning of this one, can be attributed to this separation of public and private life. Women who wished to play a part in public life were somehow 'going against nature' and were threatening the security of the family. As Stickney Ellis described the duties of the 19th century woman: 'The man naturally governs, the woman as naturally obeys.'

Nineteenth century feminists (or suffragists) argued that home and work – public and private – were inextricably intertwined: the public was private and the personal political. In our view, this is still a debate that is going on. The House of Commons debate over taxation of childcare illustrates the point.

In May 1990, the House debated a series of amendments to the Finance Bill, one of which proposed the setting of costs of non-employer nurseries against tax. Ivor Standbrook, MP for Orpington, took up the argument in a way rather reminiscent of the 19th century. He believed the proposal was anti-family and stated:

> '*I implore the Government to delve more deeply into the economic and social consequences of what they are doing and cease to be pulled along by the wretched engine of feminism.*'

Although this kind of comment is heard less frequently, it reflects the political refusal to see the private as public. We have one of the lowest levels of state provision of nurseries in Europe because of this stance. When she was a Minister of State, Edwina Curry explained:

> '*Our view is that it is for the parents who go out to work to decide how best to care for their children.*'

Not surprisingly, this separation of public and private extends to work. Women and men at work often seem to find it unacceptable to talk openly about the family. This seems to be particularly true for young women who are wishing to climb the corporate ladder. Somehow the family is in 'a different world' that should not be referred to in the workplace. A recent article in *The Times* quoted a female executive:

'No woman talks about her family at work.' (10 June 1991.)

In one organisation we have worked with, a female manager – who had been with the company for eight years – compared the feeling of having to tell her manager that she was pregnant with 'the naughtiest thing I ever did at school'. Obviously, it is childcare, and in particular pregnancy, which bring the worlds of work and family most closely together – sometimes with unfortunate consequences.

Women and childcare

If women were not supposed to be looking after their menfolk then they were supposed to be bringing up children (single-handedly).

John Bowlby, one of this century's most influential child development theorists, died in 1990. His view was that any maternal deprivation was dangerous, and that the only safe answer was 'the continuous comforting presence' of the mother. Even leaving the child with a nanny for a short time was highly risky.

In an article in the *Independent on Sunday* (9 September 1990), Christina Hardyment points out that however outdated his views may sound

'. . . they became deeply rooted in the national culture in the late 1940s and 1950s and still strike a chord with many parents. . . Mothers continue to agonise over when it is right to start work, how long should they leave their children with other adults, and alternative childcare.'

All sorts of social problems were laid at the door of the working woman. Juvenile delinquency, which actually is most convincingly linked with poverty, was attributed to maternal deprivation. The term 'Latch-key kids' signalled society's disapproval.

Today, family therapists believe that fathers, siblings, grandparents, friends and nannies, as well as mothers, may all play a role in bringing up children. A mother on her own with the children all day may well suffer from the lack of adult contact and conversation. For some, being at home all the time would mean that they would be worse, not better, mothers.

The expectations and received wisdom are changing, but the old views inevitably clash with the new, and may well cause a fair amount of confusion and guilt on the part of the mother. And for some managers it may go against the grain for them to welcome back working mothers. As far as they are concerned the mother should be with her children.

The weaker sex

Another historical legacy which still confuses thinking is the view of women as 'the weaker sex'.

In the late 19th century women were seen to be more delicate and prone to more ill-health than men. Pregnancy was treated as an illness which required *confinement*.

Even when not pregnant (which in the 19th century was rather infrequently) the menstrual cycle was seen as a time of ill-health. As Dr W. C. Taylor said in his book *A Physicians' Counsels to Women in Health and Disease*, W. C. Taylor, M. D. Springfield: W. J. Holland & Co., 1871.

> *'We cannot too emphatically urge the importance of regarding these monthly returns as periods of ill-health, as days when the ordinary occupations are to be suspended or modified.'*

The opposition to women entering politics, or being granted full citizenship, was partly explained in terms of health. For example, a Massachusetts legislator proclaimed:

> *'Grant suffrage to women, and you will have to build insane asylums in every county... Women are too nervous and hysterical to enter politics.'*

This may seem rather extraordinary now, but possibly explains some views still evident at work. It is not unusual to hear senior managers arguing that promoting a woman after her return to work after giving birth is not done *for the woman's sake*. As one woman executive put it:

> *'And even when you've only taken six months off to have three children... they say "It must affect you", and can make all sorts of excuses for not promoting you for your sake'*

In short, some men still patronise women because subconsciously they still perceive them to be 'the weaker sex'.

Conclusion

History has left us, therefore, with three interrelated strands of thought:

(1) that public and private worlds are separate;
(2) that young children depend upon the 'continuous comforting presence of the mother'; and
(3) that women are weaker and should be protected from the rigours of working life.

■ SOCIAL TRENDS – THE STATISTICAL EVIDENCE

In reality, when one starts to look at the statistical evidence, it is apparent that life isn't actually like that. Working for many women is not a matter of choice but of economic necessity. The typical family was seen to consist of: working father with mother at home looking after dependent children. This is under pressure from all directions. As we shall see, the nuclear family exists mainly in the imagination of the advertisers.

The family

Only 5 per cent of households conform to the image of working father with mother at home looking after two children under 16. The husband is the sole earner in only 27 per cent of families.

It is anticipated that the divorce rate will reach 50 per cent in 1995.

The percentage of one-parent families has now reached 14 per cent – with the vast majority of these being families headed by the mother.

Women and work

As we saw in Chapter 2, the percentage of adult women under retirement age who are economically active is 70 per cent. Of those even with dependent children 60 per cent are economically active. Eleven per cent of mothers with a youngest child below two years old work full-time and 19 per cent part-time.

Figure 3.1 is reproduced from the EOC survey 'Women and Men In Britain, 1991'. It graphically illustrates the pattern of work for husband and wife in the family. The most common combination

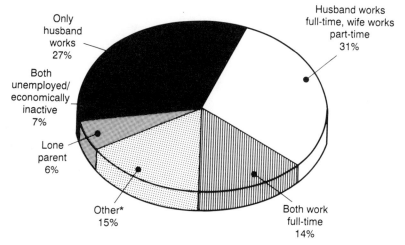

Only
husband
works
27%

Husband works
full-time, wife works
part-time
31%

Both
unemployed/
economically
inactive
7%

Lone
parent
6%

Other*
15%

Both work
full-time
14%

*Includes only wife works, husband part-time, wife full-time

Source: Family Expenditure Survey

Figure 3.1   Who works?

(31%) is of both partners working, with husband working full-time, and wife working part-time. A further 29 per cent of couples either equally share the work (both full-time), or the wife works full-time and husband part-time.

Women and childbirth

A survey in 1988 by the Office of Population and Census showed that the average age of the mother at the birth of the first child was 24. For women with higher education qualifications, and those from non-manual socio-economic groups, the age tended to be higher.

Giving the lie to the view that women are only really interested in working until marriage and childbirth, the number of years in the average woman's working life (i.e. after completing education and before retirement) when she is without a job is just seven.

Conclusion

What these figures indicate is that the simplistic notions of the nuclear family, and women's role within it, need to be completely revised. For the older generation of managers – men who themselves have relied upon wives who stayed at home – this may prove difficult. For the younger generation, the necessity to combine work and family responsibilities is self-evident.

■ NEW ATTITUDES TO WORK AND THE FAMILY

The 'two separate worlds' of work and home have become blurred as women have entered the labour market, and as men have started to play a more important role in the upbringing of their children. It is no longer a question of public or private but public and private.

Working mothers

Working mothers are trying to maintain a balance between work and home. They see work as an important part of their lives — enhancing their quality of life by both developing their full range of skills and contributing to the family finances. On the other hand, they want the world of work to be able to adapt to their domestic needs. Hence the demand for, and increasing appearance of, flexible working arrangements.

The view that it is only possible to be a successful mother *or* a successful executive is not a position many young women seem prepared to accept. We have already seen that 60 per cent of mothers with dependent children are economically active.

In June 1991, Libby Purves reviewed a novel by Maeve Haran which portrayed a woman TV executive who decided to give up working because she realised it was damaging her family. Libby Purves was very dismissive:

> *There is no suggestion that it is possible to make both television programmes and apple pies; no space for women who run businesses with crooked hems, or dare to own both Agas and briefcases... Doing justice to children and a career is not easy. But then nor is it easy to mix a job with a passion for ocean-racing or local politics. Adult mothers apply the same intelligence to their life as to their job. Any fool can see that small children will not thrive if they never know when they will see their mother: any fool can see the drawbacks of jobs without boundaries.*

The need, therefore is to be able to combine sensibly both family and work responsibilities. The days when working women had to be tougher than the men, when they had to behave as if they had no home life, may be on their way out.

Working fathers

There is also increasing evidence that some fathers are looking to move away from an exclusive concentration upon their role at work. In 1991, the Working Mothers Association has called their guide the 'Working Parents Handbook' in recognition of the increasingly active role being played by fathers.

For women, pregnancy can be the point where work and family commitments most obviously clash, for men it can be relocation. There is evidence that men are increasingly prepared to turn down job moves for family reasons.

In 1987, 33 per cent of managers and professionals in a survey had rejected job offers because they involved relocation. There is some evidence that the new GCSE exams, with their increased reliance on course work, are causing parents to think twice about moving children between schools. Moreover, given the percentage of women who now work, a promotion for the husband loses its attraction if it means his wife has to go out and job hunt. In short, there is no reason to suppose that a man is any more 'mobile' than a woman.

There seems to be a general shift towards men placing more emphasis on their lives outside work. Research by the Henley Centre for Forecasting, 'Planning for Social Change' looked at what men considered to be important to their pride.

'Family' came out top of the list (77) with 'Health/Fitness' second (61) and the 'Job' third (46). As the Associate Director of social research at Henley put it:

'Work is no longer the fulcrum of their lives. Men are starting to define themselves in terms of their family and their interests rather than their jobs. The job is dropping down the list as a source of pride.'

Not surprisingly, therefore, men too are questioning whether the advantages of working the long hours demanded are worth the huge cost to family life. Norman Fowler is probably the most famous example of this (he resigned from the Cabinet in order to spend more time with his family). However, he is far from being on his own.

A survey of 118 chief executives in European companies was carried out in 1989 by Professor Cary Cooper and Valerie Sutherland of UMIST, in order to explore the impact of work pressures on home life.

The same survey had been carried out in 1984, and comparison between the two revealed a dramatic change in views over those five years. In 1984, 24 per cent of British chief executives saw job interference with social/private life as a problem. This figure increased to 50 per cent in the 1989 survey. Almost a quarter were considering leaving the boardroom to spend more time with their families (and this was before the current recession began to bite).

The younger generation

It is not just working mothers and fathers who are exerting pressure on the prevailing attitudes at work.

The sheer business of living, now that neither servants nor non-working wives are common, creates its own domestic demands. As one young man put it, in Victoria McGee's article in *The Times* (17 April 1991):

> '. . .I don't have a single female friend who doesn't work full-time, so nobody has the sort of support that the men who were sole breadwinners, like my father, used to expect.'

These days, people with the appropriate skills are in the fortunate position of being able to be concerned about the quality of their lives. They can satisfy their basic economic needs relatively easily, beyond that they have a choice about how hard they work.

There is a questioning by people of what 'quality of life' actually means. The balance seems to be shifting away from income alone, and loyalty to one organisation for all one's working career, towards recognising the value of life outside the workplace, and of other outside interests (including the family). Work and other interests both form part of what is seen to be a high quality lifestyle.

It is not an issue that employers will be able to ignore. As Peter Herriot points out in his book, *Recruitment in the 1990s*, 1989, Institute of Personnel Management.

> 'The relationship between the employer and employee is shifting; it is becoming a sellers' market for young skilled people, and they will be able to demand changes to meet their own needs'.

■ IMPLICATIONS FOR EMPLOYERS

In Chapters 6 and 9 we specifically discuss policies organisations may choose to introduce in order to help employees combine family and work commitments. In this chapter, we will simply draw out the principal implications of the changing attitudes that we have outlined above.

Working hours

In the United Kingdom, we seem to believe that it is necessary to work 60-hour weeks in order to be a competent manager. The UMIST survey discussed earlier, found that British managers worked 'always' or 'frequently' at weekends. The exceptions in Europe were the Germans: they worked less than anybody else at the weekend, and had more outside work interests. This indicates that it is perhaps not a valid indicator to judge managers on input rather than output.

Balance is the key word. There is a growing realisation of the importance of leisure and time spent outside work to working peoples' health. Putting in 12-hour days, with long journeys at either end of the day, may help people believe that they are valued and are keeping up with their peers, but this clearly puts a strain on their health. Many people are recognising that it does them and their organisations no good at all if they are constantly under pressure from work. As Professor Cary Cooper puts it:

> *'Forty-year-olds now want to spend more time with their families than those who set the pace in their fifties and sixties. They have seen too many colleagues burnt out or having heart attacks, and they have a healthier attitude to work which is going to make their companies healthier.'*

Flexible working

The Government is becoming increasingly aware that employers need to take steps to help employees balance home and work respon-sibilities. In the summer of 1991, the Secretary of State for Employ-ment, Michael Howard, said at an employment conference that

> *'Employers should tailor jobs they offer to fit in more with their workers' life-styles.'*

In announcing a new Employment Department guide to flexible employment, he said

> *'Family-friendly policies are a means of enabling any employee, male or female, to balance his or her commitments.'*

This message echoes the conclusions in the NEDO RIPA publication 'Women Managers: The Untapped Resource'. This suggests that current managerial careers often make unreasonable demands on men as well as women, and as long as complete geographical mobility, and continuous full-time employment remain as unquestioned assumptions, organisations will lose out on scarce talent.

Signs of change

Some enlightened organisations are moving ahead and responding to these changing values. British Petroleum includes the following in its statement of values to its employees:

> *'We encourage our employees to strike a balance between their responsibilities to BP and their home life.'*

Kent County Council was recently cited by an employee as having the positive attitude that if the employee is committed and conscientious, there is no need to work 'ridiculously long hours'. The Council wanted people to be fresh, rather than overworked and stressed.

British Home Stores introduced term-time working into its 137 branches in January 1992. Eighteen months ago the company dropped its mobility clause from all staff contracts, as this seemed to prevent married women with children getting promoted. As a direct consequence, the number of female store managers dramatically increased.

■ CONCLUSION

In this chapter we have looked at some of the historical reasons why there has been a clash between old and new views about work and the family. What is clear is that the status quo is being questioned and challenged, by working men and women, and that the expectations for a more sensible balance between home and work will grow as younger people put further pressure on the system.

In this new era, organisations will need to be adept at developing the so-called psychological contract. This is defined by Peter Herriot as:

> *'an agreement by organisation and employee based on each party's expectations of the other at any particular point in time.'*

47

The psychological contract is not explicit, and it has no status in law, but in the tight labour markets of the future it is the strength of the psychological contract that matters.

The labour market changes make equal opportunities a business issue, the changing attitudes to work and family make it absolutely vital that organisations look again at this topic.

Chapter 4

A REDEFINITION – FROM EQUALITY TO DIVERSITY

In the Introduction we argued that despite more than 15 years of equal opportunities legislation, little has fundamentally changed. In general, employers have embraced the letter, not the spirit, of the law.

In our view, we have an opportunity now to take a very different approach. The changes that we have outlined in the previous two chapters – both in the labour market and in attitudes to the work/home balance – provide a powerful incentive to employers to look again at what we know as equal opportunities. Instead of looking at it as something that is imposed on them from outside, by for example legislation, employers will find competitive advantage in encouraging diversity at work.

This fundamental shift in perspective brings with it a wholly different set of operating principles that will make more rapid change not only possible, but also inevitable.

It is this shift and these principles that we will discuss in this chapter. In summary, an equal opportunities programme becomes:

- Internally driven, not externally imposed
- Focused on individuals not groups
- Concerned with diversity, rather than equality
- Addressing the total culture, not just the systems
- The responsibility of all, not just personnel

We will explore each of these areas in turn. Taken together, however, we believe that they add up to a fundamentally different approach to this issue.

■ INTERNALLY DRIVEN, NOT EXTERNALLY IMPOSED

Equal opportunities has, in the main, been seen as something which has been imposed on employers. For some, it has been about doing something for 'them' at the expense of 'us'.

The law enshrined the moral case for equal opportunity. Employers had a responsibility to help create a fair and equal society. If they failed to do so, then they could end up in court. Somehow or other, there seemed to be a whiff of confrontation about it all.

The moral (or political) case was most warmly embraced by local authorities. To them, it was obvious that they served their communities and equal opportunities was a value that should be enshrined in the way they operated. They saw the example of the United States, and became enthusiastic advocates of contract compliance. This only seemed to reinforce in other employers' minds that equal opportunities was an external issue: something to be supported in principle but resisted in practice.

Another aspect of the same thinking was the proliferation of legalistic equal opportunities policy statements. It was important to be 'seen' to be doing the right thing. A policy statement was for public consumption, internally it was, at best, in the 'pending' tray.

We know, however, that imposed change is likely to be resisted and causes a 'backlash'. Equal opportunities programmes which relied upon the law and ethics were primarily externally driven and hence 'imposed'. We should not have been surprised that equal opportunities was seen to be the province of the 'looney left' and that we ended up with legislation in the late 1980s which restricted the enthusiasm of the local authorities. The issue was being tackled from the wrong end.

The shift that was necessary was one away from external drivers, towards internal *economic and business* ones. There is an ethical argument for equal opportunities. It is these principles which led to the legislation being enacted in the first place. There is also, however, an unquestionable economic and business case for change.

The projected need for skills and the sheer number of women and ethnic minorities who will be qualifying over the next few years and entering the work force, will mean that the labour market will dictate the need to review recruitment methods. Practical business sense will mean that organisations will need to widen the recruitment pool to include 'non-traditional recruits'. The truth is, young white men are in the minority.

Moreover, because the labour market is tight, employees will be in a powerful bargaining position. People who find that their careers are blocked by out-dated prejudices will simply leave and join the competition. In addition, employees will be in this more powerful position just at the time that they are increasingly challenging the traditional trade-offs between home and work.

There is an internal momentum that means employers have to take these aspirations seriously. Women and minorities are not transient features of the labour market – they are increasing their representation among those potential recruits with the appropriate skills. Inevitably, they will be recruited in greater numbers, and as existing employees change their attitudes, an irresistible force for change builds up.

In this way, equal opportunities will shift from being imposed on organisations for external political, ethical or legal reasons and will become driven by the economic and business needs of the organisation itself. It will no longer be about being a 'good employer' and will instead have everything to do with long-term survival.

■ FOCUSED ON INDIVIDUALS NOT GROUPS

One of the consequences of the emphasis placed on external influences was that organisational change in this area simply mirrored the structure of the legislative changes. The law defined discrimination by defining its causes – for instance, prejudice against women or minorities – and so did employers. The law established two 'single issue' Commissions and so employers looked at discrimination against these groups. Discrimination was not something to tackle 'holistically' in the round, it was about achieving parity between groups. The very term '*equal* opportunities' seemed to lend its weight to this interpretation.

The danger associated with tackling the issue piecemeal, one group at a time, is that one group, often women, receives a great deal of attention and little thought is given, for instance, to people with disabilities, ethnic minorities or older people. Moreover, equal opportunities seems to be no longer about fundamental principles (such as appointing the best person for the job) but is instead seen as 'special pleading' for minority groups.

'Tokenism' follows directly from this approach. Recruiting and developing members of a minority group becomes an end in itself. This has been a particular feature of experience in the United States, where managers would boast of their equal opportunities performance. Recruiting a black female became colloquially known as a 'twofor'. This meant two points for one recruit: one because she was female and another because she was black.

51

In reality, what is important is focusing on the individual rather than the group. From a selection point of view, the important thing about a female recruit is not that she is a woman, but whether she has the skills to do the job. Putting people into 'boxes', seeing them as representatives of a particular group rather than as one particular individual, is profoundly counter-productive.

The need is for objective selection systems to be in place and applied. This will be to the benefit of everyone in the organisation: it is as much to the advantage of the white male that selection decisions are made on the basis of skill, as it is to any member of any so-called minority group. As many men lose out as women when decisions are made on the basis of who you know rather than what you know.

In essence, if organisations can ensure that they are able to treat individuals fairly and they are able to respond flexibly to individual needs, then they do not need to worry about groups. Equal opportunities should look after itself.

■ DIVERSITY RATHER THAN EQUALITY

When the focus is on individuals rather than groups, then there is a corresponding shift away from equality towards diversity.

Every individual is, by definition, unique. The organisations that will succeed in the future are those that can harness this human diversity to advantage. The focus is not on equalising the differences between groups, but on responding to individual needs and aspirations.

Once again, we find the term 'equal opportunities' unhelpful. 'Equal' seems to suggest that everyone should receive exactly the same treatment. This can be interpreted as meaning: 'they' have to fit in with the way 'we' do things. In other words, women and minorities are free to join us, we will make all decisions based on merit, but we insist on them conforming to our 'norms'. Women therefore felt obliged to dress in severe suits and to be tougher than the men. Black people had to laugh along at the office 'banter' in order to show that they did not have a chip on their shoulder.

Therefore, despite the increasing representation of women in managerial positions, there was no change in the prevailing attitude to work and family commitments. In order to succeed, women simply limited their outside commitments – as we highlighted earlier, women managers were less likely to be married and to have children than their male colleagues.

Diversity is the opposite to all of this. Instead of trying to eliminate differences, it positively welcomes them. After all, the more diverse the individuals within an organisation, the greater the potential for creative problem solving. Moreover, the so-called 'male' management style, adept at working in hierarchical structures, may not be best suited to the changing organisational environment. For instance, gaining commitment across departments and managing cross-functional teams requires the 'softer' interpersonal skills often associated with a 'female' management style.

We should not deny that individuals are different and therefore have different strengths and different needs. In itself, therefore, simply ensuring that there are objective decision-making processes in place is insufficient. If an organisation is really concerned with diversity rather than just equality, then it needs to look at its total culture – not just its systems.

■ TOTAL CULTURE NOT JUST THE SYSTEMS

The question therefore is not: 'Which of the rules need reviewing?' but: 'Is this the game we should be playing?'

Unless the overall culture is responsive to different needs, then progress will be very limited. Recruits might be selected from non-traditional sources, but they will not stay if they do not feel they can succeed.

If 'blue' jokes are still the order of the day at the office party, then will women (and increasingly some men) actually believe that this is the organisation for them? If access to the building represents a series of obstacles, will wheelchair users feel welcomed? If being black is still all that people notice about ethnic minorities, will they feel that they can develop long-term careers? If 'fitting in' is what matters, how responsive is the organisational culture to individual needs?

The most obvious challenge to the traditional organisational culture is the increasing importance that people are putting on their lives outside work. As we saw in the previous chapter, men as well as women are beginning to challenge some of the more out-dated shibboleths:

'If promotion depends upon 60-hour weeks and continuous geographic mobility then count me out'.

In earlier days, child rearing was dismissed as the 'woman's problem'. The UK Government is still resisting parental leave (which

53

would be three months available to either father or mother) but society has moved on. Many fathers will want to play an active role in bringing up their children, just as some women will decide not to have children. Yet, as was pointed out in the NEDO and RIPA report, there is a clash between the life-cycles of the typical managerial career and the typical family.

> *'If the pacing of managerial careers poses problems for women, it should also be said that it also poses problems for men. They are expected to have bound-less energy and commitment at work at a time when they have young families.'*

The reality is that, at different times in their careers, employees will have different needs to balance work and family commitments. With the tight labour market for skills, the successful organisation of the future is the organisation that can adapt to and meet these changing needs.

If an organisation is committed to equal opportunities, then it is not enough to review the current systems and check that they are 'fair'. It means taking a hard look at the organisation and ensuring that it supports cultural diversity rather than a mono-culture.

■ THE RESPONSIBILITY OF ALL NOT JUST PERSONNEL

Perhaps it speaks for itself that if an equal opportunities programme is about organisational culture, then there is a responsibility upon everyone in the organisation to help make it happen.

Earlier, when equal opportunities was seen to be purely about meeting legal requirements and getting the systems right, it seemed to be the natural province of the personnel department. As far as the average white male was concerned, it was not something he had – or wanted – to make happen.

The consequence of this, naturally, was 'lip service'. Managers would mouth the words, but they knew that this was really for public consumption. Even where organisations began to take actions and introduce policies such as Career Break schemes, people did not believe it was for 'real'. After all, in some ways a Career Break scheme hardly challenges the division between home and work, it could be seen to actually reinforce it. The message is: 'Come back to us when you're ready to join us full-time.

We should not be surprised, therefore, that a recent survey found that equal opportunities officers were among the most stressed at work. They must have felt that they were taking on the rest of the organisation! The last thing that an equal opportunities programme needs is one person to be given total responsibility for it. If it is to have any chance of success, then responsibility must be seen to be at the individual level across the whole organisation. Only in that way is sustained change a real possibility.

This wider 'ownership' for equal opportunities becomes possible once the issue is seen as a business issue – essentially about ensuring that the organisation has the skills it needs to grow and develop. At this point, it must be a concern for the whole management team. Moreover, once it is seen to be about organisational culture as well as systems, then everyone has a role to play. The immediate colleagues of a new recruit are as important as the manager. Suddenly, change is not something that only personnel are concerned with, it affects every employee. Equal opportunities is not just about selection decisions it is about creating the appropriate environment so that each individual can fulfill his or her potential.

In time, equal opportunities will therefore not be a topic of controversy and debate. It will not be viewed as something in favour of minorities and against whites. It will, however, be normal to be different and equal opportunities principles will be integrated into the values of organisations.

■ CONCLUSION

So, to summarise, the equal opportunities programme of the future will be:

- Internally driven, not externally imposed
- Focused on individuals not groups
- Concerned with diversity, rather than equality
- Addressing the total culture, not just the systems
- The responsibility of all, not just personnel

There is a logical flow between these pairs of characteristics. Once equal opportunities is seen to be internally driven rather than implementing legislation, then it can be seen to be about meeting individual rather than group needs. Once it is seen to be about individual needs, then clearly it must be concerned with cultural diversity rather than equality between groups. At this point, it must be about organisational culture rather than just systems and therefore the responsibility of all, not just personnel.

In our view, it is absolutely fundamental that equal opportunities is seen to be business driven. So long as equal opportunities was equated simply with complying with legislation, then it was always going to be about group parity, and getting the numbers 'right'. This was a recipe for inertia and, over the last 15 years, this is pretty much what we have experienced.

We have attempted in Part 1 of this book to present what we believe are some of the business incentives for taking equal opportunities seriously. With these in mind, we can then go on to Part 2, which is concerned with building the business case for change and describes ways in which organisations can create diversity at work. Our starting point is that the redefinition of equal opportunities that we have outlined in this chapter has itself made it possible to approach the topic in a wholly new (and more productive) way.

Part 2

ACHIEVING CHANGE

Chapter 5

A STRATEGIC APPROACH TO EQUAL OPPORTUNITIES

We have argued in the preceding chapter that equal opportunities needs to be redefined. One consequence of this is that it makes it possible to manage an equal opportunities programme in a rather different way.

Once equal opportunities is no longer seen to be about winning 'rights' for the minorities at the expense of the majority, then it is possible to conceive of a broad-ranging change programme which has the support of the whole organisation. Once equal opportunities ceases to be seen as something that is imposed upon the organisation by external forces, then it can be seen to be a 'business' requirement, deserving active commitment. In effect, equal opportunities becomes a major change programme, just like Total Quality Management, and it represents just as much of a challenge to integrate it into the organisation's culture.

If this is indeed the case, and we would argue that it must be in order to take full advantage of the business benefits available, then an equal opportunities programme must be managed strategically. It is no good looking for 'quick fixes' or launching a random series of initiatives, there needs to be a coherent, long-term strategy.

The purposes of this chapter are:

(1) to put the case for managing equal opportunities strategically and
(2) to outline our own approach.

Accordingly we have split the themes into these two parts. First we will tackle:

- What is meant by strategy?
- Strategy and equal opportunities
- The need for a strategic approach

We will then:

- Introduce our strategic approach and define each of its five stages
- Explore the interrelationships between the stages

In the following five chapters we will then explore each of these stages in more depth. In the final chapter of Part 2 of this book, we will bring these themes together as we consider how to manage an equal opportunities programme in order to sustain its momentum. Only by doing this will an organisation really integrate equal opportunities into its culture.

■ WHAT IS STRATEGY?

Strategy is a much used word in organisations, and can become rather downgraded to mean 'any piece of planning'.

The etymology of the word is military, in which field it means: 'planning to ensure that the place, time, and conditions (in the case of warfare), are imposed or chosen by oneself'. One of the characteristics of strategy as we use it, taken from this military legacy, is, therefore, that it means the choice of approach to an issue or event. This is opposed to being buffeted about by changing events and coping as best one can.

A strategic approach to an organisational issue implies making measured progress towards predetermined and agreed aims, as opposed to reacting to the latest 'flavour of the month' and developing a policy 'on the hoof'.

Having a strategy means that discussions about *principle* take place firstly at a senior level and secondly early in the process before decisions are made about particular *practices*. This establishes firm foundations upon which to build for the future. If there is a strategy in place, based upon clear principles and supported by senior management, it should not be necessary to have continual 'battles' each time a new initiative is proposed. It should be possible to have the principle debate once, and thereafter for discussion to revolve around practicalities of proposals rather than whether they are a good idea in principle.

What this amounts to is spending more time at the initial stages in order to save time later. A strategy involves spending time achieving understanding and agreement so that a map can be drawn up, by which an organisation can navigate itself. In this way a carefully articulated strategy can reduce a programme's dependence upon key individuals. The map can continue to be a guide, whoever happens to be in charge.

A strategy represents a conscious choice, made by senior management, about how to tackle a particular issue and what the ultimate destination is. It should put people within an organisation in a position whereby they can make decisions about issues as they arise based on some clearly established principles.

■ STRATEGY AND EQUAL OPPORTUNITIES

Although putting together a business strategy is commonplace for most organisations, strategic thinking has not traditionally been applied to managing equal opportunities. This issue has been approached, with a very few exceptions, as a one-off initiative, often as a reaction to a particular problem, with a short time-span.

Not surprisingly, equal opportunities has therefore been the province of the personnel department and relatively starved of resources.

In fact equal opportunities, as we shall see, desperately needs to be managed strategically. Because it can represent a significant challenge to the existing culture, an equal opportunities programme needs to build support from a wide range of people across the organisation in order to stand a chance of making any progress at all. Without a conscious strategy in place there is no vehicle for rallying this support and focusing effort.

The nearest parallel is with project management. Here a group of people from across an organisation are brought together in order to develop a project and bring it in on time, to specific standards, on budget. The project may well run over a number of years and it will be absolutely vital to have a project strategy in place so that resources can be allocated and decisions taken at the right time. This is even more so for equal opportunities, which is a project that spans the whole organisation and has a longer time-scale.

■ THE NEED FOR A STRATEGIC APPROACH

There follows below a summary of the benefits available and the pitfalls to be avoided, if an organisation adopts a strategic approach to the introduction of equal opportunities.

Equal opportunities linked to the business

In order to develop a strategy, people first of all need to decide where they are heading. A strategic approach ensures that at the start of a programme there is an assessment of how equal opportunities supports the business objectives. Then, clear aims can be set for an equal opportunities programme. Instead of being seen as a specialist topic, to be dealt with in isolation from business needs, equal opportunities becomes like any other major change programme – Total Quality Management, or Customer Care – a means to particular organisational ends. It is not an end in itself.

Leading from the top

It will not be a topic left to middle managers or 'personnel', but will receive the real commitment of the top of the organisation. Because they are required to set the strategy, the top team will be tied in from the start, and will see that they have a critical role to play, both as role models for the rest of the organisation, and in setting direction and reviewing progress. This support and commitment from the top remains one of the most critical prerequisites to a successful programme.

Pulling the right levers – directing effort

As with any change programme, a deliberate channelling of organisational effort is needed to make progress. A strategy ensures that this effort is being directed at the areas that are priorities for the organisation at that time. Any investment made will be reviewed with these priorities in mind, and a particular 'lever' can be pulled to shift the emphasis from one area to another and keep an overall balance. The alternative of firing hopeful 'shots in the dark' is all very well, but the shots may well miss their target.

Coherent direction

Rather than a series of separate initiatives which, in the minds of employees, seem to be unrelated, there will be a coherent programme of actions which link back to the strategic direction set at the start of the process. Initiatives will be seen to have a logical base, and come about as a result of an identified business need, rather than someone's personal perception that there is a need. Above all else, a strategy should provide coherence.

Proactive not reactive

Without a strategy, issues can appear to come 'out of the wood-work'. All of a sudden, there is a shortfall of middle managers, because some of them have left, having given up the unequal struggle to balance career and home. Or, the company finds itself being taken to court by a disgruntled applicant. With a strategy, the organisation should be ahead of the game. A strategic approach should mean that potential problem areas are brought to light, before they develop into real problems.

Broad-based support

In many organisations the progress of equal opportunities heavily depends on a small number of nominated officers, trying to bring about monumental changes on their own. Not only is this an unrealistic way of seeking to bring about change, it also means the programme grinds to a halt if the equal opportunities officer leaves. An additional disadvantage is that the programme runs the risk of being highly influenced by a personal agenda.

A more business-like strategic approach avoids these problems. Taking the parallel with project management again, the so-called project manager may well have some resource and budget, but he or she will need to bring people in from different departments and gain their support. Together, they can develop an agreed strategy and this provides the framework for further broadening the level of support.

Conclusion

These, then, are the benefits we see that accrue from embracing a strategic approach. As will be plainly evident from these arguments it is our view that the redefinition outlined in the previous chapter actually *demands* a strategic approach. The benefits that we have listed here are an integral part of how we see equal opportunities in the future. It must be: integrated into the business, led by the senior management, targeted to the achievement of particular objectives, proactive rather than reactive, and broadly supported throughout the organisation. All these things depend upon equal opportunities being managed strategically.

■ OUR STRATEGIC APPROACH

As illustrated in Figure 5.1, there are five stages to our strategic approach. We have developed this model empirically, as we have

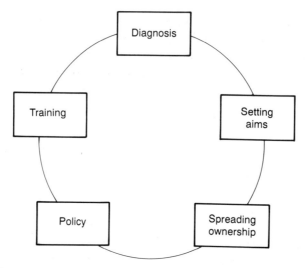

Figure 5.1   A strategic approach

worked with organisations helping them to manage equal opportunities programmes, but the influence of mainstream OD thinking
is fairly clear.

We have started with the standard OD model – identifying the
'current state' (or State A) and then the 'desired state' (or State B) –
and called the first stage 'diagnosis' and the second stage 'setting
aims'. With these definitions in place, and some idea of the extent of
the change in mind, organisations can then turn their attention to
how they can make the transition from the 'current state' to the
'desired state'.

We see three separate strands of activity: 'spreading ownership'
'policy development' and 'training'. Spreading ownership is a continuous activity, it begins with the launch of the programme and
remains a central feature throughout the life of the programme. Both
policy development and training initiatives are more focused tools.
They can be, and should be, targeted to meet specific needs. We
would envisage that they would form the content of both
organisation-wide and departmental action plans.

In what follows, we will describe each stage in more detail.

Diagnosis

This is an essential first step in the strategy. Conducting a diagnosis,
means working in three areas: analysing the statistical profile of the

organisation, reviewing the personnel policies against legal requirements and best practice, and holding discussions with a cross-section of employees to gain an impression of the organisational culture. In this way a diagnosis can clarify the 'current state' of equal opportunities in the organisation. It specifically aims to:

- Look at the facts as well as the opinions
- Highlight the areas where changes are needed
- Establish a starting point, from which to measure progress.

Setting aims

With the current state clear, it is then possible to establish the 'desired state'. This task must lie with senior management because they are in the best position to link equal opportunities with the overall business goals. By setting some aims for equal opportunities they should be able to:

- Convey a 'vision' of what equal opportunities means for everyone in the organisation
- Identify the business purposes for pursuing equal opportunities
- Establish standards against which progress can be measured.

Spreading ownership

To be successful an equal opportunities programme requires behavioural change from people at all levels in the organisation and this requires active and willing support from the majority of people in the organisation. We call this process 'spreading ownership'. It does not happen by chance and the process is best initiated by running a series of workshops, involving everyone in the organisation. By spreading ownership in this way, it is possible to:

- Advance beyond lip service to actual changes in behaviour
- Ensure equal opportunities enters the organisational bloodstream
- Gain input to the policy development process.

Policy development

This stage draws on information from the preceding stages. It depends upon the diagnosis to reveal the potential problems, the declared business aims to focus attention, and the process of spreading ownership to provide policy makers with a ream of practical proposals. Policy proposals should feature in both organisation-wide and departmental action plans. The aims at this stage are to develop policies that can:

- Improve the personnel systems, so that the best people are recruited, developed and rewarded
- Create a supportive environment so that all employees can develop their full potential.

Training

Again, just as with policy development, training depends upon the preceding stages in order to identify which initiatives to put in place.  Well-designed training programmes can help people manage the transition from one way of doing things to another. Again, training initiatives should feature in both organisation-wide and departmental action plans. Training can:

- Help minorities to compete on an equal basis
- Help managers apply selection and development policies effectively
- Equip people with the skills to manage diversity.

■ THE INTERRELATIONSHIPS BETWEEN THE STAGES

The sequence

We have dealt with the five stages of our strategic approach in a particular order because we believe this is the sequence in which they are best tackled.

Where else is it sensible to start if not with a diagnosis? Until there are firm facts, everything else is opinion, and a dangerous basis upon which to act. It is only with some sense of where one is, that one can sensibly plan where one would like to go.

Does it make sense to 'set sail' without first deciding where the ship is? The process of setting aims is dependent upon the diagnosis, but must precede policy and training initiatives. Not only does it help to decide which initatives to develop, it also ensures that the senior management have agreed the principles before they are being asked to agree particular proposals.

How can any initiative succeed unless the organisation has been prepared to receive it? Policies will be policies on paper only. Equal opportunities is not something that can be imposed on people, because it is so easy to find ways of tacitly blocking progress. Yet, the process of spreading ownership cannot really start until there are some programme aims which are based on real business needs. Only then will it be possible for people to 'buy in' to the programme and see what is in it for them, and the organisation. Therefore, the stage of initiating wider 'ownership' needs to be positioned after the stage of setting aims and before the policy and training stages.

At this point in the life of an equal opportunities programme, we believe it is possible to generate a series of action plans – and it is at this stage that the policy and training initiatives fit in. At the top of the structure, there would be an organisation-wide action plan. This would include policy or training proposals that need to be managed across the whole organisation. There would then be a series of action plans generated by each of the departments, which would contain local policy and training initiatives.

Policy development and training are therefore the last two stages of our strategic approach and, in this case, they do not need to be tackled in sequence. Indeed, they are probably best addressed together as part of a combined approach to a particular issue. For example, at the same time that the recruitment policy is reviewed, it would be sensible to review and run some training courses for those involved in the selection process.

In our view, one of the causes of the failure of equal opportunities programmes to date is that many have jumped straight in at the policy development and training stages without doing the necessary preparation. We call this solution-oriented thinking: the 'We've got a Career Break so we must be an equal opportunities employer' syndrome. Where managers are so used to problem solving, the temptation is to throw a solution at the issue so that the next problem can be addressed. A strategic approach offers a framework within which to channel this energy to the appropriate issues at the appropriate time.

A cyclical model

Certainly there is a sequence to our strategic approach, but it is also a cyclical model. It is not the end of the programme when the training stage is reached. As we describe in Chapter 11, the programme manager will be monitoring the impact of the various action plans and their associated policy and training initatives. At some point it will then be important to conduct a second diagnosis – maybe in order to take account of a significant change in the business environment, or maybe simply to re-focus effort after the completion of the initial action plans.

This second diagnosis, therefore, takes the organisation back into a second cycle of the strategic approach. On the basis of the information from the diagnosis, new programme aims may be set and new action plans devised to help make the transition from this 'current state' to the new 'desired state'.

In this way, an equal opportunities programme is not a one-off event. It is a continually evolving programme that is designed to help the organisation achieve particular business needs. Embracing equal opportunities means embracing a continual process of change.

Cycles within cycles

At the risk of added complexity, we would also offer our strategic approach as a tool during the stage where organisations are putting their action plans together.

It is probably most helpful to illustrate this with a typical example:

Diagnosis: A review of applicants for engineering vacancies in a particular company reveals that only 5 per cent come from women.

Setting aims: The aim is to increase the total number of quality candidates. Within this overall aim, it is hoped to increase the proportion of applicants, and recruits, from women to 10 per cent (this vacancy) and to 25 per cent (within three years).

Spreading ownership: All those involved in the recruitment process, including the advertising agency, are invited to a meeting to discuss the situation and put forward ideas for achieving the stated aims.

Policy development: In the light of the recommendations from the meeting, a specification of the skills required for the job is drawn up and a positive action advertisement drafted. The selection procedure is reviewed and panel interviews are introduced.

Training: Interviewers go through a three-day selection skills course. With an eye to the longer term, the company offers sponsorship for women to attend an engineering course at a local college.

Diagnosis: Response to the advertisement leads to an overall increase in applications of 50 per cent. The proportion of women applying rose to 15 per cent. Of those eventually recruited, 10 per cent were women.

In other words, in order to tackle any particular issue there will need to be some sort of activity at each stage of the strategic approach, hence our title 'cycles within cycles'. It acts as a tool to ensure that all aspects of a problem are being examined.

■ **CONCLUSION**

In this chapter we have argued that a strategic approach to equal opportunities is not only desirable, but essential if organisations are to realise the potential business benefits. We have introduced the five stages of our strategic approach and indicated how the stages relate one to another. In the chapters that follow we will explore each of these stages in turn and then return to consider how to manage the overall programme in the final chapter of Part 2 of this book. Here, we will show how an equal opportunities programme manager can use the various stages of our strategic approach to ensure that sustained progress is achieved.

Chapter 6

DIAGNOSIS – DEFINING THE STARTING POINT

Should we go to the doctor, complaining about a persistent symptom, for example a stomach ache, we hope that he or she conducts a proper diagnosis before making out a prescription. This will be done by asking pertinent questions about symptoms, lifestyle, and carrying out an examination before drawing conclusions about the causes of the illness.

There are many possible causes for the same symptom, and the effectiveness of the treatment depends upon identifying the particular cause. If the pain in the patient's right leg is caused by a sprain, then a resumption of exercise can aid recovery. This would hardly be the case if the leg were broken. The same is, of course, true of organisational life. Unless we are clear about the real causes of a problem, all our solutions are, at best, inspired shots in the dark. In general, however, organisations in the United Kingdom have approached equal opportunities without conducting a full diagnosis.

For instance, to great acclaim, organisations have announced the introduction of 'career break' policies, pronounced themselves 'equal opportunities' employers, and then been confounded by the fact that the representation of women at management level has remained remarkably static. Bandaging a cut, however, will not be enough to revive a patient who is suffering from internal bleeding! Organisational life is a good deal more complex than we give it credit for, and we are apt to address the surface issues, without necessarily seeing those that lie beneath. There has been much 'solution-oriented thinking'. Perhaps due to a creditable desire to *do* something concrete and get something going, people latch on to potential solutions. They are clear about the 'whats' but not necessarily the 'whys'. In their haste, however, they may end up taking two steps back for every three they move forward.

This chapter, therefore, is concerned with

- Explaining what we mean by an equal opportunities diagnosis and providing a framework
- Highlighting the benefits of conducting a diagnosis, and the parallel risks run if no diagnosis takes place
- Illustrating the sorts of issues and causes that should be explored in a diagnosis: looking at the statistics, personnel policy framework and the prevailing culture

■ EQUAL OPPORTUNITIES DIAGNOSIS: A FRAMEWORK

One of the main symptoms associated with the lack of equal opportunities within an organisation is relatively easy to see – the skewed distribution of women and minorities in many organisations is fairly self-evident. The causes, however, will vary from one organisation to another, as will the type and extent of the problem. Indeed, it is quite possible for an organisation to have made considerable progress with attracting women to work for them, but have done very little to help them progress. At the same time, it is quite common for the same organisation to have revised their recruitment procedures without even considering whether they could do something to increase the number of applications from ethnic minorities.

Furthermore, in reality, things are more complex than this and some of the symptoms are not quite so immediately evident, and require further information and discussion. An organisation could be progressively helping the well recognised 'minorities' succeed, while actively discriminating on the grounds of age. Does this mean that they are an 'equal opportunities employer'?

Clearly, there is a need for a framework which is able to identify issues systematically and help managers gain a better appreciation of the scope of equal opportunities. It cannot be switched on or off – on for one group, but off for another – it has to be more integrated than that. An equal opportunities diagnosis is the tool we use to help organisations assess how far they are towards being an 'equal opportunities employer'.

Working with clients we have identified three areas that need to be included in any diagnosis:

(1) the statistics;
(2) the personnel policy framework;
(3) the prevailing culture.

There is an obvious interplay between the three areas and we have found that they are best worked through in this order, with each area of inquiry identifying more issues to be explored at the next.

They start with a firm quantitative foundation – for instance, hard information about the profile of the organisation – and become progressively more open and qualitative.

Statistical information

This can be very powerful because, above all, it provides the hard facts. To take the most obvious example, there may be all sorts of reasons why the representation of women among managers is so low in the United Kingdom, but what cannot be denied is that it is low.

On their own, however, statistics can lead to oversimplification. Over 30 years, the focus in the United States on 'the numbers', and the associated use of quotas for minority groups, has caused a certain amount of progress. It has left, however, significant areas unaddressed. Only more recently are some of the policy issues (such as childcare) and cultural issues (such as managing diversity) being worked. Moreover, in themselves, statistics seldom provide sufficient information upon which to base judgements and follow-up actions. Numerical goals set in the absence of a wider diagnosis, lead only too easily to positive discrimination.

Personnel policy framework

Exploring this can begin to make some sense of the figures. Traditional recruiting patterns, for example, can severely limit applications. If apprenticeships are limited to sons of fathers, what chance ethnic minorities? Or, as emerged in a large public sector employer, should managers have been surprised that many women did not apply for promotion, when the policy was to post vacancy notices in the gents?

Prevailing culture

Perhaps the most significant piece in the jigsaw. Whatever policies are in place, they rely on people to implement them and people are inevitably influenced by the working culture that surrounds them. Certain patterns of behaviour are accepted as the 'norm' and become, quite simply, the way things are. In one company, women going off on maternity leave were all given a farewell party, complete with fluffy toys, and taken off the payroll. Is it surprising that 80 per cent of those going off on leave in that company did not return to work?

Looking at all three areas – statistics, policies and culture – it is possible to build up a picture of the state of equal opportunities. We believe that progress in all three areas needs to be kept in step. It is all very well having progressive policies, but if there has not also been a supporting shift in organisational culture, the policies will simply not be used. Similarly, a concerted effort may be made to attract more women and minorities into an organisation, but if the policy framework is not in place, or the culture remains hostile, then they will probably fail and leave. Therefore, the diagnosis needs to explore the relationships between progress in these three areas and by so doing may well highlight one particular area where progress is out of step.

Some of the information needed to conduct this sort of diagnosis is readily available. For instance, much of the statistical analysis is relatively straightforward. Most organisations have databases that can identify the distribution of employees between grades. There is also usually a personnel policy manual ready to be inspected and here the formal policies can be found. In order to discover how these policies are actually implemented in practice, however, it is essential to carry out some face-to-face discussions with employees. By providing illustrative detail, these discussions are the main vehicle for exploring an organisation's culture, and therefore making sure that any actions address the core, rather than the peripheral, issues.

■ BENEFITS OF CONDUCTING A DIAGNOSIS

In Table 6.1 we have highlighted the benefits of conducting a comprehensive diagnosis and contrasted them with the risks facing organisations which ignore this stage.

■ A DIAGNOSIS: ISSUES AND CAUSES TO BE EXPLORED

As suggested earlier in the chapter, in order to carry out a full diagnosis, there are three areas to explore: the statistics, the personnel policy framework and the prevailing culture. In the remainder of the chapter, we explore each of these areas in more detail and provide examples of the sorts of issues that should be explored.

Table 6.1 Diagnosis

Benefits of diagnosis	Risks without diagnosis
• Provides the hard facts	• Plenty of room for opinion
• Identifies causes, not symptoms	• Work on 'gut feel'
• Identifies business costs	• No business logic for change
• Policies that meet real neeeds	• Hit and miss policy development
• Tool to keep progress in step	• Running before you can walk
• Establishes a starting point	• Difficult to measure progress

■ LOOKING AT THE STATISTICS

Statistics provide the best starting point. Without some fairly basic information it is impossible to draw reliable conclusions. For this reason, we believe that it is essential that organisations are able to monitor not only on the basis of sex, but also for ethnic origin and disability. These are not the only people who suffer discrimination, but their situation may well identify the need for actions which will have universal benefits.

If organisations do not already have information on ethnic origin and disability, then – in our view – this is best gathered by asking people to self-certify. Providing sufficient time is put in to explaining the purposes for gathering this information, it should be relatively easy to get a high level of returns. Now that most people have answered a question about ethnic origin in the National Census, perhaps organisations will be less squeamish about asking their employees for this information.

Looking at the statistics: the current profile

A good starting point is to draw up a profile of the organisation. How many women are employed? How many ethnic minorities? How many disabled? Where are they in the organisation? What does the age profile look like?

These figures can then be compared against both national and local figures, as well as those for similar organisations. (In Chapter 2 we look in detail at how the UK labour market has changed and the direction that this change is taking.) This information, in turn, is likely to generate further questions to explore.

How many women in the organisation are in management grades? Nationally, it is estimated that only 9 per cent of managers are women. This reduces to 3 per cent at senior executive level. How do the male and female grade profiles compare Furthermore, the majority of women who have made it to management tend to be concentrated in 'support' functions and therefore are not eligible for the top jobs. How many are in the high profile, core jobs? Is there a so-called 'glass ceiling' beyond which women do not progress? Comparing male and female grades may also begin to raise questions about equal pay for work of equal value.

An organisation might be relatively pleased with the fact that 12 per cent of its employees come from ethnic minority groups (versus the 5 per cent estimated in the United Kingdom population) but how many are in management or supervisory grades? Again, how satisfactory is this percentage if the organisation is based in Hounslow where there is a high Asian population to recruit from?

There is legislation in the United Kingdom that requires employers to have at least 3 per cent registered disabled among its employees. Very few organisations meet this requirement – not least because many people who could do so choose not to register. A question that might be worth asking of the medical department, however, is: what percentage of employees could register? Again, are they concentrated in the organisational back waters? Low profile jobs where they are not very visible?

Just looking at the age profile can be instructive. In one small financial services organisation, the average age in the clerical functions was well under 30. Not surprisingly, they suffered from relatively high turnover. Not surprisingly, it became apparent during discussions that the managers did not believe that an older person would 'fit in' with their young teams, and were therefore ruling out any applications from candidates over 25 years old.

One final thing to look for (and it is often ignored) is evidence of success. There will be some parts of the organisation that have a more balanced profile than others. They can be very fruitful sources for further exploration: if the causes of success can be identified then there is no reason why they cannot be applied elsewhere in the organisation. We devote the whole of Chapter 12 to an example of such a success.

Looking at the statistics: recruitment, promotions and leavers

It is essential to look at the 'pushes' and the 'pulls' – the recruitment, promotions and leaving trends. How is the current population changing? Who is coming into the organisation? Who is getting promoted? Who is leaving? What is the distribution of performance grades and potential assessments?

The critical question for recruitment campaigns, of course, is the extent to which they mirror the rapidly changing labour market. A good example is the recruitment of graduates from universities and polytechnics. In 1989, 45 per cent of those awarded first degrees were women. Of course, the percentage of women varies according to degree discipline, but it represents a good starting point for organisations looking at the effectiveness of their graduate recruitment campaigns.

Looking at the detail of recruitment campaigns can also be highly instructive and pinpoint the real causes of discrimination. Any campaign can be split into the component parts – developing the job profile, attracting the applicants, short-listing and selecting candidates – and discrimination can occur at each and every stage. Right at the beginning of the process, stressing particular aspects of the job – for instance, the need to work very long hours, or the likelihood of the need to relocate – will put off many otherwise able candidates. Does the job really need to be done in this way, or has it simply always been done like that? Similarly, it is no use training interviewers to be more objective when, for example, the recruitment agency continue to send along almost exclusively white males (because they think that is what is wanted).

Analysis of performance and potential gradings can also highlight some interesting issues. We have increasing evidence which seems to suggest that men and women are awarded similar performance grades, but that the women lose out as far as the assessment of potential is concerned. One of the issues here is that while assessment of performance is relatively closed down (someone has or has not achieved their objectives) the assessment of potential is much more open (with a corresponding increase in the scope for personal 'gut feels'). The thinking seems to be: **'she's** good at her job, but **he's** a safer bet for a long-term career.' Given the profile of most organisations, it is, of course, primarily men who are making these judgements. Perhaps this partly explains the existence of 'glass ceilings'.

Leaving trends may also have a story to tell. If a disproportionate percentage of women and minorities are leaving, why is that? These statistics, coupled with exit interviews (where they happen), can cast significant light upon the prevailing culture within an organisation and, in particular, its ability to tolerate diversity.

Looking at leaving trends can also touch another taboo subject. What is the average age of people retiring? Throughout the 1980s and into the early 1990s, it has been common practice for organisations to slim down, particularly during recessions, by offering attractive terms for employees to retire early. In some organisations, employees know that they are unlikely to last beyond the age of 55. While for some people this is their definition of paradise come early, others may think differently. Is it healthy for organisations to lose all this experience at once? Why should fit and sharp managers retire at an age where their bosses, the directors, reckon they still have another 10 good years?

Looking at the statistics: cost and potential for savings

There is another set of information which is worth exploring: how much is all this costing the organisation? In total quality terms this would be called the 'cost of non-conformance', and just as with quality, many of the costs may be relatively hidden.

In Chapter 7 we will explore examples of the sorts of cost savings that organisations have been realising. Our purpose in this chapter is simply to indicate the sorts of statistical questions that might be helpful in establishing the current costs or potential for savings.

Attrition of young women who leave to have children is an obvious starting point. How many women do not return from maternity leave? How many years service have they put in? How much has it cost to train and develop them? What are the costs associated with recruiting their successors? For each percentage reduction in attrition, how much would this save?

Some organisations remain painfully unaware of their employee profile. Again, in terms of total quality, what are the costs of doing nothing? Significant cost savings became clear to a small financial organisation we worked with who suddenly realised that 44 per cent of all their employees were women aged under 30.

With a combination of the introduction of more flexible options for return (for example, part-time working) and a change in attitude (managers wanting and expecting their people back), attrition due to maternity leave can be dramatically reduced. Typically, this has been reduced from as high as 80 per cent leavers to a complete reversal with about 80 per cent returning. There will always be some women who want to leave their job completely, but it seems that the majority wish to combine in some way having a job and raising a family.

Another cost of 'non-conformance' to high quality policies and practice is the potential legal cost of cases being brought against the organisation or of formal investigations by either of the Commissions.

Financial costs can be significant – while they have not reached the figures attained in the United States (where compensation to some appellants has reached £250,000) the Commission for Racial Equality is currently lobbying to increase the maximum fines from just under £9,000 to £30,000. Of course, the financial cost is only part of the total costs. The cost in management time and the dent in the corporate image are even more damaging.

Looking at the statistics: conclusion

Clearly, gathering statistical information is a highly valuable starting point. It can begin to provide the facts rather than the opinions by:

(1) revealing the current profile of an organisation;
(2) examining the recruitment, promotion and leaving trends; and
(3) establishing costs and potential savings.

Arguing and debating opinion may be interesting but remains pure speculation until the facts are presented. What the statistics can often do is highlight the areas that need further investigation.

■ PERSONNEL POLICY FRAMEWORK

Personnel policy framework: examining the policy documents

If an organisation sets itself the aim of having high quality human resource management, and policies which are up with the best or 'at the leading edge', then in some way or other, equal opportunities needs to be incorporated into the thinking of all personnel policies. If affects employees 'from cradle to grave', from initial application for employment all the way through to retirement.

The intent in this chapter is not to describe these policies in depth – in Chapter 9 we address policy formulation in some detail – but to indicate the sorts of factors that can be taken into account in assessing the current state of equal opportunities within an organisation.

There are two obvious measures for assessing an organisation's personnel policies with regard to equal opportunities: do they meet legal requirements and how do they compare against best practice? In what follows, therefore, we have examples both of things to avoid (policies or procedures that run the risk of being in breach of the law) and things to consider in order to avoid being left behind. In Chapter 9 we will provide detailed examples of best practice, so the discussion here of particular policies is no more than cursory.

Personnel policy framework: equal opportunities policy

An obvious place to start is with the equal opportunities policy. Not all organisations have one, of course, but where they exist, they say a lot about how the issue is regarded. We explore this further in the next chapter.

At one extreme there is the 'we don't discriminate on the grounds of. . .' followed by an exhaustive list of all sorts of groups who could be, or have been in the past, discriminated against. The emphasis is on selection and promotion decision making. Many of the policies developed in the 1970s, as a response to the legislation, were cast in this style. The overriding message is primarily a negative one: we don't discriminate.

At the other extreme, there are the policies that are much more open – there is no list of 'non-discriminates' – and put the emphasis on the right of each individual to fair and equitable treatment. Here policies not only address the selection process but also the sort of day-to-day working environment that should be encouraged. These tend to be more recent policies.

Personnel policy framework: recruitment

Most organisations will have a set of recruitment policies and procedures which grow up over time and may well become outdated.

Many organisations, for example, still have some form of staff introduction scheme. This means that current employees encourage their friends or acquaintances to apply for vacancies. In some companies there is still an unwritten rule that prefers employees' relatives over other external applicants. There can be some short-term savings – for instance in the speed and cost of the recruitment process – but there are longer-term debits. Is it really sensible to close down the potential pool of applicants so greatly? Moreover, both these practices can result in the perpetuation of the existing employee profiles (because we often socialise with people like ourselves) and for this reason were explicitly discouraged in the Codes of Practice issued by the Commissions in the mid 1980s.

In quite deliberate contrast to the staff introduction schemes, a number of leading employers have embarked on 'outreach' programmes in order to attract applications from people who would not normally apply. Some of these have been very successful as discussed in Chapter 9.

The content of an application form can also say a lot about the state of recruitment thinking. Many will still include personal information – such as marital status and number of children – which encourages interviewers to ask potentially discriminatory questions. Conversely, many still do not gather information about the ethnic origin of applicants. If they do not, how can they determine whether they do or do not have a problem attracting and selecting ethnic minorities?

Obviously, a critical part of the recruitment process is being clear about the skills required to perform the role: job descriptions and interview assessment forms give a good indication of the state of this thinking. In a number of organisations, candidate profiles take over from skill profiles. Job descriptions bristle with experience that applicants 'must' have and interview assessment forms record factors such as 'personal circumstances'. In these instances, rather than thinking about the sort of skills required (which is admittedly complex), recruiters think about the sort of track record candidates ought to have. Usually, their starting point is existing employees. Not surprisingly, this reinforces the tendency for like to recruit like: 'If you went to the same school as I did, or play the same sport as I do, then you must be alright.'

Personnel policy framework: combining job and family responsibilities

Gone are the days when employers could disregard the impact of the home on work. As we saw in Chapter 3, women, and increasingly men, expect their employers to help them combine job and family responsibilities.

The most obvious point at which there can be a clash between organisational and domestic lives is in the early years of bringing up children. Some employers have seen this as an inevitable conflict, resigned themselves to the loss of their female employees, and adopted maternity leave provisions that meet the minimum legal requirements. Others have deliberately adopted policies that encourage women to return to work, and we discuss some of these in Chapter 9.

Obviously, maternity leave is itself just a relatively short period and organisations need to think much more long-term than this. For example, much has been made in recent years of the introduction of Career Break Schemes, initially by National Westminster Bank, and subsequently by a vast range of 'blue chip' organisations. Typically, this provides for an employee to take a break from work in order to meet family responsibilities and subsequently return within five years.

Evidence of even more radical thinking is the emergence of many more forms of flexible working contracts: part-time working, job sharing, term-time working, and annual days contracts to name but a few. It has often been family issues that have led employees to seek different patterns of working, and led enlightened employers to welcome them. It should be emphasised that these organisations do not regard their employees on flexible contracts as 'second-class' employees to be exploited. As decisions in the Europe Court are increasingly making clear, part-timers should have equal access to all benefit schemes (in particular pension schemes from which they have traditionally been excluded).

The existence and the extent of flexible working policies are good indicators of the degree to which organisations are genuinely 'putting individuals first' and integrating equal opportunities into the way they work.

If non-standard hours contracts represent one of the greatest challenges to organisational culture, the area that requires the greatest financial commitment is the provision of childcare facilities. In the private sector, Midland Bank have been very publicly leading the way. In Chapter 9 we explore the different options that are available to organisations: from setting up their own crèches, through going into joint partnerships, to issuing childcare vouchers.

There are other issues, however, apart from the raising and looking after children which may bring work and domestic responsibilities into conflict. One of the most obvious of these is the request to an employee to relocate. In years gone by, an employer's request was a command and to deign to refuse a relocation was to wish upon one-self immediate 'career blight'. Values have changed and enlightened employers know they cannot treat employees in isolation; they have to consider their domestic considerations. These days, the need to relocate is itself being questioned, and where it is considered neces-sary, help is offered with managing the resultant domestic issues. This may well involve job counselling (if not job offers) for spouses.

Personnel policy framework: training courses

In Chapter 10, we discuss the sorts of training issues that leading edge organisations are beginning to take into account.

During the diagnosis, the main priority is to see whether (and how) equal opportunities is integrated into the ongoing training courses that are run. To what extent are people helped to put policies into practice? Are interviewers trained, if so is equal opportunities directly addressed? What help is given to managers so that they can meet all the needs expected (by both the organisation and the employees) of the appraisal process?

Positive action – initiatives designed to help those in a minority compete for jobs on equal terms with the majority – may often take the form of providing training courses and this too can be explored at the diagnostic stage. Assertiveness training and language training are two of the more obvious examples.

Personnel policy framework: positive approach to disability

With about 10 per cent of the working age population having a disability that could adversely affect their chances of employment, it is surprising that so few organisations have seriously looked to tap into this potential. Those that have are reaping the rewards of a particularly loyal, hardworking group of employees.

As far as policies are concerned, the first issue to examine is what happens to employees who become disabled – all too frequently they are immediately 'counselled out' of the organisation or the first to go in any cut-backs. Some employers take a more enlightened approach. For example, at Esso every effort was made to redeploy those employees who developed a medical condition that prevented them from continuing to do their job. Seafarers and tanker drivers, for instance, were offered retraining and redeployment to other parts of the company.

The next issue is whether any positive steps are being taken to attract people with disabilities to work for the organisation. The majority of organisations ignore the 3 per cent quota of employees that legislation requires and they do not even bother to apply for an exemption certificate which would enable them to carry on recruiting able-bodied applicants.

Another indicator, of course, is the ease with which people in a wheelchair, for example, are able to get about in the office. While building regulations and local authorities now try to ensure that employers and architects take into account the needs of disabled people when they design new offices, this has not always been the case. The vast majority of buildings present a series of obstacles to be overcome. Moreover, there is the issue of access to information as well as physical access. How do people who are deaf or who have a visual impairment gain access to information? At the most pragmatic level, how do these considerations affect the application form?

Nowadays, there are a number of specialist companies who will carry out audits of office premises in order to identify problems and suggest solutions. Governmental funding can be obtained for making alterations to buildings or purchasing specialised equipment, so making these changes need not send office costs rocketing.

Personnel policy framework: career development and reward systems

It is all very well to have progressive recruitment policies and procedures, but these will be ineffective if the career development and reward systems are unable to identify skills and support the development of each individual's potential − wherever he or she may be in the organisation.

When discussing career development, we frequently hear the phrase: 'It's not what you know it's who you know that matters.' Playing golf with the right people seems to be more important than performance in the job. This may, or may not be the case, but the comment certainly reflects uncertainty about what the criteria are for promotion, and what you have to do in order to get on.

In a real 'equal opportunities' culture, where the best person for the job is appointed, the criteria and procedures for appointment have to be clear and open. Managers will always have personal preferences but good personnel systems will minimise their influence by helping managers to make consistent decisions based on accurate information.

In this regard, an appraisal scheme is a fundamental building block. An organisation needs some way of assessing skills, measuring performance and gaining some input from employees about their aspirations. Because an appraisal scheme can meet these various needs, it also needs to be carefully managed. The manager needs to be 'coach' as well as 'judge'; the danger is that either role becomes the exclusive focus.

In some way or other, the appraisal process needs to be able to meet all these various needs. The paper work needs to reinforce this, and also the way in which the appraisal discussions are conducted.

Equally as important as an appraisal system, at least as far as larger organisations are concerned, is a career planning system. One of the reasons why managers may appoint people they play golf with, is that these are the only people they actually know. Openly circulating vacancy notices is one way of helping overcome this problem – so that anyone who is interested can apply and ensure that they at least get cursory consideration – but it leaves a lot to chance (not least that the manager has not already made up his or her mind and that the interviews are therefore anything more than a sham).

A career planning system provides the missing rigour. It usually consists of two interlocking parts – a critical job plan and personal career plan – and both look over approximately a five-year period. The former ensures that each critical job has a number of people who are fit and able to take over if the designated incumbent falls under the proverbial bus. The latter indicates the potential career moves for the employee and provides for individual input to this form of planning.

Not surprisingly, for it to be effective, career planning requires a great deal of effort from top management. Unless plans are updated they become potentially as discriminatory as any other form of ad hoc decision making. People identified as 'stars' in their early career may go off the boil, while others may be late developers.

Personnel policy framework: equal pay

Appraisal and career planning systems will help ensure a fair deal for each employee within an organisation. In themselves, however, they are unlikely to address any gross historical anomalies. There has been equal pay legislation in the United Kingdom since the 1970s, but women's pay still lags significantly behind men's. Although the legislation is complex, and the process of seeking legal redress inordinately drawn out, organisations are fooling themselves if they believe they can go on ignoring this issue for ever.

Part of any diagnosis of the current state of equal opportunities, therefore, needs to examine the potential for equal pay problems. (After an initial analysis, it may well in fact warrant a full-scale report which a number of specialists are able to carry out.)

In time, we would hope that the traditional issue of equal pay will disappear, along with the traditional division of jobs into men's and women's work.

Meanwhile, the statistical analysis may well throw up issues to be explored. From a policy aspect there are a number of steps that organisations can take to minimise their exposure to legal action.

The first step is to ensure that there is a proper job evaluation system in place – an objective way of deciding which salary grade is appropriate for each job. This means that it needs to be an 'analytical' rather than a 'whole job' evaluation system – in other words, one that breaks each job down into its component parts rather than one that considers the overall job and seeks to compare it with others. The latter allows far too much room for opinionated debate: 'Of course being a warehouseman is a more demanding job than being a secretary.'

Even with an analytical system, however, it can be very easy to weight the various factors in a discriminatory way. If physical strength and working in a hazardous environment are particularly valued, for instance, then it will not be surprising to find men, on average being paid more than women.

It is also quite possible to have a generally robust system, but for people to run it in a discriminatory way. Many companies have a job evaluation committee, ensuring that a number of views can be taken into account when deciding the grade to be awarded to any particular job, but many do not happen to include any women among these assessors. Nor frequently, have those involved, got much idea about equal pay legislation. Perhaps it is not surprising that the legislation has had little discernible impact on the differential between men's and women's pay.

A more recent, but no less significant development in this field of equal pay, is the movement towards equal retirement ages, and pension benefits, for men and women. Many companies have already amended their pension schemes to enable women to carry on working to 65 years of age, thus providing equal retirement ages. There are still, however, wide discrepancies in pension benefits and this may well remain the case so long as the state pension scheme continues to discriminate. The Equal Opportunities Commission, however, is currently taking the Government to court on this very issue and employers may well see some advantages themselves for moving towards a more flexible system that gives both men and women more choice. A flexible decade of retirement – for example, between the ages of 60 and 70 – might make a lot of sense as the number of youngsters coming into the labour market declines and the percentage of older people in society increases.

Personnel policy framework: harassment and disciplinary and grievance procedures

Sexual and racial harassment are an unfortunately common feature of organisational life. It can be extreme – the sort of behaviour that has led to lurid reports in the tabloid press – more often, however, it is subtle and frequently unintentional.

We will examine this issue in more detail when we discuss conducting interviews as part of the diagnosis. From a policy perspective, however, organisations can, and should, signal what is or is not acceptable. For that reason, many organisations have incorporated sexual and racial harassment as examples of gross misconduct in their disciplinary procedures. Moreover, the usual grievance procedure may not be appropriate in the case of harassment. If the boss is doing the harassing, then working the issue through the normal line structure may not actually get past the first post. Where organisations are handling these issues sensitively, and a sufficiently open climate has been created, these problems can be tackled early – well before disciplinary action is appropriate.

Personnel policy framework: conclusion

Examining the personnel policies provides a vital element in our emerging picture of the state of equal opportunities within an organisation. At one level, this review is able to identify whether there are any areas where the law is being infringed. At a deeper level, by making comparisons with best practice, it gives us one way of measuring the degree to which an organisation has integrated equal opportunities into its formal thinking. The next stage is to see how this actually translates in practice.

■ THE PREVAILING CULTURE

Carrying out interviews with a cross-section of employees

With the statistical analysis and policy review completed, there will be a number of questions that can only be addressed through the process of face-to-face discussions.

So far, we have gathered a lot of factual information – we know what the profile of the organisation looks like and we know what policies it has in place. We do not know, however, what is happening on a day-to-day basis; we do not know much about the prevailing culture. We do not know much about what people think, believe or feel about equal opportunities. Given that this subject is one that will inevitably engage people at the emotional level – it is one of the few issues at work that directly addresses personal values and has immediate relevance to home life – we ignore these sentiments at our peril. One of the pieces of information that organisations need at the start of an equal opportunities initiative is an indication of the current level of resistance or support for the subject.

In particular, discussing issues face-to-face with employees is an opportunity to try to shed some light on some of the anomalies thrown up by the statistical analysis – why does assessment of potential grades differ between men and women? Why is the level of attrition among ethnic minorities unusually high?

Or, conversely, the statistical analysis may have highlighted departments where significant progress has been achieved. Why can they bring on minorities when others fail? This cannot only help to spread understanding about how to achieve success, it can also stimulate renewed interest. Finding concrete examples where managers are realising business benefits can act as a valuable spur to others in the organisation.

In addition, people may well raise concerns that could not be detected through the statistics or the review of policies. It can indicate the extent to which the formal policies are actually being implmented in practice. How are selection decisions actually being made? How are policies being used? Do people know about the policies at all?

The main purposes for holding the discussions are, therefore, to:

- Gain an impression of the degree of support or resistance to equal opportunities
- Increase understanding about the causes of any particular problems or successes already identified
- Give people, at all levels within the organisation, an opportunity to identify any issues of concern
- Gauge the effectiveness with which current policies are implemented.

The prevailing culture: conducting the interviews

Perhaps the first point to make is that holding these discussions in itself marks an important step, and setting them up needs to be managed. Expectations will inevitably be raised and there is no point holding the discussions if there is no intent to take subsequent actions. Similarly, it would be counter-productive to invite people to interviews but then give them no feed-back. If the activity is to be done, then it needs to be done well and carried out as suggested here as part of a coherent programme.

Also vital to the success of these discussions is that they are held in an open environment, where people feel free to say what they really think or feel and confidentiality is assured. Therefore, while it is possible to conduct discussions in small groups, there are advantages to holding one-to-one discussions.

We have found that it is helpful to ensure that those involved represent a good cross-section of the organisation. Managers and their staff both need to be included. Similarly, the interviews need to include a sample of women and minorities as well as white males. There is also an advantage if the age and service profile is mixed. By doing this not only does it ensure that the information base is not missing a vital perspective, it also begins to involve a wide group of people. As we see in Chapter 8, this will be very helpful when the time comes to communicate the equal opportunities policy.

Conducted in this way, these discussions can provide a rich store of anecdotal information. In what follows, we have grouped such anecdotes around the purposes highlighted earlier for holding the interviews.

Degree of support or resistance to equal opportunities

Very few people will actually resist the principle of equal opportunities. After all, how can anyone logically defend a position that anyone other than the best candidate for the job should be appointed?

Not surprisingly, therefore, in many organisations, people have said to us: 'We don't have a problem with equal opportunities'. What they actually mean, of course, is that they personally have not suffered under the current system therefore there cannot be anything wrong with it.

As we discuss in Chapter 8, the vast majority of white male managers – upon whom the implementation of any equal opportunities programme is likely to rely – seem to view equal opportunities apathetically. It is nothing to do with them and, moreover, there is nothing in it for them. One of the fundamental reasons for conducting an in depth diagnosis is in order to overcome this apathy. It starts to provide the facts to counter the charge: 'I don't see what all the fuss is about!' In addition, by involving people and beginning to get them to offer their opinions, we are embarking upon the process of gaining their ownership.

For many people, therefore, equal opportunities in the abstract, is something they are neither supportive of nor actively resistant to, they just don't see what all the fuss is about. By focusing, however, on the application of equal opportunities principles to recruitment or promotion practices, it is possible to get a much better indication of the actual level of support or resistance.

Some people will be astonishingly frank. Thinking about whether he had ever considered appointing a disabled person, one manager responded: 'I wouldn't want to sit next to someone who dribbled all day.' Stereotypical views usually abound with those who are resisting change: Asians are deemed to be good at figures, Blacks are lazy and don't want to work.

It is not a safe assumption, however, to presume that members of so-called minorities will necessarily see equal opportunities as the answer to all their prayers. There are many organisations with a 'Queen Bee' – the point about queen bees being that there is only one of them, and they are the centre of all the attention. Being in a minority of one can be alienating, it can also be quite flattering. There are many examples of older women who are proud to have made it in a man's world and are not particularly keen to see lots of younger women following in their footsteps. This is even more so, if the newcomers are challenging their assumption that they can only succeed by following the traditional male path.

There is another concern that minorities may frequently express. Just as positive discrimination is perceived as a threat by the white male population, so also can it be for minorities. Who wants to think, for example, that they have succeeded just because they are black? This, of course, is one of the problems with the quota legislation in the United States. Not only can it cause great resentment among the majority of employees, it can also undermine the confidence and legitimacy of those minorities who do make it through to senior positions.

Resistance, therefore, can come from all quarters – from black people as well as white people, from women as well as men – and the same goes for support.

The prevailing culture: causes of problems and successes

Statistical analysis may well pinpoint a 'glass ceiling': a level in the organisation beyond which minorities seem not to be able to progress. The statistical analysis in itself, however, is unlikely to be able to shed much light on why this might be.

Let us take the issue of the low proportion of women in management positions and explore the thinking that may be causing this.

In Esso UK in the mid 1980s, women were successfully entering management grades but they were not being spotted as real 'high fliers'. What was happening, and this is typical of many organisations, is that women were succeeding in the support functions – but not in the core business departments (refining and distribution). The company placed high importance on managers' abilities to handle the 'blue collar' interface, negotiating with the unions and managing the refinery operators and tanker drivers. Those who were going to make it right to the top had to be able to demonstrate that they could handle this 'macho' environment. Women were, almost without thinking, ruled out of contention. There is more than one way of handling conflict, however, and by 1988 two of the company's trickiest distribution terminals were being very successfully managed by women.

The stereotypical thinking that was getting in the way here was about women not being good at handling conflict. Another cause of the 'glass ceiling' for women, are the traditional family views prevalent among senior male managers. Clearly when key appointments are being made, judgements will need to take into account longer-term career aspirations and potential. Managers say: 'Well, there aren't that many key slots in the organisation, and we've got to make sure we choose someone who will be a long-term runner.' The assumption frequently made, of course, is that men are better long-term bets than women. After all, women will want to devote time to bringing up their children.

For some women, of course, this will indeed be the case. For many, however, it will not be. The traditional image of the nuclear family, beloved by advertisers, of the husband as the breadwinner, the wife who remains at home and looks after two school-age children, constitutes no more than 5 per cent of current United Kingdom households. Many successful businessmen, however, are themselves head of just such households. They forget the impact of the divorce rate, the number of women who head up single parent families, and they have not yet fathomed the phenomenon of dual career couples.

In one-to-one discussions, these sorts of issues become apparent. Clearly, there is not one single cause that is keeping talented women from reaching senior management positions. It is the complexity of the causes that the discussions can start to bring out into the open.

Just as with this particular example of a problem, it is essential to pursue the causes of any particular success with the same rigour. Only then will it be possible deliberately to spread this success across the organisation. In our final chapter, we examine one particular success – Rank Xerox's Customer Response Centre in Milton Keynes – in detail.

The prevailing culture: issues of concern

Sometimes discussions with employees will reveal new issues not apparent in the previous analysis. Exploration of one particular issue may expose a number of deeper interrelated causes.

If people feel relaxed, and are prepared to be open, then they will share the stories that reveal what the prevailing culture is really like... and how they feel about it.

On her first days at work in a new company, one woman attracted repeated comments about her dress. She was not dressed flamboyantly, but neither was she wearing a prim and proper suit. She concluded rapidly: 'In this organisation, as a woman, you are judged on totally different criteria from your male colleagues.' Christmas parties in this company were also infamous occasions.

The culture can also discriminate in a less overt way. For instance, in many organisations, putting in the hours may well be valued more highly than the actual output achieved. In order to get on, people need to be seen to be at work before 8 a.m. and still there at 7 p.m. A woman who was working flexibly but putting in a standard 37.5 hour week was continually referred to in one organisation as 'the part-timer'. The message is: 'If you're not married to the firm, you haven't got the necessary commitment.'

While this was obviously the same for either men or women with family commitments, many women are more directly affected. As one put it: 'Because I am a mother, they don't believe that I have the same commitment.' It sends very clear signals to women who are seeking to combine work and family commitments.

This is an example where management has itself created an unhelpful culture. The day-to-day working environment created at peer level can also create difficulties. What has passed for office banter, can actually often cause real hurt. Well established cultures will often resist outsiders: 'That's the way we are around here and if people don't like it, they know what they can do!' Teams that have existed for years on a daily diet of one-upmanship jokes may well find it difficult to adapt their behaviour.

At its extreme, office banter can actually qualify as racial or sexual harassment.

All too frequently, racist remarks and comments are quietly ignored by people – white as well as black – who find them offensive. Therefore people making the comments and setting the tone, continue to believe that they are all part of the give and take of working life.

Carried out, as part of a thorough diagnosis, discussions with employees can expose concerns about which senior management may have no idea.

The prevailing culture: effectiveness of policy implementation

One of the areas where the difference between policy intent and implementation is most marked is in recruitment.

Most organisations have formal recruitment policies and procedures that managers should follow in order to fill vacancies. Some have assessment forms that encourage interviewers to record evidence of candidates' skills. Yet, many interviewers make up their minds about a candidate within the first five minutes of an interview. Not surprisingly, research has shown that interviewing is not a particularly reliable predictor of future performance.

Discussions with those involved in the recruitment process reveal how decisions are actually made.

Asked what they think is the most important criterion for selection many recruiters identify the degree to which the candidate is likely to 'fit in'. Out of the window goes any detailed assessment of each individual against the skills required to do the job, and in comes the celebrated, much loved 'gut feel'.

Moreover, 'fitting in' can simply be shorthand for more of the same, which has some quite considerable drawbacks if organisations are trying to move towards equal opportunities. Why disrupt the harmony of an existing team? When does the first Indian get appointed to work in an all white team? The fact that the best team is certainly not one where everyone has the same skills, gets forgotten.

Of course, there are parallels between the recruitment and promotion processes. On the subject of who gets on within an organisation, it is quite apparent that in many cases the informal systems are much more powerful than the formal systems. As they say, 'It's not what you know, it's who you know.' The same considerations of 'fit' are as relevant for considering promotions as they are for initial recruitment. The health of the formal systems – the extent to which paper work is completed, kept up-to-date and used by management – is a very good indicator. If managers believe the formal systems are a waste of time, then informal systems will be filling the gap. Where this is the case, minorities often lose out.

The prevailing culture: conclusion

These are examples of the way in which an organisation's culture can either support or undermine equal opportunities. Anecdotal information builds up a powerful picture of how decisions are being made in an organisation, and what it is like to work there.

Currently, organisation's cultures are not particularly sympathetic to women or minorities or any sort of non-conformist. This is hardly surprising given that work and, in particular, management has been the almost exclusive province of white males.

The introduction of an equal opportunities programme, therefore, is a deliberate attempt to influence organisational culture. It is essential that there is some way of identifying the changes in culture that a successful programme is going to require. Conducting discussions with employees is an essential tool in measuring how supportive the current culture is towards equal opportunities. For senior managers who are trying to scope the size of the task that an equal opportunities initiative presents, this is invaluable.

■ CONCLUSION

This chapter has dealt with the part of the 'strategic approach' that we call diagnosis. By this we mean:

- Taking a thorough look at the employee statistics within an organisation
- Conducting a review of the personnel policies against both legal requirements and best practice
- Holding discussions with a cross-section of employees in order to gain an impression of an organisation's culture.

By doing this organisations can:

- Obtain the facts rather than the opinions
- Highlight the areas where changes are needed
- Establish a starting point from which to measure progress.

Furthermore, if the equal opportunities programme is not to drift, this diagnosis cannot be a one-off initiative; it must herald the start of an ongoing process. Total Quality Management has finally ushered in the age of measurement. Is the profile of the organisation changing? Are the recruitment patterns matching the changes in the labour markets? Are the personnel policies still up with the best? Do the policies meet the needs of the employees? Do people feel they are getting a fair deal? Are managers putting the formal policies into practice?

The habit of regular review, as we discuss in Chapter 11, is critical to sustaining the momentum of the programme.

Unless organisations carry out this sort of analysis, equal opportunities programmes are almost bound to fail. In the absence of hard facts and real causes, everyone is entitled to an opinion and people will rely on 'gut feel'. Because there is no information about how the lack of equal opportunities is hurting the business, the programme will be resented as an initiative imposed upon the organisation. Instead of being able to develop policies that will meet identified needs, there will be fashionable 'shots in the dark'. There will be a series of stop/go initiatives rather than a coherent planned process of change. Because there is no clear starting point, progress will not be measured.

For us, therefore, a 'strategic approach' to equal opportunities must begin with a diagnosis. It represents the foundation upon which all the other initiatives can be built. In particular, as we discuss in the next chapter, a thorough diagnosis enables the top management team to set some credible aims for an equal opportunities programme.

Chapter 7

SETTING AIMS – IDENTIFYING THE BUSINESS BENEFITS

Conducting an equal opportunities diagnosis can only do so much – it describes the current state of equal opportunities in the organisation. Once this starting point is clear, then the next step for an organisation is to decide where it should be heading. We call this process 'setting aims' and we see this as the province of senior management. It sounds simple, but the clarity with which the aims are set will, to a large extent, determine the degree of support an equal opportunities programme can attract, and thus the degree to which it is successful or unsuccessful.

As we argued in Chapter 4, a central element of our redefinition becomes internally led rather than externally imposed or driven. The key to this is the process of setting aims.

If the aims, or the drivers of the change, are all conceived as being external – the need to conform to legislative requirements, or to be seen to be a 'good' employer – then the whole programme will be understood in this light. Therefore, it should not be surprising that equal opportunities has frequently been seen by employers as a political or ethical issue, to be dealt with by the public relations or personnel departments but very rarely as a proper subject for serious business discussion.

Conversely, we would argue that if the aims are primarily seen as being internal – related to the current and future needs of the organisation – then equal opportunities suddenly becomes a much more significant issue. It ceases to be peripheral and becomes a central business concern for senior management.

The first challenge therefore is to establish whether there is in fact a business case for equal opportunities. If so, what are the internal aims that could be set? We will then turn our attention to how top managers can set these aims and what actions they might take to get an equal opportunities programme off to a good start.

So, in this chapter we will:

- Examine the business case for equal opportunities
- Explore the significance of setting equal opportunities aims
- Consider the role of top managers in setting aims
- Define what we mean by developing a vision
- Suggest actions to signal their commitment.

■ EXAMINING THE BUSINESS CASE FOR EQUAL OPPORTUNITIES

As suggested above, all too frequently equal opportunities programmes have been politically or ethically led. Tackling the issue in this way, senior managers often found that they were forcing it onto a reluctant organisation. Having not given themselves the chance to think the topic through, they were then thrown off balance when the reaction to a programme launch was negative.

In our view, it is imperative that top managers take exactly the reverse approach and identify very carefully the internal benefits for embracing equal opportunities and ensure that they link into the mainstream business goals.

Making these links between equal opportunities and the business becomes increasingly self-evident. In 1990, a survey of chief executives of major UK companies ranked in order of importance the issues that they believed would preoccupy them for the 1990s. Human resources matters – specifically *availability of people* was ranked as the single most important key issue for the 1990s. This came ahead of (in this order) '1992', customer care, and competitiveness.

The links between equal opportunities and human resources concerns are self-evident. In addition, we would contend that equal opportunities can make a significant contribution to the other three areas as well.

At Rank Xerox (UK), for example, they identify the so-called 'vital few' objectives which drive the overall business goals. Among these objectives are 'customer satisfaction' and 'employee satisfaction'. During a workshop we ran for the UK Board in 1990, it did not take the directors long to work out that equal opportunities could play a key role in achieving those objectives and it has now itself become one of the 'vital few'.

In the following discussion of the link between the business and equal opportunities, we have grouped the business links into the following categories:

- Equal opportunities and managing change
- Equal opportunities and Total Quality Management
- Equal opportunities and customers
- Equal opportunities and choosing the best
- Equal opportunities and keeping the best
- Equal opportunities and productivity
- Equal opportunities and the bottom line.

Equal opportunities and managing change

The one thing that we know most organisations have in common is the need to respond to, and somehow manage, the change that is going on around them – in society's values, for example towards the environment; in their markets, among their employees. As Charles Handy says in his book *The Age of Unreason* Business Books Ltd, (an imprint of Century Hutchinson Ltd), London, 1989:

> *'Change isn't what it used to be. It has accelerated to such an extent that it doesn't make patterns any more. Change is radical, random, or discontinuous.'*

It is true that assumptions that previously looked fairly solid are now being questioned. It was not long ago that the manufacturers were telling us that there were no sensible alternatives to the use of CFCs.

With '1992', the domestic market is going to take on a whole new meaning. The United Kingdom, and UK companies in particular, can no longer sustain an insular attitude. The ability to work across different cultures will be valued highly, as Europe (and now the former USSR as well as Eastern Europe) become 'open for business'. Certainly this ability to work across cultures will be relevant to both managing the changing makeup of the organisation's external markets, and to managing the changing makeup of the internal market (i.e. as the work force itself becomes increasingly diverse).

In this ever-quickening state of flux, organisations that are straight-jacketed by traditional ways of thinking are unlikely to survive for long. New ways of thinking are not so much a luxury as a necessity. Handy calls this 'Upside down thinking' and claims:

> *'New ways of thinking about familiar things can release new energies and make all manner of things possible.'*

Working with organisations and asking their managers to identify the sorts of cultural benefits that they see equal opportunities providing, it is clear that they are beginning to see these links: 'Gives us a chance to get different thought patterns into the company', 'Moves us away from a mono-culture'.

If 'upside down thinking' really is what is required, the very last thing organisations need is to be peopled by a series of 'clones'. If people have been through the same experiences, recruited and trained in order to 'fit the mould', they lack the stimulation of new thinking, will not challenge each other and are likely to repeat the same tired old solutions.

In an article prior to his retirement, Judge Pickles – not always viewed with equanimity by equal opportunities practitioners – was berating the legal profession, and its limited horizons:

> *'I am very much opposed to the self-perpetuating oligarchy consisting of Oxbridge, public school people, which runs the legal system and the judiciary. I think it's suffocating, it's incestuous.'*

This area is one where equal opportunities can make a significant contribution. By broadening the recruitment net, and bringing in people who are 'different', an organisation is helping itself to change, become more flexible and adapt to new environments. Creative thinking and radical new ideas will be required to deal with the increasing pace of change affecting all organisations, and diversity of thinking within the organisation will be an important factor enabling this to take place.

Looked at in this light, adopting equal opportunities policies becomes a vital part of a long-term competitive strategy, a vital part of an organisation's ability to thrive on – as well as just manage – change on a large scale.

Equal opportunities and Total Quality Management

If equal opportunities can, therefore, help organisations manage change, there is one particular challenge – becoming a 'quality' organisation – that it specifically supports.

As the pace of technological change further increases and enables those with the finance to invest with the ability to reduce costs still further, competitive pricing is being taken as the norm. For example, manufacturing organisations that are thriving are those that compete on price. However, they are also able to: adapt their products to particular markets, guarantee the quality of their products, and meet tight delivery deadlines, and thereby meet the increasing demands for high quality goods and services of the customer base.

It is becoming increasingly likely that in the 1990s purchasers will insist that their suppliers have embraced 'total quality' before they are allowed to bid for the business. It is becoming a pre-qualification for entry. Currently this has been interpreted as gaining certification either under the British Standard (BS 5750) or the International Standards (IS 9000). Of course, these standards just ensure that the bureaucratic processes are in place, and certain quality hurdles are overcome. Total quality goes much further than this; in essence, total quality is about 'delighting' the internal and external customers.

Systems and technology can go some way to helping organisations meet customers' needs, but it is people who make the difference. Machines cannot anticipate customer requirements. Systems cannot overcome the 'its's more than my job's worth' attitude. In a total quality organisation employees cannot treat their own jobs in isolation – everyone is part of a customer-supplier chain. Rather than inspecting for quality at the end of the process, it needs to be built in as part of the thinking right from the start.

In our view, creating an equal opportunities culture is part of becoming a total quality organisation. Total quality requires the best people and needs them to be working in the most effective way. *NB*

At one level, it is common sense: the best person must be appointed to the job, there must be 'round pegs in round holes', then there is a chance that people really will 'Get it right first time'.

Moreover, a Total Quality approach would ensure that functional boundaries do not impede the 'right' decisions being taken. People from production, finance and sales each need to appreciate what the others bring to the party. Segregation of the organisation, among other things into men's jobs (say in production) and women's jobs, (say in clerical administration), will be replaced by increasing reliance on cross-functional project teams who form and disband when the job is done. How can this happen successfully if gender or race issues get in the way and cloud the discussions? Where individuals are not allowed to be themselves, and make their own unique contribution, where there is not mutual respect, work cannot be carried out effectively.

By ensuring that the best people are appointed, and by creating an environment where employees can work together as effectively as possible, equal opportunities can play a significant part in helping organisations embrace total quality. It goes further than this, however, because it also enables organisations to re-orient themselves successfully around customer requirements.

Equal opportunities and customers

The link between equal opportunities and 'customers' is usually conceived negatively. It is either a concern about how the customer might react ('They won't want to deal with a black person'), or a resistance to local authorities seeking to carry out contract compliance ('Asking us a whole load of irrelevant questions about the makeup of our organisation').

In fact, contract compliance is only one particular form of a customer requirement. While legislative changes have blunted those local authorities who were very actively delving into the affairs of their potential suppliers, it does not mean that the issue has completely gone away. Just as some purchasers will insist that their suppliers are environmentally 'green', or have BS 5750, thereby ensuring that the supplier reaches the standards they believe to be appropriate in the area of the environment and TQM, so others will want to see that their suppliers are actively seeking to embrace equal opportunities. Such values may have been out of fashion in the 1980s, but they look like they are back with a vengeance in the 1990s.

The link between equal opportunities and 'customers' can be looked at more positively. It is not just that some purchasers may insist on seeing how you are progressing in this area, it is that equal opportunities can actually be a powerful force for bringing organisations closer to their customer base. For instance, B & Q found that their Macclesfield store, staffed by over-50s, was gaining higher customer satisfaction scores than their other stores.

After all, just as the labour market is changing, so too is the customer base. This applies to both sorts of 'customers' – both the immediate purchasers in other organisations (the people who decide whether to buy your product or service or a competitor's) and the public as the eventual consumers.

Long gone are the days when business deals were simply conducted between men. Advertisers too, are becoming increasingly aware of the growing buying power of, for example, older people with healthy disposable incomes, and have altered their advertising strategy to this end. While there is still much to do, the larger employers have begun to be more open-minded about recruitment, and as a consequence, the representation of women and minorities among the decision makers for orders has increased. A chauvinist, golf-playing salesman will not necessarily get the best results.

Moreover, perhaps because they have suffered discrimination elsewhere, women and ethnic minorities provide an increasing proportion of new start businesses. In 1989, women represented 25 per cent of the self-employed in the United Kingdom. Banks have become increasingly aware of this, as they need to be. Women entrepreneurs have frequently berated the high street banks who seemed unhelpful and uncomfortable about funding new businesses being started up by women. (Anita Roddick tells the story of the difficulties she had in getting the finance to get started.) Research by Stirling University among 60 women entrepreneurs revealed that 40 per cent would use a woman-only bank if there was one in their area. The changing profile of the business community has profound implications for organisations.

Equally important, and feeding this change in the business community, is the shift in the demographic profile of the United Kingdom. For London Weekend Television, who have estimated that by the year 2000 about 25 per cent of their audience will be from ethnic minorities, this brings into sharp focus the fact that minorities only make up 5 per cent of their employees. Not only is this difficult to justify from a moral perspective, but it also means that they run the very real risk of losing touch with what their customers want. Nor should we forget that about 14 per cent of the public have a disability – and they too are customers.

The changing profile of the customer base is as inevitable as the changing profile of the labour market. The one is simply a different aspect of the other. Most of us are both employees and consumers. Organisations that positively address equal opportunities can put themselves at a competitive advantage by being able to anticipate and meet the changing needs of their customers.

Equal opportunities and choosing the best

We have argued that as organisations need to become increasingly outward looking and responsive to their customer needs, equal opportunities can play an important role by ensuring that their employees are able to do this. When we were discussing total quality, we also alluded to the fact that equal opportunities ought to ensure that organisations choose the 'best'. We would like to explore this issue in more detail here.

It is, of course, mainly a matter of common sense (which is not to suggest that it therefore automatically happens). With the changing profile of the labour market, as described in Chapter 2, organisations that continue to look to white males under 28 years of age, as the exclusive source of their recruits, are ignoring well over half the potential applicants. They cannot be getting the best.

The employer's legitimate concern is to choose the candidate that has the best fit to the organisation, with the skills required. Unfortunately, there are a lot of factors that interfere with this judgement, not least issues of race and gender. There is one area, however, where the focus is very clearly on skill, and that is in sport. Decisions about whether to include someone in a world-class sporting team will be made purely on merit. For instance, it does not matter what you look like, the question is whether you can or cannot run a mile faster than anybody else.

Is it therefore surprising that sport is the area where ethnic minorities have made their most obvious breakthroughs? This summer's series of Test matches against the West Indies – with Philip DeFreitas, 'Syd' Lawrence, Chris Lewis, Mark Ramprakash, and Devon Malcolm playing their part in the England team – prompted a *Times* editorial: 'Fair Play For Blacks'. It concluded:

> *'The team that does not pick on merit will be, ultimately, a loser. A more potent force for equal opportunities is hard to imagine.'*

The same is true, of course, of the office 'team' just as much as the sports team. Imagine the England cricket team without these five black and Asian Britons. Widening the pool of recruits is a vehicle for raising, not lowering, standards.

Esso's graduate recruitment campaign is a case in point. In the mid-1980s, the company was becoming increasingly concerned about the supply of scientific and engineering graduates. They were specifically aware that the supply of chemical engineers from tertiary education was probably insufficient to meet oil industry's needs (let alone to provide for those students who chose to leave engineering behind for a career in the City). One contributory cause of the problem was the fact that not many women were choosing to study for science and engineering degrees. Esso realised that it had to widen its responsibilities beyond the post-university stage in a young person's decision making process. It therefore played an active part in encouraging women to consider science and engineering as a career, playing a high profile role in the 1984 WISE campaign (Women Into Science and Engineering). In the early 1980s, the percentage of female graduate recruits entering Esso each year fluctuated between 10 per cent and 15 per cent. Since 1986 this figure has fluctuated between 35 per cent and 40 per cent. Clearly, there has been a significant change – and this has not led to a reduction in quality. Quite the reverse, when ranked in order of perceived quality, more women were typically at the top of the lists. Perhaps the fact that women generally had to struggle against the odds in order to be allowed to study traditional male subjects, led to this consistently high quality.

In addition, all this obviously applies equally to promotion decisions just as much as to recruitment selection. One of the very real benefits that an equal opportunities programme can provide is sweeping away the 'jobs for the boys' mafias. There is no room for decisions that are not based on merit. Equal opportunities ought to:

(1) force into the open the selection criteria for each vacancy;
(2) ensure that these criteria are based on skill; and
(3) help managers apply the criteria objectively.

Equal opportunities and keeping the best

It is only the first step to recruit the best. The challenge is to keep the best. What equal opportunities can do is make the organisation much more responsive to the needs of individual employees. If total quality is about being responsive to customer requirements, equal opportunities is about being alert to employee needs.

We are no longer in the era when organisations can simply choose their pick of the best. As we argued in Chapter 2, even in recession, we have skills shortages. As jobs become more knowledge-based, those with the relevant skills become even more sought after.

This is a central theme in Peter Herriot's book *Recruitment in the '90s*, Institute of Personnel Management, 1989. He states:

'It is the central argument of this book that it is only when organisations agree contracts with individuals which take account of their specific needs that they will be able to meet the human resource challenge of the '90s.'

In other words, if there is not sufficient flexibility within an organisation, the best will go elsewhere. Gone are the days when the contract of employment bound employees to the employer from 'cradle to grave'. The balance is shifting in favour of the employee. Why, for example, should women return from maternity leave to an organisation that gives them the stark choice between full-time work or a Career Break, when they know that they have highly marketable skills? Conversely, the organisation tuned into the individual's needs, might be keen to discuss a more flexible return to work, rather than lose that individual's skills altogether. This is what the psychological contract, as we described in Chapter 3, is all about.

All the HR systems need to be finely tuned in order to identify and address individual needs. As we suggested when we were discussing diagnosis, there need to be sophisticated appraisal and career planning systems. Only then can organisations really demonstrate that they can help individuals fulfill their potential.

Equal opportunities and productivity

Equal opportunities should not only ensure that organisations are staffed by the best people, but also that they get the best out of them.

Again, at one level this is common sense. If people feel discriminated against, or just not supported, their confidence will fall off, and they are unlikely to give of their best. If people feel sidelined, or that they have nowhere to go, they are unlikely to show much drive and energy. If, on the other hand, there are 'round pegs in round holes' then people are likely to be good at their jobs and be happy to get on with them. If there is potential that is not being tapped, then the organisation must be losing out – it is not making use of those assets that are represented by its employees. In these days when employees are no longer to be regarded as inefficient machines, but as the source of much of the 'added value' that is so critical to profitability, this can be a fatal flaw.

Indeed, motivated, committed employees can achieve remarkable feats. Can the growth of 'The Body Shop' be entirely divorced from the way in which it treats its employees and the commitment this generates?

Flexible contracts, perhaps surprisingly, can also be another source of increased productivity. In Rank Xerox's supply company, the two saleswomen who job share were top of their sales league in 1990. They and their managers have seen the real advantages of job sharing. Often, people on flexible contracts, because they are at work for a limited time, are more determined to pack things in. For one thing, many have remarked to us that they simply do not spend the same amount of time at the coffee machine!

Equal opportunities and the bottom line

We have no doubt that all the above represent significant benefits for organisations. More importantly, perhaps, we have worked with directors and managers who clearly believe so too. Moreover, they see that equal opportunities is helping them create the right organisation for the future.

To an extent, however, there must be a degree of conjecture. The benefits may seem to accrue logically from pursuing equal opportunities, but where is the evidence? Indeed, in some cases, it may well be difficult to separate out the effect of equal opportunities from the effects of other changes being introduced.

That is not to say, however, that there are not some tangible bottomline benefits that can be directly traced back to the introduction of equal opportunities policies. In our experience there are, and they can be grouped into two main areas: reducing *attrition costs* and reducing *recruitment costs*. People understandably need good hard facts before they will fully support what is perhaps a major shift in culture, and there is an old pragmatic American saying: 'If it ain't broken, don't fix it!'

This is where the diagnosis, as described in the previous chapter, should come into its own. As far as *attrition* is concerned, it should answer questions such as: Who is leaving and why? How much training have we invested in people who leave? How can equal opportunities help us reduce attrition? What level of attrition do we believe is appropriate for our organisation? For instance, we have already noted the high level of unemployment amongst people with disabilities. Given that 70% of those who become unemployed have had five years' service, or more, with their employers, this also represents a significant source of attrition. With a bit more imagination, employers should be able to reduce this waste almost entirely. As far as *recruitment* is concerned, it should provide information such as: How much do we currently spend on recruitment? How much can we save in recruitment costs with each percentage point reduction in attrition? How will equal opportunities make it easier for us to fill vacancies and what will this save us, for example, on the cost of extra recruitment campaigns, and advertising?

For some organisations, it is enough to look at the current situation, for others it might be prudent to carry out some projections into the future. When we were doing some work in a relatively small financial services company, we were able to point out to them that 44 per cent of all their employees were women under 30 years old. To date, maternity leave had not been a big issue – they only had two mothers among their 60 employees – and they had a very conventional maternity leave policy, meeting the statutory minimum only. It did not need much further analysis to realise that, in the near future there could be real problems of continuity, that a great deal of experience could drain out from the organisation, as well as soaring costs of recruitment and training, unless active steps were taken to encourage mothers to return to work.

In this organisation, they were taking action to avoid a potential problem, others have acted in order to tackle particular problems they were already facing. The most obvious examples are where companies have set up childcare facilities.

In 1988, Midland Bank announced that it was embarking on an ambitious programme of providing workplace nurseries. The initial investment of £350,000 was justified on the basis of the need to increase staff retention. Training costs for each staff member were estimated to have reached £8,000 and £10,000 at the point that they left, and, at Midland, 58 per cent of all employees were women.

The London and Manchester Group relocated its head office from London to Exeter in 1975 and in 1979 they opened a nursery. This is now seen as a core benefit and plays a significant part in the company's high staff retention. Spencer, a clothing company in Banbury, providing 20 nursery places in 1987 developed from having difficulty attracting trained machinists to having a waiting list of eager applicants.

The same logic seems to apply where organisations choose to make childcare provision during school holidays. Target Group, a financial services company based in Aylesbury, runs a successful holiday play scheme and finds that they no longer have staffing problems in the summer. The National Savings Bank in Glasgow found that its Christmas holiday scheme resulted in savings of £4,000 per week. B & Q have also shown us that employing older workers can have direct bottom-line benefits. Their Macclesfield store, staffed by people aged over 50, produced award-winning sales over target performances in both 1989/90 and 1990/91. Their labour turnover was nearly six times less than comparison stores.

The business case for equal opportunities: conclusion

In our view, equal opportunities is – and should be – linked to the widest organisational issues. In short, equal opportunities makes business sense. It enables organisations to:

- Manage change by attracting people with new and different ways of thinking
- Create a working environment where total quality can take root
- Anticipate and meet the changing needs of customers
- Recruit and promote the best people by widening the traditional sources of candidates
- Retain the best people by ensuring that their needs are fully taken into account
- Increase productivity by raising motivation and commitment
- Increase profitability by reducing attrition and recruitment costs.

Equal opportunities is no longer represented by a series of pressures from outside the organisation. It is to these internal needs that organisations should turn when they are seeking to develop their aims for an equal opportunities programme. Perhaps it is now time, however, to return to why we believe this process of setting aims to be so important.

■ EXPLORING THE SIGNIFICANCE OF SETTING EQUAL OPPORTUNITIES AIMS

In order to explore the significance of setting aims, we will cover two areas:

(1) a definition of what we mean by setting aims;
(2) the consequences of being clear or unclear about aims.

Definition of setting aims

There are a whole series of words and expressions that people use when they discuss the way in which we seek to shape the future within organisations: 'goals', 'targets', 'objectives', 'purposes', 'mission', 'strategy' and 'vision' to name but a few. For us, setting aims encompasses all these. In our thinking in this area, we have been influenced by the work of The Coverdale Organisation, and we will use their terminology. They have distinguished three aspects of aims:

Purpose: the reasons for the proposed change and the benefits envisaged. This sets direction and is an essential point of reference when it comes to decision making. Will or won't a particular proposal help us achieve our purpose?

End result: this is the description of the future. If the desired changes come about, what will the organisation and its culture be like? The more compelling the description, the easier it will be for people to see what the fuss is all about.

Success criteria: these identify the parameters within which to work, the standards to be attained, and the measures of progress. The criteria can be linked to the purpose (a measure of the extent to which the benefits have been realised) or to the end result (specification of the quality standards to be met).

A well thought through equal opportunities programme will have clearly identified all three sorts of aims:

(1) a set of purposes for beginning the programme;
(2) a description of what the organisation would be like if equal opportunities were a reality; and
(3) success criteria, relating both to the benefits and to the end result, which can be used to assess progress.

It is our contention that many of the equal opportunities programmes launched to date have not had clear aims and this has fundamentally, and fatally, undermined them.

The consequences of being clear or unclear about aims

Purpose

All too frequently, equal opportunities programmes have not had any meaningful organisational purposes. Conceived as responses to external influences, the business benefits – in so far as they exist – are about minimising the potential cost of litigation, or about being perceived publicly as a 'good employer'. Often purposes are expressed negatively: 'We will aim to reduce litigation'. The consequences of this are outlined below.

Because the business purposes are unclear, equal opportunities does not merit the attention of senior management. The topic never gets on the business agenda and it becomes the province of specialists and lacks the active commitment of the senior management. Because the specialists do not know the overall business well enough (they are not close enough to it), they do not themselves set programme aims, and they concentrate on the 'hows' rather than the 'whys'. They launch a series of unconnected initiatives, which are received with apathy by the vast majority of the management population, because they do not seem to link to the rest of what is happening within the organisation. Equal opportunities is seen as some kind of side issue, separate from mainstream business and day-to-day management. There is a brief flicker of life, then equal opportunities goes the way of all other 'flavours of the month' and is discarded in favour of the next 'brand'.

It is almost impossible to generate genuine enthusiasm and commitment in the absence of purpose. How can people become enthusiastic about something that seems to come out of the blue, without an obvious business rationale? How can people judge how worthwhile it is? In many cases, as we shall see in the following chapter, in the absence of declared purposes, people will draw their own conclusions about the reasons for the initiative. The average white, male manager will feel threatened and will therefore resort to a highly effective form of passive resistance.

The converse is true, of course. As people become clear about purpose, then the issue gets onto the business agenda, and becomes the concern of all managers and, in time, of all employees. Policies can then be introduced and people understand *why*. They can be supported and intelligently applied. Moreover (and, as we shall see in the following chapter, this is fundamental to gaining wider ownership) people can take their own local initiatives.

Once the real business needs have been communicated, people can begin to think about the implications for themselves in their own jobs. If one of the purposes is to reduce attrition due to maternity leave, a manager can look again at the situation prevailing in his or her department. Rather than accepting the 'inevitable', managers could seek to help women return. For instance, if an individual is due to go on maternity leave, the individual and manager could discuss ways of helping her return to work: different work patterns, or other proposals could be considered well ahead of time.

As we have seen above, there are plenty of business purposes that an equal opportunities programme can pursue. For instance, one might be: *to ensure that we utilise the full potential of all our employees.* This can be contrasted with the political or ethical purpose which might have been: *to promote more women so that they have a fairer slice of the cake.* They send fundamentally different messages.

Being clear about purpose is absolutely critical. Unless we know why we are being asked to do something, we can be suspicious of the motives. Moreover, purpose sets direction and without purpose it is difficult to set meaningful criteria to measure progress.

End result

In our experience, equal opportunities means very different things to different people. What does an equal opportunities organisation look like? Somehow, if misinterpretation is to be avoided, each organisation needs to define what it means by equal opportunities.

Where this does not happen, people are left to interpret the programme as they see fit. Some will see it as being about women's rights and they envisage an organisation in a few years that has at least as many female managers as male managers. Others will state that they see it as nothing other than the status quo – we already appoint the best person for the job – and therefore that the organisational profile is likely to remain pretty much as it is.

The end result is the outcome of meeting the business purposes. It visualises the organisation as it will be, for example, 'an organisation which will be as diverse as the customer base we sell to'. Business benefits can be very dry, whereas a description of the resulting organisation can express much more about what it will actually be like. It can start to ease some of the concerns: 'Oh, if that's what you mean, I'm a bit more relaxed about it.' For that reason, as we describe below, it needs to be a fundamental part of any equal opportunities policy statement.

Success criteria

The success or otherwise of most equal opportunities programmes is not measured. Moreover, where organisations have actually set measures – for instance, about the future profile of the organisation – they are related to the end result rather than the purposes. (Primarily because they do not actually have declared business purposes.)

The absence of success criteria linked to purposes are the most likely cause of the 'drift' of an equal opportunities programme. If there is no anchor to the business needs of the organisation, then a series of loose initiatives can continue for as long as somebody at the centre of the organisation has the will and the budget. Moreover, how can the success of any initiative be established? If a Career Break Scheme has been introduced in order to reduce attrition of maternity leavers, it is essential that these statistics are monitored.

Alternatively, if there are no criteria, managers may well feel free to ignore the whole subject and the programme will never get off the ground. After all, if they are not being measured on their performance in this area, why should they put in any effort? As Denis Oliver, the Finance Director of Rank Xerox (UK), put it:

'If we can't measure it, we know it won't happen!'

It is not that the criteria will enable managers to give a huge sigh of relief and exclaim 'Right, we've hit all those targets, we're there now.' Any numerical criteria will continue to be reviewed. Rather, what criteria do provide is a tool for testing the temperature. Top management (in particular) can review and assess whether progress is on track or whether they need to take some further action.

Criteria can, and should, be set for each of the areas that emerged in the diagnosis as requiring attention.

Setting aims: conclusion

As stated above, we believe that an equal opportunities programme should have declared purposes, end results and success criteria. Clearly, these three aspects of aims interrelate – but they are different and top managers need to be careful about the terminology they use.

The best example of this – and one which might shed some light on a particularly thorny debate – is the confusion that surrounds the decision to set equal opportunities 'goals' or 'targets'. Typically these take the form of numerical targets for the number of women, for example, in management roles. The confusion stems, we believe from a failure to distinguish between purpose and criteria.

Essentially, these 'goals' are in fact criteria – measures of the effectiveness of the programme. They are not, and should not become, purposes: in other words, ends in themselves. The purpose is to promote the most able people into management positions. One criterion is that we would expect a proportion of these to be women.

We explore the need for setting and reviewing equal opportunity goals further in Chapter 11. The point we want to make here is simply that it is vital to be clear about your aims and to be able to distinguish their three aspects.

In Table 7.1, we have contrasted the effects of being clear, or of being unclear, about the aims of an equal opportunities programme.

In the absence of aims there is no clear direction. Each of the separate equal opportunities initiatives may be worthwhile in themselves, but do they logically relate, one to another, and do they add up to a coherent programme? Overall what are we trying to achieve? What will the future organisation be like? How will we know when an initiative is having a positive effect, and that we are making progress? How is the effectiveness of the programme to be measured? All these are legitimate questions, and each is the province of aims. Without answers to these questions any equal opportunities programme is bound to drift.

Table 7.1 Aims

Benefits of having aims	*Risks of not having aims*
• A clear vision	• Managers form own interpretation
• Business reasons for change	• Seen as political or irrelevant
• Senior management commitment	• Province of specialists
• Seen to benefit all	• Seen to benefit minorities
• Generates enthusiasm	• Encounters passive resistance
• Firm basis for decisions	• Ad hoc decision making

■ ROLE OF TOP MANAGERS

As stated at the beginning of the chapter, we believe that setting aims is the province of top management. We meant this partly negatively – in other words, they should concentrate on setting aims and not interfere in other issues that are the proper province of the people who report to them. We also wanted to emphasise, however, that they should not passively approve someone else's set of aims, but rather that they themselves should set them.

The reasons for this are as follows:

• Top managers are in the best position to relate equal opportunities to the overall aims for the organisation
• Their active support is required, not just their acquiescence, so they must fully 'own' the aims

- They must speak with one mind on this – if they start to give mixed messages, they will be unable to provide a sense of steady direction

A shift is taking place from seeing equal opportunities aims as externally driven to internally generated. Most directors, however, will be familiar with the former, where equal opportunities remains the province of public relations and human resources specialists, and will need to take time to make the links with the future health of the business, and the role they will need to play.

Unless the senior management team are genuinely 'bought in' to the concept of equal opportunities – that is to say they want it because they see that it is good for the business, and they are prepared to pay for it – then they can easily undermine any programme.

Sooner or later, support at the top of the organisation is going to be needed to approve a policy change – for example, the extension of flexible working contracts. If they withhold that support, unless there are compelling business reasons for rejecting any particular proposal, they will be seen to be paying 'lip service' to equal opportunities. The message from the top will be seen as: 'Espousing equal opportunities is good for the corporate image, but don't expect us to do anything about it internally.'

It goes further, because this 'buy in' is also required at a personal level. Given that they are who they are, the impact of the behaviour of top managers is disproportionately great. They set good, or bad, role models. An inappropriate joke from a director at a conference or a Christmas function can seriously derail a patiently developed equal opportunities programme in an instant. Equally, a refusal to countenance sexist or racist 'banter' can effectively redraw the line on what is considered acceptable behaviour.

In our view, it is vital that the top managers of an organisation set the overall aims for the programme. For these reasons, it is essential, therefore, that a decision to embark upon an equal opportunities initiative is not rushed through. Time needs to be taken so that each member of the senior team feels comfortable with the approach and has real understanding of, and commitment to, the task ahead.

■ DEVELOPING A VISION

In our view, the first step the top managers need to take is to develop a 'vision' for equal opportunities that they all share and support. This sounds very grand, but in reality all we mean is that they should agree, among themselves, what they believe the aims of the equal opportunities programme to be. This may well simply take the form of a policy statement, although it should be far removed from the bland, legalistic documents of previous years.

In the 1970s and 1980s we were all very clear about what being an equal opportunities employer meant – it meant *not* doing a lot of things. It meant *not* discriminating against women, and people from ethnic minorities. It meant *not* sacking women when they became pregnant. It meant *not* rejecting a black applicant because you thought your customers might object.

This approach is exemplified in the typical policy statements at the time which refer to equal opportunities 'irrespective of sex, marital status, creed, colour, race or ethnic origin' and suggest 'staff who believe they have been denied equality of opportunity may pursue their complaint through the appeal and grievance procedure.'

The emphasis is unfailingly on the negative and it sets the scene for a minimalist approach. It is rather like the organisations that Tom Peters castigates for claiming that they are: 'No worse than anyone else' – this is hardly likely to be the source of great inspiration and drive.

Nowhere is the case for equal opportunities linked to the business objectives. It tells you what not to do, but not what to do. What is more, the focus is on selection decisions – whether that be at the recruitment or promotion stage – and it ignores the vital part organisational culture plays in creating the environment for success. As a consequence of this, the responsibility for the policy is seen to lie with personnel and the line management. Seemingly, equal opportunities has nothing to do with anyone else in the organisation.

An organisation with a traditional policy statement will usually concentrate on doing the minimum in order to meet the letter of the law. A modern policy statement should be the absolute reverse. The following are the sort of criteria we would expect it to meet:

- It should link equal opportunities to the core business objectives
- It should express what will be done, rather than what won't
- It should be phrased inclusively rather than listing potential groups suffering discrimination
- It should state how the policy will benefit individuals and their changing needs at various points in their career

- There should be emphasis on the provision of a supportive environment as well as the use of fair selection processes
- All employees as well as managers should have responsibility for the policy.

As we argued in Chapter 4, we need to turn the traditional interpretation of equal opportunities on its head. It should not be about avoiding discrimination against particular groups, it should be about ensuring that each individual is able to realise his or her full potential. This therefore needs to be reflected in the aims and, in turn, in the 'vision'.

The 'vision' can be long- or short-term, but what it needs to do in some way is convey:

(1) *why* equal opportunities is important;
(2) *what* the desired end result is; and
(3) how the effectiveness of the programme will be *measured*.

Of course, each organisation will want to express this differently. There cannot be such a thing as a 'standard' equal opportunities 'vision'. The aims for any particular organisation will vary according to their own assessment, at the diagnosis stage, of their current needs and how they relate to the business aims it is pursuing. A critical role for the top management team is to digest what equal opportunities means for them, as a particular organisation, and to shape their policy statement accordingly.

A good example is the BP policy statement. Here there is a very deliberate emphasis on the family and work balance:

'For every employee our values mean a trusting, equal opportunity, non-discriminatory working environment. Our company offers challenging and exciting work. We will vigorously promote career development and we will aim to offer all employees a challenging career. We will seek to recognise both individual contribution and collective team-work. We encourage our employees to strike a balance between their responsibilities to BP and to their home life.'

The top management team must use the opportunity of communicating the vision to convey their key messages to the organisation. It is their opportunity to show how equal opportunities fits with the way in which they see the organisation developing. It can make clear how the values that are expressed in the equal opportunities 'vision' support the overall business goals. In this way, it is possible to develop a policy statement which conveys the *positive values* that the organisation desires while not putting off the majority of its employees. As we shall see in the following chapter, this sort of a 'vision' is essential if there is going to be any real success in gaining widespread ownership across the organisation for equal opportunities.

■ ACTIONS TO SIGNAL COMMITMENT

Up to this point, the top management have reviewed the business case for equal opportunities and developed their own policy statement. In the next chapter we will explore what they might do to successfully launch an equal opportunities programme (as well as what they could profitably avoid doing).

There remains, however, one further consideration that they should take into account at this stage. The vision represents a consciously long-term goal. There will be a need to convey a sense of momentum and to take some short-term actions; to scope some longer-term projects, so that people recognise that it is not just 'jam tomorrow'.

The starting point here must be to return to the diagnosis. If this has been well conducted it should have:

• Described how the current situation does or does not support equal opportunities
• Identified the potential savings from an equal opportunities programme

It should not be difficult to identify the priority actions. These are likely to fall into two groups:

(1) areas where the organisation is in danger of infringing legislation; and
(2) areas where there are potentially high savings.

In our view, the two groups also need rather different treatment. Where there is a danger that current practices or procedures are potentially illegal, then it is obviously appropriate for the top management team to adopt a strong stance. They can actively use these issues to show that they mean business.

An example of a stand that could be taken here is on harassment. If the diagnosis suggests that sexual or racial harassment, while predominantly of a mild kind, are prevalent then the top management need to send a signal that this is not acceptable behaviour. One way of doing this would be to change their own behaviour. That is not to suggest that top management are themselves always perpetrators of 'problem' behaviour (although this is certainly possible) but it is highly likely that they will witness it. In raising their own awareness of the issue, they begin to see the potential harassment for what it is, then they can ensure that they themselves do not silently condone it. As suggested earlier, the behaviour of top managers is critical in setting good – or bad – role models.

Inevitably, however, not everyone in the organisation will come into contact with the top management. The inclusion of harassment, therefore, in the examples of gross misconduct in the disciplinary procedure would be one way of sending a clear message across the whole organisation, and signalling a resetting of the standards of behaviour at work. This can also be supported by changes to the grievance procedure to accommodate one of the more typical forms of harassment – boss to subordinate – by allowing a by-pass through personnel, avoiding the immediate line management. In themselves, these procedural changes are unlikely to change behaviour, although they may have some impact, but they set the framework for subsequent discussions. They cannot ensure organisations do not end up in court, but they mark the beginning of the process of tackling the issue openly and sensibly.

The second area for action is where the diagnosis has identified considerable scope for savings. The need here is not to take a strong stance and issue a revised policy. In fact, what is required is for the top management team to indicate first of all that they believe that a particular topic needs to be addressed and to propose a way of involving the rest of the organisation in the development of the ideas. As we explore in the next chapter, it is absolutely critical that widespread 'ownership' is gained for the equal opportunities programme and hence for any proposed policy changes.

This is most easily illustrated if we take a particular example. It may well be that a diagnosis will reveal that over 50 per cent of those who go on maternity leave do not return. This contributes significantly to attrition and costs the organisation dearly. It is tempting, therefore, for the top management team to call in the people in the personnel function and ask them to draw up some policies which will help reduce this attrition. The expectation is that these will be launched on a duly grateful organisation.

In reality, however, the vast majority of the organisation will not know what all the fuss is about and the people who ought to have the most influence over the policies are the people who will be the users – the women who are taking maternity leave and their managers. Gaining their constructive input will take time and should not be rushed.

At this stage, therefore, it would be inappropriate to take a stand and rush out a policy. It would be enough to indicate that this is an area for priority action and that proposals will be developed involving those most directly affected.

All in all, the top management team need to balance their follow-up actions. They need to include changes that can be rapidly implemented as well as projects that will require patient staff work. All the actions need to be consciously linked back to the 'vision', and to the preceding diagnosis.

Inevitably, at this time they will also need to consider:

(1) how to communicate both their 'vision' and also the follow-up actions; and
(2) how (and by whom) this programme is going to be managed and monitored.

The first is the subject of the next chapter – Spreading ownership – and the second is covered in Chapter 11 – Sustaining the momentum.

■ CONCLUSION

The setting aims stage of our strategic approach is critical in determining the level of support that an equal opportunities programme attracts. The programme should:

- Demonstrate the links between equal opportunities and business performance
- Identify the business purposes for pursuing equal opportunities
- Establish some standards against which progress can be measured
- Convey a 'vision' of what equal opportunities means for everyone in the organisation.

These are issues for top management to address and decide. They cannot delegate responsibility for developing these aims without undermining the importance of the topic.

If they have been clear in their thinking, these aims will give top management the ability to determine the direction of the organisation without them having to tell people what to do. This is their critical role in the evolution of an equal opportunities programme. From here on they may play a monitoring role, but their real concern should be to get these aims 'owned' by the rest of the organisation. If they can do this, they will be able to let go and simply wait for the policy changes to come back up to them for approval.

Chapter 8

SPREADING OWNERSHIP

In the last chapter, we dealt with the need for clear aims as a fundamental stage in tackling equal opportunities in any organisation. This chapter will explore the need for these aims to be communicated to the organisation as a whole, in order to move to the vital stage of achieving ownership.

This chapter will focus on the following issues:

- What we mean by 'ownership'
- Why widespread ownership is so important
- Equal opportunities and leadership styles
- What sorts of things to avoid
- Ways of gaining the appropriate degrees of ownership
- Reasons for running a programme of workshops
- Specific workshops for human resources
- Other ways of spreading ownership
- Signs of increasing ownership

■ WHAT WE MEAN BY OWNERSHIP

'Gaining ownership' and 'getting people to buy-in' are phrases that crop up frequently these days in literature about organisational change, but what do they actually mean? Both, of course, have their origins in property transactions – for example, you buy a house and you are then its owner. This implies a deliberate choice – there are plenty of other houses you could have chosen, but this is the one for you: you have weighed up the cost against the value of the purchase and decided to go ahead.

It is this essence of positive choice that we mean by stressing the need for 'ownership'. There is nothing lukewarm about ownership. It implies full and active commitment. The Coverdale Organisation have a framework for examining what they call 'degrees of agreement'. Obviously, at one end of the spectrum an initiative can be met with rejection and active opposition. What we sometimes forget, however, is that at the other end of the spectrum there are varying degrees of acceptance. An individual could:

Acquiesce: 'I am indifferent to your intentions'

Sympathise: 'I respect your intention and will not stand in your way, though I do not feel obliged to help'

Support: 'I shall willingly help you to pursue that aim'

Share: 'I am fully committed to that aim and will do everything in my power to achieve it with you'

It is our contention that for equal opportunities to have a real chance of taking root, people need to be at the 'support' and 'share' end of the spectrum and this is what we mean by 'ownership'. If top management only succeed in gaining acquiescence and sympathy for equal opportunities, this is insufficient. What is actually required are changes in behaviour, people doing things differently – for instance, managers need to interview differently, staff need to think twice before cracking a joke – and this requires active support.

■ WHY WIDESPREAD OWNERSHIP IS SO IMPORTANT

As we saw in the last chapter, it is essential for top management to be clear about the aims they have for an equal opportunities programme, but it is obviously impossible for them to do anything more than convey this 'vision' and to set the appropriate standards. Cultural change can be led from the top – perhaps *has* to be led from the top – but it cannot start and finish there. The grand policy intentions depend upon the actions of a host of individuals lower down in the hierarchy to translate them into reality.

The added twist, so far as equal opportunities is concerned, is that those who are charged with making a reality of the policy – overwhelmingly white males – may well be precisely those who feel that they will 'lose out' most in the new order of things. In their own minds, they become the 'newly oppressed' group. Not surprisingly, many equal opportunities programmes have failed to win the 'ownership' of this critical group. By not being clear about the aims, and therefore not being able to communicate them, organisations are almost guaranteeing problems for themselves.

We can best see the significance of this if we explore what happens if this 'ownership' is lacking. In the absence of real information, and without clear aims, managers will make assumptions about an EO programme. The sorts of assumptions they are likely to make are:

- 'This is not in my personal interest' – this leads to resistance (usually passive)
- 'While it is not in my interests, the boss wants it to happen, so I had better do something to show that I am supportive' – this leads to lip service (doing something for the sake of being seen to do it)
- 'Equality means treating everyone exactly the same, and women and minorities are going to have to fight with the rest of them to get on' – this leads to a lack of support for people who face additional barriers to progression
- 'Equal opportunities goes against the grain – *I'm* certainly not going to make any attempt to change'.

What follows are some examples of the difficulties that this thinking can cause.

Passive resistance

Recruitment provides some of the best opportunities for passive resistance. The mindset works as follows: 'My priority is to find someone who will *fit in*, this means someone who shares my interests and outlook.' In practice, this actually means 'someone like me' – maybe to the extremes of recruiting someone who went to the same school or belongs to the same rugby club. There does not have to be anything overt about this resistance – after all, there will be plenty of good reasons for selecting the chosen chandidate – it is, however, fairly fundamental. Unless managers are prepared to widen their thinking about who should be recruited, and who gets on in the company, an equal opportunities programme must remain a sham (or, at best, wishful thinking).

A steady blocking influence exerted by middle management is the usual cause of equal opportunities programmes running into difficulty.

Lip service

When managers feel they ought to do something for the sake of pleasing the boss, they usually go for the most tangible act – promoting a woman or a minority working for them. Something as overt as this is sure to earn 'brownie points'.

This positive discrimination or 'tokenism' does no-one any good. The woman or minority promoted may well not be ready for the job, and may feel that she/he has only been promoted because of his or her gender or race. Colleagues are almost bound to reach this conclusion and are therefore unlikely to be supportive. When the whole experiment is deemed to end in failure, which is not surprising if the individual appointed bears the double burden of being 'the first' and also having to win round unsupportive colleagues, this adds fuel to the fire of cynics. They cry: 'I told you so. They're not up to it!'

Moreover, the cynics are able to assert that equal opportunities is all about promoting women and minorities to meet the targets set by senior management, and has nothing to do with promoting the best person for the job. A fundamental element of an equal opportunities programme is undermined.

When a manager strives to do the right thing, and promotes a woman or a minority simply because of the equal opportunities policy, both the individual appointed, and the organisation as a whole, lose out.

Lack of support and training

One attitude managers can take is to decide that recruiting women and ethnic minorities is fair enough, but that they will have to struggle just as much as the white men to climb the ladder. This has all the hallmarks of 'equality', but, on further inspection, what it means in practice is that women and minorities actually have to struggle much harder than their colleagues. They face barriers that do not exist for the majority.

As Rosabeth Moss-Kanter points out in her video *The Tale of O*, there are added pressures if you are different and, in some way or other, stand out from the crowd. If you are the first woman to become a manager, or the first minority to join a department, all eyes are on you to see how you will turn out. The high profile, if you are robust enough to take the pressure, can be advantageous. This, in part, accounts for the rapid progression of the 'star' woman or minority. For the rest, however, it can lead to overload and very public failure.

White men, of course, have had their informal support networks (not that they would call them that) for years: playing golf together or just drinking in the evenings in the pub after work. Woman and minorities may well feel excluded from these sorts of activities, and lack more of their 'own kind' to network with. It is essential that managers take account of this and provide some of the missing support.

Often when the awareness of these types of issues is raised, the informal networks which operate among employees do make an effort to include women and minorities in their weekly bowls match, or visit to the pub.

The 'let them tough it out with the rest of them' attitude ensures that managers do not see the need to help people make the most of their potential. 'You've either got it or you haven't.' Let us take the example of a woman who has been a secretary for years and is now promoted into a more broad-ranging role. She is bright, articulate and a good organiser. The sink or swim attitude means she is offered no help in managing the transition. From having had years of implementing someone else's ideas, she is expected to come up with ideas of her own. From years of dealing with relatively 'closed' problems, where someone else has defined the scope and decided what needs to be done, she has to grapple with 'open' problems where it is up to her to make these decisions. Unless the manager is supportive, and understands the issues involved, very soon there are complaints: 'She just won't use her initiative, I don't know why she took the job!'

In Chapter 10 we highlight some of the ways in which well designed training programmes can help men and women develop the skills appropriate to dealing with new situations, and realise their *full* potential.

Equal opportunities is not going to change the way we work here

This sentiment is often expressed by employees who feel discomfort at the prospect of change they see that equal opportunities will mean.

Individuals are happy to support the progression of women and minorities, so long as it does not interfere with the way things are. It is the responsibility of the women or minorities to 'fit in' – if they don't like our banter, that's their problem.' Or 'We have always had pin-ups in the mailroom. If they don't like them, they don't need to look at them!'

Often the concern comes from people with a strong sense of tradition, who may well come from very traditional backgrounds themselves. Deep down, for example, an older traditional male (or female) may believe that for instance, women should not really combine a career with a family. Another may voice concern that 'the lads wouldn't like to work for a woman.' Beneath this statement maybe there is another: 'I don't want to work for a woman, because fundamentally, I believe it's the man who is the boss.'

To summarise, with anything less than a high degree of ownership, an equal opportunities policy will remain a platitudinous statement of intent. There are too many ways for people to block change – both overtly, or more subtly – for there to be a short-cut to achieving ownership.

Further purposes for gaining widespread ownership

As far as equal opportunities is concerned, passive acquiescence or sympathy are not enough. Positive actions are required to overcome the forces of inertia and make any progress at all. Organisations work on the basis of procedures and custom and practice, but equal opportunities requires *habitual challenging* of the way things are done. Unless people embrace the need to change and do things differently, there cannot be equality of opportunity.

'Ownership' is achieved where there is genuine understanding and active support for the aims expressed in the equal opportunities policy statement.

Gaining this ownership, on a widespread basis, is a lengthy process. The purposes for going through this stage are:

- To avoid the otherwise inevitable passive resistance or acquiescence
- To avoid the likely misunderstanding of the true nature of equal opportunities
- To remove the fear of threat and replace it with a sense of opportunity
- To create a climate where people can constructively challenge the status quo
- To gain commitment to, and input to, potential policy changes and therefore:
- To ensure that equal opportunities is integrated into the culture of the organisation.

In our view, the stage of gaining widespread ownership of an equal opportunities programme is a pivotal one for its success. With this everything becomes possible, without it there is little point trying to progress any further. It is, in effect, a precondition for achieving sustained change. Without gaining widespread ownership, it is impossible to address the cultural issues identified at the diagnostic stage. There is no point developing leading edge policies, or indeed appointing significant numbers of women and minorities, if the organisational culture does not move in step.

In Table 8.1 at the end of the chapter, we contrast programmes where widespread ownership has, and has not, been achieved.

The question now becomes: 'How can we gain this ownership?'

■ EQUAL OPPORTUNITIES AND LEADERSHIP STYLES

In his book *Organisation Renewal* (Meredith Corporation, New York, 1969), Gordon Lippitt talks about the appropriate styles of leadership, depending on the situation. If there is a continuum of leadership (decision-making) styles from 'tell' through 'sell' to 'consult' and 'share', then those managing an equal opportunities programme are going to have to think very carefully about which styles to use when. It is our contention, that all too frequently, they are at the 'tell' and 'sell' ends of the spectrum. To achieve genuine ownership, they need to be predominantly at the 'consult' and 'share' end of the continuum. That is not to say that there are not times when people need to be 'told', just that these instances need to be well judged.

There is a good parallel here with health and safety at work. The emphasis here has traditionally been on the 'tell' style and regulations are issued such as: 'All employees in the laboratory will wear safety goggles.' Employers have legal responsibilities and they are obliged to issue mandatory instructions. On the other hand, enlightened employers, who want to influence the subconscious thinking and ingrained habits which are the cause of most accidents at work, will spend time and effort trying to create a wider safety awareness among employees. Their aspiration is not just that employees wear the appropriate safety equipment and follow the prescribed regulations, but also that they work in a way that anticipates danger and minimises the risk of accidents.

The same is true with equal opportunities. The 'tell' style is wholly appropriate where top management need to wear their values on their sleeve. We believe they should issue, for example, a disciplinary procedure which makes explicit reference to sexual and racial harassment as examples of misconduct. Nevertheless, merely issuing the procedure is unlikely, in itself, to have much impact (other than driving underground some of the more overt forms of harassment). Nor should the procedure specify in great detail what constitutes harassment. People need time to consider the issue and understand the problems harassment can cause, before they are likely to change their behaviour.

There is however, a major difference between equal opportunities and safety policies. Employees will see for themselves the need for progress and vigilance on the safety front. An individual will personally relate to the topic. 'After all I want to work in a safe environment too.' However, although for some employees, equal opportunities will be seen as important, it is, for the average employee, not as easy to relate to as, say, the safety initiative. For many there will be no obvious personal motivation for change. So again, time will need to be spent in getting the message across, and emphasising the purposes and need for change.

Therefore, in what follows we explore the impact that differing leadership styles can have on the degree of ownership that is gained for an equal opportunities programme. In some ways, it is easiest to begin with how not to do it: after all, it is the way many organisations still seem to be tempted to proceed.

■ HOW TO ENSURE YOU NEVER GET OWNERSHIP

What follows is a recipe for disaster, and we do not contend that any single organisation has, or indeed could, make *all* these mistakes. Each of these instances, however, has occurred and is caused by a misunderstanding about what equal opportunities is and hence the inappropriate or ineffective use of leadership styles. By going to the extreme, however, we hope that we are able to make a point and that the subsequent thoughts on how to get ownership are all the more powerful. As Ralph Coverdale said:

'There is no perception without contrast'.

Develop the whole programme in isolation and launch it with a roll of the drums and a major fanfare
There is nothing more likely to cause suspicion and cynicism. On the one hand, there is the 'here we go again' syndrome: 'The Chairman must have read something in the paper.' On the other, there is the natural concern: 'What does this mean for me?' However good the fanfare, it does not create the right environment to encourage a sensible and mature debate about the issues. In itself, it is likely to raise

more issues than it can address and cause people to brace themselves for, and to resist, change.

Don't tell people why equal opportunities is important or focus entirely on the external pressures for change
Of course the law is important, but it hardly represents sufficient reason, in itself, for embarking upon a major programme of change. Unless the business reasons are clear, people will assume it is all being done for PR reasons – looking good to the outside world – and all that is required is a bit of 'window dressing'.

Play on the rights of minorities and women, to the exclusion of white males
If the changes are all to the advantage of particular 'minority' groups, then why should the 'majority' want to do anything about it? If this is how equal opportunities comes across, then it will be impossible to get widespread ownership.

Tell the white men they have to do all the changing and make them feel that they are entirely responsible for 2,000 years of oppression
There are no end of reasons for why we are where we are, focusing on the past raises the level of emotion and is a highly ineffective way of seeking to create support. As we know from Total Quality Management, fixing the blame rather than the system may be easier, and a well practised art in some organisations, but it does not fundamentally solve the problems, merely finds excuses for them.

Tell the minorities that they are welcome, but that they are the ones who will have to do the changing
This is the opposite to blaming the majority; here the fault clearly lies with the minorities. They need to change and subvert their 'differences' as far as possible to fit in with the company culture, and be 'like us'. It is, of course, a great message of support for those in the organisation who do not want anything to change: 'We can just sit here, behaving as we have always behaved, and the minorities either make it or they don't.'

Issue a policy statement to be filed in the personnel manual, appoint an equal opportunities officer and hope that the whole thing will go away
Managers are used to this, with more than enough to do, their bottom drawers are full of low priority 'nice-to-dos'.

■ WAYS OF GAINING OWNERSHIP

As discussed above, ownership cannot be thrust upon an unwilling recipient. Genuine ownership implies choice, and a 'tell' style will not get very far. Moreover, if the 'sell' style is adopted, then it is imperative that the reasons for the changes are based upon sound logic and are clearly expounded. Woolliness leads to misunderstanding and room for people to put their own gloss on events.

It is for these reasons that we believe that it is imperative for organisations to go through a diagnostic stage, and an aims setting stage, before they seek to gain widespread ownership. If there has not been a diagnosis, there will not be a demonstrable logic for the programme. If there is a weak legalistic policy statement, this will leave ample scope for people to read in their own interpretation of top management's thinking.

Not surprisingly, the correct principles to work with constitute a complete reversal of the ways of avoiding gaining ownership.

Develop the programme with the active involvement of people at all levels in the organisation
This is one of the key advantages of conducting interviews with a cross-section of employees at the diagnostic stage. 'Big Bang' launches are probably best avoided (asking people lower down in the organisation what they think about such events is usually sufficient deterrent). Instead, find several different ways to explore equal opportunities issues. If an equal opportunities programme comes 'out of the blue', then this is a clear sign of lack of preparation.

Explain clearly the equal opportunities programme aims and link them back to the business
Based on the information gained in the diagnosis, the top management should have been able to develop a credible policy statement. They should never tire of referring back to this document, it must remain the touchstone of the whole programme. Emphasise the benefits to the business and the working environment, in achieving diversity across groups, departments and the organisation.

Stress the benefits for all employees and give them time to see this for themselves
If the policy is about appointing the best person for the job, then the only people who could lose out are those who have been coasting on

an easy ride. Equal opportunities *acts as an audit of the existing systems* – for instance, increasing the clarity around the criteria for progression will be of benefit to all. In addition, equal opportunities can act as a catalyst for change – for example, in creating a much greater balance between home and work. Because equal opportunities is so associated in people's minds with positive discrimination, these wider benefits for all are not immediately apparent.

Avoid allocating blame and emphasise that we have all got to change
It is not up to one group or another to do all the changing. We are breaking into new ground, working cultures are evolving, and we all need to re-orient ourselves. We all have our prejudices and being aware of this is the first stage to doing something about them.

Develop a comprehensive system for spreading awareness and understanding of the programme, which allows people to make a conscious choice to 'buy in'
People at work have a great deal to do, and they will need a conscious signal from top management that equal opportunities has a business priority. Only then will the majority take it seriously. This does not mean, however, that the issue should be forced on people in an aggressive way. Quite simply, equal opportunities is common sense and there is no doubt that people will come to this conclusion themselves – providing they are allowed to do so in their own time.

Clearly, the diagnosis and setting aims stages set the context for gaining widespread ownership. What is needed, however, is a vehicle for communicating the logic and the nuances associated with an equal opportunities programme. A large-scale launch seems as inappropriate as informing people by circulating a memo. It is for this reason that we believe organisations need to design and run a programme of equal opportunities workshops.

■ REASONS FOR RUNNING A PROGRAMME OF WORKSHOPS

A workshop, involving some of the key people who have developed the policy to date, is probably the most successful vehicle for beginning this process of gaining ownership. If the number of attendees is kept small enough, in our experience 12 is about right, then individuals will have sufficient opportunities to air their views. The workshop can then genuinely be used as a two-way communication process, and once people have begun to input their thinking, the process of transferring ownership has itself begun.

Each workshop could address the following aims:

- To send a signal from top management about the priority of the issue
- To allow people time to air their concerns and get them addressed
- To provide an opportunity to explore the overall aims for the policy
- To raise people's awareness of the issues involved
- To begin to get some input to the policy development process.

What follows are some examples of the way in which we have seen workshops address these aims.

Send a signal from top management

Simply holding the workshops, and dedicating time to the issue, in itself sends a powerful signal throughout the organisation. When the Board of Esso UK and the managers who directly report to them took a day out in 1985 to look at equal opportunities, it was a highly unusual step. When they subsequently decided that all employees should go through a similar workshop the message was clear: this issue is important and must be taken seriously.

Supplemented by good pre-briefing, so that the reasons for the workshop programme are clearly understood, this puts the issue firmly on the business agenda.

This impression is further enhanced if top managers introduce each workshop. This gives them the opportunity to indicate their commitment and begin to put across the business rationale. For Dennis Oliver, the Finance Director of Rank Xerox (UK), this means linking equal opportunities and total quality. 'Quality is all about working on fact rather than gut feel or tradition, and that's what equal opportunities is about.' Top managers, just by being there, and taking time out to make an introduction, get people sitting up and taking notice.

Time for people to air their concerns

We have not run a workshop where at least a third of the attendees did not have significant reservations about there being an equal opportunities policy at all. Sometimes it is expressed directly: 'We've got better things to do with our time than worry about equal opportunities' or other times more obliquely: 'I don't think we've got a problem, I think we're very fair.' There is also the usual expression of cynicism that meets any organisational initiative: the 'here we go again' syndrome. People need to be able to let off steam in this way: they can then settle down and look at the issues.

At the centre of the concerns is usually the question: 'How will equal opportunities affect me?' It is absolutely essential that people are given time to express their concerns about positive discrimination. This fundamental fear – that recruitment and promotion decisions will be on the basis of gender or colour rather than skill – is the reason for much of the resistance.

There is another concern that frequently comes up: 'It's not me who is prejudiced, it's the customer, and I've got to do what the customer wants.' Another version of the 'it's not me, it's them' syndrome, is to blame the team. 'Will *they* fit in to the team?' 'I need to consider the team's views.'

Sometimes people express fears based on previous limited experience: 'I don't take on women in their late twenties because they represent a risk.' The fear, common among many managers, that young women will up and leave in no time to have children means that many women do not stand a chance of getting past the first post. They are weeded out before the interview stage. There is also a fear that ethnic minorities somehow have more 'rights' and that it is therefore difficult to dismiss them if they prove to be incompetent. The solution? – obviously, there's no point hiring them in the first place! As for people with disabilities – wouldn't they be better off in sheltered employment?

All these concerns can be addressed – in the main by being clear about the aims for the policy and sharing some factual information – but they must not be simply swept aside. It is of paramount importance that these concerns are treated seriously. Before people can themselves listen, and take in new information, they need to feel that they are being listened to.

Explore the aims of the policy

In Chapter 7 we discussed what the aims for an equal opportunities programme might be. The workshops are the opportunity to start to get the rest of the organisation to 'buy in' to these aims.

The starting point here must be to go back to what equal opportunities is (and is not). If equal opportunities is not about positive discrimination, then what is it about? Allowing people to define equal opportunities themselves, provides the right context for an explanation of the proposed policy statement. This has worked so well in Rank Xerox (UK) that Viki Ford, the manager of the programme, intends to use many of the ideas from the workshops in a revised policy statement. Ownership really does become very tangible when people can see their own words incorporated into formal policy documents.

In itself, however, a policy statement is far removed from the day-to-day reality of organisational life and it is important that people have time to make, for themselves, links between equal opportunities and the business goals. Every benefit that is identified represents another opportunity for people to 'buy-in' to the programme. Some people are switched on by the bottom line benefits – reducing attrition and recruitment costs, for instance – others by what they see as the forthcoming cultural shift – with people from differing backgrounds lending their different perspectives to decision making. Of course, most people will sign up to clarifying promotion criteria and opening up career paths – there are not many organisations where career progression would not benefit from a thorough in-depth review.

During this discussion of the aims, the organisation's ideas and plans for equal opportunities can be outlined. If there is an overall programme, who is its custodian, what are the short- and longer-term overall objectives for progressing the issue? At this early point, it is important to stress the long-term nature of an equal opportunities programme and to ensure expectations are realistic.

Raise awareness

An invitation to one workshop we were running began 'gentlemen. . .' – which was all very well but the sales manager issuing the invitation had forgotten that there was a female manager in his region!

As organisations begin to change, people's lack of awareness can cause them excruciating embarassment. A woman was being shown round an office and introduced to staff. One young man inquired: 'Are you the new personnel girlie?' He subsequently learnt that she was a newly-appointed director.

Once people are in a mood to listen, the workshops represent a one-off opportunity to help individuals make real headway in re-examining some of their basic assumptions and habits. It starts to open minds – thereafter people are more open to change and steadily continue the process once back in their normal working environment. It represents the key to unlock the issues associated with the organisation's 'culture' identified at the diagnostic stage.

This opening of minds during the workshop is reinforced if there is a mixed group of attendees. Given the right environment, people who would not have had the courage to talk openly, start to discuss their views with colleagues. Eyes can be opened – very often people are simply not aware of problems that they are causing.

The first need is probably to share some basic factual information. Most people have only an inkling of the changes occurring in the labour market which we described in Chapter 2. What is more, the labour market also represents the customer base, and its changing composition alters some of the old assumptions about who customers actually are.

Some of the other concerns can also be addressed by providing facts. In most organisations, women put in over six years service before they go on maternity leave – hardly the overnight desertion expected by some managers. Addressing concerns by providing factual information represents the first step to raising awareness. Once people feel their own concerns are being addressed they can start to open up to other people's concerns.

A particularly common complaint from professional women, for example, is that they get treated as if they are secretaries if they pick up a call. The caller, usually male, will say: 'I don't want to talk to you, I want to talk to the manager.'

The prevailing working environment and 'office banter' regularly get raised as issues at workshops. What to the average white male seems to be all in good, harmless fun, may actually be resented by others. In order to be accepted, women and minorities often suppress their true feelings about these issues, but workshops give them an opportunity to be more open and be heard. What is more, in such a situation, many of the average white males express similar discomfort with the banter.

Workshops often provide the first opportunity for these issues to be discussed and enable people thereafter to work the issues in a mature way to a satisfactory resolution for all concerned. As Diane McGarry, the Sales Director for Rank Xerox (UK) pointed out in her introduction to a workshop:

'Things will be different in the future: working with people from different backgrounds will be the norm. We need to raise our sensitivity.'

Providing input to policy development

We explore the process of policy development in detail in Chapter 11 and we discuss the policies themselves in Chapter 9. The general point to be made here is that any policy making – whether it is broad consideration of the next steps, or detailed review of operating procedures – is improved by involving those who are going to be responsible for implementation.

In some ways it turns on its head the job of those in the centre charged with policy development. Rather than coming up with the bright ideas themselves, they are the recipients of the ideas and can then push forward the ones that best seem to meet the organisation's needs. In this way there is ready-made support for the emerging policies.

One example here will serve to make the point. At their Board workshop, the directors of Rank Xerox (UK) thought that maybe equal opportunities should be included in managers' objectives for the forthcoming financial year. At a subsequent workshop, opening up this whole issue of 'how should we measure the progress of the equal opportunities programme?', managers themselves not only suggested that equal opportunities should be included in their own objectives but also that it should appear in the objectives for all employees. Quite properly, the managers followed through the logic, that everyone has a responsibility for making equal opportunities a reality, to its proper conclusion, and proposed a step beyond that hesitantly suggested by the Board. In addition, they went on to suggest a host of further ways that progress could be measured.

Conclusion

Precisely because everyone has a responsibility for the implementation of the equal opportunities policy it is essential that all employees are involved in the workshop programme. That is not to say, however, that all employees should go through exactly the same sort of workshop. All the above purposes need to be met, but the sorts of issues addressed would be dependent upon the attendees. In general, we have found that there are three separate groups of attendees: line managers, human resources staff, and all other employees. Each of these groups has distinct responsibilties and therefore it is appropriate to focus the workshops accordingly.

As far as the line managers and general employees are concerned, their workshops would have a great deal in common. They would address the purposes as outlined above – all that would differ is the actual issues discussed. There would be no point in spending a great deal of time discussing how to select candidates fairly, if those involved in the workshop are not expected to be involved in the recruitment process. Taking down the pin-ups in the mailroom, however, is another matter.

The group that probably does need a rather different workshop contains those who work in the human resources department. They have a particular role to play and their active support is required early on in the programme.

■ SPECIFIC WORKSHOPS FOR HUMAN RESOURCES

'Human resources' or 'personnel' are often seen as the 'custodians of policy' or the 'conscience of the organisation'. This does not mean, however, that they are necessarily more likely to be supportive of equal opportunities than anyone else in the organisation. Some will be, some will not be. Members of the department will have their own personal views, because just like everyone else they are moulded by their own personal experiences to date.

Those in the human resources department, however, do have a particular role with regard to equal opportunities. At a strategic level, the department is often charged with ensuring that the human resources policies and systems support the overall organisational strategy. Clearly, equal opportunities must be part of this picture. On a more pragmatic basis, much of their day-to-day work can have a huge bearing on the effectiveness of an equal opportunities programme. If all the women and minorities are weeded out of the selection process before the manager gets to see the papers, where does the problem lie? Alternatively, who is in the best position to challenge the traditional manager's thinking if not personnel?

It is quite possible that people in the human resource function will regard equal opportunities with some hostility. After all, it requires them to review long established custom and practice and think again about almost everything they do. What is more, if policy development really is gong to be opened up to greater involvement from the rest of the organisation, this can be seen as a challenge to personnel's specific expertise. Therefore, it should not be surprising that human resources do not necessarily welcome equal opportunities with open arms.

In practice, however, it is essential that those in the human resources function are seen to be ahead of the game. They need to be up–to–date and able to advise line managers about the changing composition of the labour market, or the legal framework. They need to know how other organisations are responding to these issues so that they can take account of best practice in their advice. They represent a vital layer of support for the equal opportunities programme manager. They should be an informed body of people with whom those responsible for the equal opportunities programme can readily exchange and try out new ideas. In essence, they are the group from whom early 'buy-in' is essential.

With all this in mind, the workshops for the human resources staff need to be run in a slightly different way. People will still need time to explore the issues, air their concerns and understand the formal policy and its objectives. They also need time to consider the functional implications of equal opportunities and to digest additional information that would not be relevant for line managers. The additional purposes for a workshop for human resources are therefore:

- To explore how the equal opportunities strategy relates to the overall human resources strategy
- To increase understanding of the external factors influencing developments: the legal framework, the labour market, and best practice
- To build understanding of the implications of equal opportunities for the work of the department
- To exchange ideas and build support for the equal opportunities programme manager.

When an organisation is trying to get ownership among line managers and their employees, it is critical that those in the human resources function are seen to be supportive. If the 'conscience of the organisation' is seen or heard to be acting at odds with the policy, this can undermine the entire process. What is more, because of the nature of their jobs, and the role they are seen to have in the organisation, rather like the directors, they have a disproportionately greater impact on the success of an equal opportunities programme.

Those responsible for driving the equal opportunities policy (often people themselves with a human resources background) need to be able to rely on a forward-looking, progressive human resources function as active allies in the process of change. This level of support and commitment cannot be taken for granted or rushed. We believe that running specially designed workshops for the human resources function is the most effective way of gaining their essential 'ownership'.

■ OTHER WAYS OF SPREADING OWNERSHIP

The workshop programme in itself only represents the start of the process of spreading ownership. There are many other ways that this process can be continued, and these are specifically dealt with in Chapter 8. Without these workshops, however, many of the other initiatives run the danger of falling upon fallow ground. Unless the soil has been properly prepared, the seeds of growing awareness cannot take root.

■ SIGNS OF INCREASING OWNERSHIP

It is appropriate, therefore, to ask what are the signs that the ground has been adequately prepared and that 'ownership' is spreading? As we discussed right at the start of this chapter, 'ownership' implies that people are prepared to *do something differently*. The following are the sorts of indicators that can be found if behaviour is beginning to change. In essence, they are the opposites to the passive resistance, lip service, and lack of support that we earlier identified as the consequence of a lack of ownership.

Change in language
Habitual references to 'salesman' become 'salesman or, of course, saleswoman' and perhaps 'salesperson'. It may not be very elegant, or doing much for the English language, but this sort of change illustrates that people are beginning to think more broadly.

Managers questioning their own assumptions
For some, this may be as simple as doing their share of getting the coffee instead of expecting their secretary to do so every time. Or, it may lead to managers questioning some of their selection criteria. One manager called personnel to ask: 'Do you have a problem if I want to recruit someone who is aged 57?' (This was in an organisation where most people expected to receive early retirement terms by the time they reached their mid-50s.)

People being prepared to challenge potentially discriminatory behaviour
This might mean, for example, teams curbing their habitual office 'banter' or deciding not to hire the traditional 'dancing girls' for the Christmas party.

When asked, managers are able objectively to justify appointments
Appointment decisions should be objectively justifiable with no suggestion of positive discrimination 'in either direction'. It could also lead to a good deal more healthy exchange between employees and managers about their skills and their prospects for promotion.

Managers positively supporting policy proposals
Apathy and resistance are replaced by positive support. The spread of flexible working contracts is a good indicator of the degree of line management ownership – the more widespread, the more managers are being prepared to look again at how work is structured and how they can keep the skills of key employees.

These are some of the more obvious, short-term changes in behaviour that can become apparent if ownership is genuinely spreading through the organisation. In time, of course, this will also start to have an impact on the profile of the organisation. Longer term, this remains the fundamental test: how diverse is the organisation? It is essential, however, that the cultural issues begin to shift first – then the ground will be prepared for new policy initiatives.

■ **CONCLUSION**

During this chapter we have:

- Defined 'ownerhip' as: 'genuine understanding of and support for the aims expressed in the equal opportunities policy statement'
- Argued that passive resistance or acquiescence are the usual causes of the foundering of an equal opportunities programme
- Suggested that top managers need to choose their leadership styles carefully and contrasted the impact of different approaches on the success of the programme
- Proposed running a series of workshops as the vehicle for initiating the process of gaining widespread 'ownership'
- Illustrated the sorts of behaviour that would suggest the process of spreading ownership has begun.

This process of spreading ownership can never be considered 'finished'. If equal opportunities is not seen as something separate from good management practice, but as an essential aspect of it, then it must become integrated into everything that happens in organisations. It must become part of the evolving culture of any organisation.

As far as our model for managing equal opportunities is concerned, this is the central stage. 'Spreading ownership' relies upon the success of the previous stages. At its foundation lies a comprehensive diagnosis which provides the factual basis for discussion. It also needs to build upon a vibrant interpretation from top management which links equal opportunities with the organisation's wider objectives. With these stages complete, and the process of gaining widespread 'ownership' initiated, then at last it is time to develop some new policies.

Chapter 9

POLICY DEVELOPMENT

Without formal policies (and sometimes even with them) individuals feel free to make up policy as they go along. This is fine in small organisations where the key decision makers can easily get together and they face issues of policy relatively rarely. As organisations grow, however, there is an increasing need to ensure that there is a consistent basis for decision making. This is what the formal policies provide. In some ways the company policy manual is an organisation's Bible. If people are in need of guidance they turn to the formal policies to see what they say. Some policies offer detailed advice, others simply indicate the desired direction and leave open areas of discretion.

With consistent treatment being such an important factor in achieving equality of opportunity, it should not be surprising that early enthusiasts have been great policy makers. Without any formal policy, how can there be consistency of treatment? What better place to start then with the organisation's Bible?

There is no doubt that there is an important role for policy making. We believe, however, that it needs to be positioned appropriately. Policies should not be an end in themselves, they must be stimulated by real business needs and they should be drafted in a way that reflect the needs of those affected. It is for this reason that we have only turned our attention to policy making following chapters on diagnosis, setting aims and spreading ownership. Each of these earlier stages will demonstrably shape the policies that organisations choose to develop and introduce. Unless the ground is adequately prepared, the policies will not be able to bear fruit.

In this chapter, therefore, we will seek to explore:

- the positioning of policy development within an equal opportunities programme
- the policies that need to be in place in order to support an equal opportunities programme.

The majority of the chapter will be devoted to the discussion of specific personnel policies. The intent is not so much to offer prescriptions – policies need to be designed afresh for each organisation – as to establish the options that need to be considered and to display the underlying principles upon which they are based.

■ POSITIONING OF POLICY DEVELOPMENT

As we saw at the diagnostic stage, equal opportunities affects the personnel policy framework in a couple of ways:

(1) it may bring to light the need for completely new policies; and
(2) it requires the existing policies to be reviewed in the light of equal opportunities themes.

To summarise, this may mean that some policies will be introduced, or revised, in order to comply with legislation or to keep up with best practice in the employment market. Legal considerations may expose, for example, the need to do something about an organisation's approach to people with disabilities. The increasing number of women within the organisation may lead to a review of flexible working provisions.

In this way, organisations should be able to ensure that they both comply with the law and also meet the changing needs of their internal (current employees) and external (potential recruits) labour markets.

It is tempting, once the diagnosis has exposed the need for a particular policy initiative, to get on with it and develop the policy. In practice, however, there will be a number of considerations that need to be taken into account.

Personnel policies represent some of the steps that organisations need to take in order to make the transition from the organisation they are, to the organisation they wish to be. There is little point issuing policies if people are still unclear about the future to which they are aspiring. The policies must actively support the business goals and must be driven by organisational priorities. In other words, policy making can only take place once the top management group have set their aims and decided how equal opportunities fits in with the business.

Moreover, developing and issuing a new policy will have minimal impact unless people have had time to think about equal opportunities and what it means for them. Effective implementation of equal opportunities does not mean simply issuing a whole set of new policies and procedures. People cannot be simply 're-programmed' to work in a new way. There is a great danger, therefore, in getting ahead of the organisation and developing policies that will not be implemented.

By issuing policies too early, policy makers also miss the opportunity of gaining significant input from those who will be most affected by the changes. Who knows better about what changes are required in the maternity leave policy than the mothers who have taken leave and their managers? However good the research, policies developed in isolation by a head office function will almost inevitably miss the mark. This thinking was taken to its logical conclusion at the Ove Arrup Partnership. Two women were pressing the organisation to introduce a Career Break Scheme, so they were charged with doing the research and their proposals were then implemented.

Furthermore, as discussed in the last chapter, actually involving people in developing policies is the surest way of gaining their 'ownership'. This is one of those seemingly rare instances of 'win/win'. The organisation develops better policies and increased commitment from employees to making these policies work. Employees get policies that meet their real needs. It goes almost without saying that, where necessary, organisations will have to provide information on any financial constraints before letting employees loose.

The principle of getting people at the 'sharp end' involved in policy making can be formalised to the extent of deliberately launching 'pilot schemes' and experiments. Viki Ford, Personnel Programmes Manager at Rank Xerox (UK), deliberately set about this when seeking to develop a flexible working policy. The working culture was traditional ('If you didn't work 10 hours a day, five days a week, you were seen to lack commitment') but a few individuals with particular domestic needs were able to agree experimental contracts with their managers. On the back of these highly successful experiments, a formal policy has been introduced (x number of non-standard hours contracts). Going about policy development in this way has enabled assumptions to be broken and thus the formal policy has been drafted as an enabling, rather than constraining, document. Practical experience has realised opportunities rather than fears.

Every preceding stage of the strategic approach has therefore a role to play in policy development.

At the diagnostic stage, the policy development needs can be identified. At the setting aims stage these can then be integrated into the overall business approach. The process of gaining ownership can then be used as a vehicle for widening the involvement in policy making (and for deciding which policies are required).

■ THE PRINCIPLES OF GOOD PRACTICE

There is no such thing as an 'ideal' personnel policy, or a model policy that can be simply taken from one organisation and applied in another. The essence of good policy making is to ensure that the policies reflect the current, and projected, business needs of the particular organisation in question.

In what follows, therefore, we seek to draw out the principles that organisations need to consider in their policy making. We have found it convenient to group the policies into two separate categories:

(1) those concerned with human resources 'systems'; and
(2) those concerned with enabling change and creating the appropriate environment.

The policies concerned with systems are: recruitment, career development, reward, and pension schemes. The essence here is ensuring that the systems are sophisticated enough to recruit, develop and reward the best. These policies are the basics. Even without equal opportunities as a concern, organisations should be looking to do these things.

The policies concerned with creating the appropriate environment are: balancing home and work, people with disabilities, sexual and racial harassment. The emphasis here is on being proactive and ensuring that the organisational culture does not act as a barrier to change.

Excluded from this chapter is the equal opportunities policy statement itself, which of course reflects both the 'systems' and 'environment' dimensions. This policy was discussed in depth in Chapter 7.

■ SYSTEMS: RECRUITMENT

The essence here is that both the systems themselves and the way that they are used should reflect the fact that the applicants, as much as the employers, are in a position to choose.

Specifying the job requirements

Getting this stage right is essential to the whole process of recruitment – job requirements must be the continual reference point for selection decisions, and if they are written in too exclusive a style then inevitably large numbers of suitable candidates will be ruled out. As the mismatch grows between the skills in demand and the number of people who have these skills, devising arbitrary ways to rule out suitable candidates will be seen to be the damaging pastime that it is.

With the current age profile of the working population, those who continue to specify an upper age limit of 40, are already immediately ruling out the majority of potential applicants.

Another supposed job requirement used in this way to reduce applications is: 'must have a degree'. Certainly, there will be jobs and careers where qualification at degree level is essential. There can be a danger, however, that this is used as a job requirement simply to cut down on the number of applicants, or because it is seen to be fashionable. In reality, where graduates are recruited to jobs that actually do not require graduate skills, they soon find that their expectations are not being met and they leave. This gets no-one very far.

The reason why recruiters do not give much thought to this stage of specifying the job requirements is that they are usually under pressure to fill the vacancy rapidly. Anyone is better than no-one. Rather than conducting a review of the genuine job requirements, recruiters are tempted into short-cuts and working to person specifications. This means that rather than concentrating on the skill requirements to do the job, recruiters think about who could do the job. More specifically, not so much who *could* do the job, as who *has* done the job. Not surprisingly, this leads simply to 'more of the same'. If the job of Prime Minister had been advertised, would John Major have been disqualified because he did not have a degree?

There can often be a confusion between what are 'essential' and what are 'desirable' requirements. This may well arise when considerations from the person specification cloud the thinking about the actual job requirements. Working in one organisation, we were reviewing a particular internal vacancy notice and concluded that we could ourselves apply for the job. We met all the 'essential' requirements – these were all personal characteristics: age ranges, sense of humour, willingness to work in a team – although we had none of the technical know-how required for the job which was listed under 'desirable' qualities. Obviously, people can be trained 'on the job' to develop the appropriate technical skills, but there must be limits to what is sensible.

In our view, the whole concept of person specification gets the recruitment campaign off to the wrong start. It encourages people to conjure up an image of the 'ideal' candidate – and this will inevitably carry with it unhelpful assumptions. At this point in the recruitment process it is essential to:

(1) revisit the basic objectives of the job; and
(2) specify, in some detail, the essential skills required to carry out this job.

Rather than seeking to exclude potential applicants, the incentive should be to include anyone with the suitable skills.

Outreach policies

Once the job requirements are clear, they need to be communicated to potential applicants so that they can decide if they wish to apply. This is where 'outreach' policies come in. They are the opposite to the old 'staff introduction' or kinship recruitment policies – rather than playing safe with more of the same, outreach is all about getting applications from people who would not have normally applied. At the diagnostic stage it should have been possible to identify whether particular minorities seemed to exclude themselves from consideration by not applying.

There are three main strands to outreach policies:

(1) revising existing PR material and activities;
(2) developing positive action adverts; and
(3) developing positive action training.

Looking again at PR (Public Relations) may well identify why applications are not coming in, for example, from women, minorities and people with disabilities. The usual reason is that these people do not feel the organisation is 'for them'. School leavers surveyed in 1986 felt that the Civil Service was a white, middle-class and male organisation. This is equally true of many other organisations – which is not particularly surprising because, if you look at the employee profiles, the majority would fall into this category. Therefore, actions need to be taken to overcome the resistance to apply –

who wants to set themselves up for failure by applying for something they know they will not be allowed to do? The message needs to be: 'We might be overwhelmingly white and male now, but we don't always want to be.' In 1990, the Metropolitan Police targeted a recruitment campaign at ethnic minorities and generated an additional 1,000 responses. B & Q's adverts in summer 1989 ("we're looking for older staff to make us a wiser store") generated over 5,000 responses.

When the applicants do not come to you, you can still go to them. One of the most powerful steps that an organisation can take is simply to increase the face-to-face contact with any under-represented groups. If women are not applying, then it makes sense to get out to the schools and find out why. Littlewoods have done a lot in the North West to try to increase the applications they receive from ethnic minorities. One of their actions was to support South Liverpool Personnel – an employment agency focused on people from ethnic minority communities. Similarly, companies have approached a number of the disabled charities who have put them in touch with suitably qualified candidates.

This needs to be supported by changes to the overall corporate literature – so that the messages are consistent – and by producing appropriately targeted publicity material. Just to give one example, a four-sided leaflet called 'Women in Esso', featuring the career profiles of successful women in the company, obviously caught the public's imagination because it was, for a long time, the company's most requested fact sheet.

Positive action advertising takes this one step further. Rather than working on the overall image of the organisation, this is targeted to a particular vacancy. There are some legal hurdles that need to be cleared, but there is no doubt that positive action advertising can be very effective. The point is that not only can it increase applications from the targeted minority, it can also increase applications from the majority. This obviously means standards can be raised. A very good example is the advert placed by Rank Xerox's Customer Response Centre to attract more men to work in what has been a typically female area. They managed to fill all nine vacancies from one advert (which was unheard of) and recruited five women and four men. We will discuss this particular approach in more detail in Chapter 12.

Positive action training takes a slightly different approach. The philosophy here is that employers can increase the pool of talent available to them if they consciously target and train under-represented groups. Examples of these initiatives are discussed in Chapter 10.

Application form

Many organisations currently rely upon applicants to send in CVs rather than developing their own application form. We believe, from a policy perspective, this is an unhelpful trend.

A well designed application form ensures that there is enough information, but not too much, in order to make pre-screening decisions. When people send in their CVs, they usually start with some detailed personal information – most of which is irrelevant to the selection process. Information such as marital status, number of children, and (frequently) date of birth are irrelevant but it tempts recruiters to make judgements based on this information. In addition, there is an advantage, as we shall see below when we look at pre-screening, in having the information that is required presented in a consistent way.

It is also possible, if an organisation has its own application form, to include a question about ethnic origin which enables effective monitoring to take place. Otherwise, it is impossible to detect whether, for instance, ethnic minorities are proving disproportionately successful or unsuccessful. It would also be an essential tool to see whether a positive action advertising campaign was successful.

Selection processes

Once the applications are in, there are four sorts of selection processes that can take place:

(1) pre-screening, i.e. deciding who should be weeded out on the basis of the written information provided;
(2) aptitude or personality testing;
(3) interviewing; and
(4) assessment centres or simulation exercises.

Pre-screening

In our experience, pre-screening is the stage where many of the most subjective judgements are made and, given that this is also the stage where the majority of applicants can be rejected, this should be a cause of some alarm. At the diagnostic stage a few sample campaigns should have been analysed and this may have revealed specific information about drop-out rates of different groups at different stages of the recruitment process.

Sometimes there is conscious or unconscious racism – anyone with a foreign-sounding name is screened out. More often, however, the subjectivity comes simply from the fact that recruiters are working from person specification rather than job specification. As we argued above, we believe 'person specs' as a concept is poorly conceived. Bio-data screening, for example, is a systematic way of discriminating based on person specifications. What happens here is that a wealth of personal information is screened so that those candidates that best match the 'ideal' profile are selected to go on to the next stage. This can be a sure way of replicating the existing profile of the work force. At a more informal level, recruiters are tempted to draw conclusions based on very shaky assumptions. For example, a married man with a mortgage is considered to be the most 'stable' sort of employee. An example from the 1970s from the world of sales recruitment may illustrate the point.

Clearly, there is a need in many sales jobs for potential recruits to enjoy making contacts with new people and to feel comfortable in a social environment. In one recruitment handbook, this had been translated in the pre-screening criteria into an absolute requirement that candidates should smoke. Clearly, attitudes change and what was seen in the 1970s as a sign of sociability, would now be considered anti-social. The point is that the issue was not whether applicants smoked or not, but whether they had the skills to relate to other people effectively. Looking for and relying upon these sort of short-cuts to determine whether an applicant is suitable must be bad recruitment. Short-cuts are always going to be based on generalisations and hence assumptions. They are bound to reinforce stereotypical thinking.

As far as pre-screening is concerned, it is necessary to revert to the skill requirements developed at the start of the recruitment process and to score each applicant against these requirements. It is for this reason that we believe organisations should have their own application form, rather than relying upon CVs that are sent in by applicants. This ensures there is a standard basis for gathering (and hence comparing) the information and also ensures that monitoring can take place.

153

If it appears that particular minority groups are being screened out disproportionately, then something can be done about it. There are some organisations, for example, who have chosen to interview every disabled applicant who applies. In one company, where most ethnic minorities were not making it through to the interview stage, the requirement for the pre-screeners to record their reasons for rejecting a candidate had the impact of increasing the proportion of those who did.

Again, good equal opportunities is simply good selection practice. Forcing pre-screeners to be clear about reasons for screening candidates in or out is going to be good for all concerned. It will, of course, take time. The most important factor is to have been clear – right at the start of the recruitment process – about the skills needed for the job. This not only makes pre-screening easier, it should also enable potential applicants to screen themselves in or out. In the best of all worlds, if the advert or vacancy notice is clear enough, there should not be hosts of unsuitable applicants.

Unless there is a systematic, skill-based process for pre-screening application forms, the process of deciding who gets through to the interview stage might as well be decided randomly. In one company, as a trial, a proportion of rejected applicants for the annual graduate intake were re-sifted and a number were put forward for first interviews. What was interesting was that these candidates were as successful as those who had been initially screened 'in' and subsequently obtained a second interview.

Aptitude or personality testing

At first glance, aptitude or personality testing appear to be the ultimate 'equal opportunity' tools. Unfortunately, on closer inspection this is not quite the case.

Tests are based on 'norms' and the norms have frequently been set by a predominantly (if not exclusively) white, male sample. Not surprisingly, therefore, organisations have found that tests were excluding women and minorities disproportionately. Both the Civil Service and BR have recently amended their tests.

There is a role for testing intellectual or technical aptitudes – well designed numerical tests, for instance, may well be better indicators than academic results (which often say more about the school than the innate ability of the student) – but the tests do need to be checked out and reviewed to ensure that they are relevant to the job concerned and are not based on an unbalanced sample.

Interviewing

The correlation between interviewing assessment and subsequent job performance is not high. Typically, interviewers make rapid, subjective judgements and spend much of the time looking for information to support their conclusions. In Chapter 10 we discuss some of these issues and how a training programme can address them.

Training must play a part, but there are also steps that can be taken from a policy point of view in order to improve the effectiveness of interviewing. Panel interviewing rather than solo interviewing, for example, helps increase the likelihood that subjective conclusions are challenged. It also helps if those involved in interviewing are themselves as diverse a group as possible. In particular, women and minorities in suitable positions should be encouraged to become involved in the selection process. Not only will they be able to challenge stereotypical thinking or prejudice among other interviewers, they also represent role models for women and minorities among the candidates.

Paper work systems can also help. The simplest is an interview assessment form. This can be simply a list of the key skill areas down the left-hand margin, with space on the right-hand side for interviewers to add in the evidence they have gained. This can both act as a prompt – to be used as a guide about the areas to question – and also ensure that there is a record of the rationale for the selection decision.

However unreliable the interview can be shown to be statistically, it will still be with us well into the future as a selection tool. Managers need to be directly involved in the decision about who joins their teams – otherwise they may well feel little commitment to making it work – and interviewing is the most straightforward way of involving them. What is more, at its best, it is a very effective vehicle for two-way discussion with the candidate. Applicants need to know what the job is like, they want to meet the manager of the team, and the interview is as much their opportunity to find out about the organisation as it is the company's to find out about them.

The emphasis, therefore, needs to go into developing policies and procedures which facilitate objective decision making and to provide training for everyone who is expected to play a part in the selection process.

Assessment centres

Assessment centres involving job simulation exercises (a simple example would be an in-tray exercise) can play a part in a comprehensive selection process. Through interviews, recruiters can establish what candidates have done in the past and explore particular achievements in some depth, thus revealing the extent to which they have displayed certain skills. Job simulation exercises take the next step forward into the future and seek to put candidates in a position where they are able to demonstrate that they have particular skills.

The keys to success here are:

(1) the design of the exercises and the extent to which they relate to the attributes required by the job in question; and
(2) the observation skills of the assessors and their ability to assess attributes rather than simply performance in the exercise.

As part of a graduate recruitment selection process, one company developed a business game that candidates played in three competing teams of five or six people. One manager was assigned to each group in order to assess the group members. When the managers later got together, it became clear that the various attributes that were notionally being 'tested' – about candidates' abilities to work in a team – were actually merging into an overall assessment of how that individual performed during the three-hour game.

Just as with interviewing, and aptitude testing, there is a need to ensure that the selection tool is appropriately designed. Are the right attributes being tested? In addition, there is a need to ensure that those involved are adequately trained. In short, running assessment centres is not for well meaning amateurs.

Conclusion

As we have described, the whole selection process can be a fairly hit and miss affair. There is no simple way to ensure that the best people are those selected. What organisations need to do is:

(1) ensure that they are very clear about the skills required;
(2) make sure the message is communicated to as wide a range of people as possible;

(3) put in place the paper work systems (application form, interview assessment form) that support objective decision making;

(4) develop a range of selection tools that together provide a balanced picture of an applicant's skills in relation to the job;

(5) train everyone involved in the selection process;

(6) continue to monitor in order to identify any particular problem areas.

■ SYSTEMS: CAREER DEVELOPMENT

Recruiting the best people may be the start of the process, but the real challenge is to ensure that the best are then developed and promoted. Obviously, some of the needs for internal selection (i.e. promotion) are exactly the same as for recruitment. The essential ingredient remains being able to specify the skills required for the job. Thereafter, as discussed in Chapter 6, as part of the diagnosis, we believe that it is essential that organisations have well developed appraisal and career planning systems. The only other point to make here is that progression and promotion are not synonymous. As organisations remove layers of their hierarchy, lateral moves will be increasingly important.

Specifying job requirements

Just as with recruitment, there can be a tendency for inappropriate selection criteria – based on thinking about person specifications – to rule out otherwise suitable candidates.

The best example of this is when criteria related to length of service are used. The logic seems to be that a certain amount of experience is required in order to develop certain skills. The Civil Service is particularly prone to this sort of thinking. It can often be encouraged by unions, who see anything that smacks of a system being better than a manager exercising his or her unfettered discretion.

In reality, of course, what is required is a particular set of skills. Some people might take five years to acquire them, others might be rather quicker. The need is for the skill not for the 'time served'. Not surprisingly, given the traditional profile of many of our organisations, having service criteria for promotion is one way of ensuring that women and minorities do not challenge the white, male hegemony too rapidly. Because recruiting patterns have only recently changed, women and minorities will often not have the number of years' service required and will therefore be ineligible. Specifying unjustifiable length of service criteria may well constitute indirect discrimination.

Of course, the simplest way of excluding women is for managers to split the organisation's roles into men's and women's jobs. While this is unlikely to be one of the formal criteria in the job requirements, the residues of this sort of approach are still very evident. Because a job is considered to be a man's job, requirements appear such as 'must be good at handling conflict'. What about preventing the conflict arising in the first place?

A related, but separate issue is the way in which managers presume jobs must continue to be done in the way that they have always been done. Insisting upon a full-time, wholly office-based job may well rule out some of the best candidates. Later on in this chapter, we explore some of the policies that can address this sort of situation.

Specifying the job requirements in an inclusive (rather than exclusive) way is therefore one of the key factors in ensuring that organisations can promote the best people.

Appraisals

As far as equal opportunities is concerned, we believe an appraisal system is an essential tool for ensuring that the organisation and the employee are making the most of their contractual relationship. This is the formal vehicle for employer and employee to review their psychological contract.

As we suggested in Chapter 6, an effective appraisal system needs to serve a variety of purposes. An appraisal can be a means of:

(1) assessing skills and development needs;
(2) measuring and discussing performance; and
(3) gaining input from employees about their aspirations.

The manager must act as *coach* (seeking to motivate employees so that they achieve the best performance they are capable of) and as *judge* (providing valid and reliable data about current performance and future potential).

The danger is that a manager will feel more comfortable with one of these roles than the other, and concentrate solely on this aspect of the appraisal system. As the John Cleese character , Ivan the Terrible, puts it: 'This is the annual appraisal interview where the company tells you what it thinks of you.'

In our view, therefore, it is essential that the policies and procedures associated with the appraisal system should reflect these dual roles (of coach and judge) and that this should be made equally clear to managers and to their staff.

One way of doing this is to hold two separate, formal discussions. At a first 'coaching' discussion, performance can be reviewed, skills and development needs identified, and potential career moves jointly discussed. This can be followed by a subsequent interview where the manager reports a formal performance assessment.

Another way of ensuring both the coaching and judging aspects are attended to is to split off the coaching role to a 'mentor' who is not the line manager. We discuss this in more detail in the next chapter. It has some advantages but, in our view, allows the manager to avoid one of his or her key responsibilities and undermines management accountability.

However it is set up, an appraisal system needs to reflect the full variety of purposes that we outlined above. It must be able to meet all the needs of both managers and employees. Again, as with selection systems, it will be critical, when the manager is assessing performance, that this is done objectively. The key performance areas need to be related to the accountabilities of the job and the assessments need to be backed up by factual examples. Of course, the assessment should never come as a surprise and should reflect the sorts of regular discussions that have taken place over the year.

Some organisations have chosen to include a measure of equal opportunities awareness among their performance indicators in their appraisal schemes. It can send a signal (this issue is important enough to feature in the appraisal) but it can also easily be ignored. Because it is one of the categories does not mean that it gets any more than perfunctory attention: 'No problems here, let's move on to the next box'. As with so much else in this field, the paper work can say one thing, but it is the way that policies are actually implemented that counts.

For this very reason, we argue, in the next chapter, that all those involved with appraisal schemes need to go through a comprehensive training course. Only then can the formal policies stand a chance of being implemented in practice.

Career planning

There is always discussion in organisations about the promotion process and conjecture about what employees need to do to 'get on'.

In our view, it is essential that the criteria for progression are known and that there is a rigorous system which enables the 'best' to secure promotion. Otherwise, it soon becomes not what you know, but who you know. Moreover, career planning is the most effective way of taking account of individual needs and trying to get a close fit between an individual's life plan and his or her job moves.

Some organisations have a policy of openly advertising vacancies and then interviewing candidates who apply. Others run assessment centres and decide whether candidates are ready for promotion. Both these policies have the potential for opening up vacancies and, if they are well conducted (applying the thinking that we outlined above for selection processes) they can be effective. We have a preference, however, for a more sophisticated approach to career planning which ought to be able to meet organisational and individual needs more effectively. It does, however, require a great deal of effort to ensure that it functions properly and is best suited to larger organisations. It also depends upon an effective appraisal system.

A career planning system consists of two interlocking parts – a critical job plan and a personal career plan. Together they ensure that:

(1) the organisation has identified a number of people who could fill key jobs; and
(2) there are potential career moves outlined for each employee.

The logic for a job planning system is as follows. When the proverbial bus runs over one of the directors, there need to be people who are willing and able to do the job. Broad experience is likely to be essential and therefore the planning needs to start early – particularly these days if directors are supposed to be in their mid-forties when they are first appointed. In any organisation, there will be a sequence of critical jobs that need to be planned for and an adequate supply of candidates ensured.

This job planning system needs to mesh in with individuals' personal career plans. There is no point identifying someone as a potential director if that is the last thing she/he wants to be doing. This is where there needs to be an effective appraisal system which is able to feed through reliable information about individuals' career aspirations. Employees must have an input to these career plans. Only then can it be certain that these plans take account of all their needs – including, for instance, their outside needs associated with their family situation. In this way, life planning and career planning ought to be brought together. Specifically, career planning activities should include those out on maternity leave or Career Breaks.

A rigorous career planning system such as this ought to help organisations make the most of the talent available to them. It requires, however, a high degree of 'maintenance' in order to be effective – and to avoid becoming discriminatory. 'Stars' do not always remain 'stars'. Others may be slow starters, but develop into highly effective performers. At Esso UK, meetings are held by the Board every fortnight in order to review and update current career plans. After all, are there many more important tasks for senior management than ensuring the quality of employees into the future?

Conclusion

Career development should not be left to chance. An organisation needs to put the systems in place that allow it to make the most of the talent available to it. It needs to:

(1) ensure that the promotion criteria are skill-based and clearly communicated;
(2) encourage managers to 'coach' their employees to make the most of their skills;
(3) have an appraisal scheme which provides reliable information on current performance and career aspirations;
(4) develop a career planning system which regularly reviews plans for jobs and individual careers.

■ SYSTEMS: REWARD

Paying people in a way that reflects their contribution to the organisation is easy to say but difficult to do. Yet, it lies at the heart of the employment contract – an individual sells his or her labour in return for particular rewards – and is increasingly important as the United Kingdom moves towards a know-how economy. Collectivisation appears to be a dying force, as even traditional manufacturing workers are embracing individual contracts, because they believe that this can more accurately reward them for their contribution. This is even more so the case for knowledge workers who will each make a unique contribution at work.

As far as equal opportunities is concerned, this is a healthy trend. If equal opportunities is about ensuring each individual is properly rewarded (and what else can it mean?) then individual contracts must be the best way of doing this. Collective bargaining obscures differences in contribution. The outcome is not decided through any particularly logical argument but simply expresses the current state of the power balance between employers and employees. Unions have not been particularly assiduous in looking after the interests of women and minorities.

If rewards are not to be established by collective bargaining, then what factors should be taken into account in order to determine pay? There are three interrelating factors:

(1) an assessment of the individuals' performance within the job;
(2) an assessment of the job compared to other jobs within the organisation; and
(3) the market's assessment of the value of the skills required to do the job.

As explained above, we see the appraisal system as being the best way of establishing an individual's performance. There needs to be agreement about the key performance areas, about the standards that are expected in each area and regular discussions about performance. In this way, the formal annual assessment should reflect actual performance.

Job evaluation

Job evaluation systems represent, in a way, the internal job 'market' and seek to value the relativities between jobs. As described in Chapter 6, an analytical job evaluation system is an important defence in 'Equal pay for work of equal value' cases.

The first point is to ensure that it is the job, not the job holder, that is being evaluated. Job titles often indicate the sort of traps that people can otherwise fall into. A man is a 'chef', a woman is a 'cook'. A man is a 'salesman' a woman is a 'shop assistant'.

Then, as argued in Chapter 6, it is important to ensure that the various factors involved in establishing the 'value' of a job are not weighted in a discriminatory way. If physical strength and working in a hazardous environment are particularly valued, then it would not be surprising to find men, on average, being paid more than women.

Job evaluation, however, is not as straightforward as it was in the days of rigid hierarchies. As flatter organisations become the norm, some of the traditional ways of evaluating jobs need to be reviewed. How significant, for example, is the number of people working for a manager? Similarly, as organisations respond to change, some of the rigid boundaries between jobs are breaking down. For example, as people increasingly use personal computers, and produce their own memos, the traditional role of the secretary (and the skills required to fulfil the role) must change. In some way or other, this needs to be reflected in the way that jobs are evaluated.

In our view, there needs to be a formal job evaluation system which breaks down jobs into their component parts and therefore establishes a credible 'grading' for jobs. As important, however, is that this system – and the assumptions upon which it is based – are regularly reviewed and that those involved in this process represent a cross-section of managers. Only in this way will the system have the credibility that it requires in order to play its part in determining what constitutes 'fair' reward.

Market surveys

The external labour market represents the third essential factor influencing reward. However the internal market, or job evaluation system, values a job, actual rewards need to respond to and be in line with market valuations. In the 1970s and 1980s the peaks in demand for IT people, for instance, forced up salaries. Similarly, the 'Big Bang' led to a leap in City salaries in the mid and late 1980s.

There is a need, therefore, to take the internal job evaluations and compare rewards for key jobs across organisations. In this way a check can be made against the external market.

One point to make from an equal opportunities perspective is that the external market is not adequate justification for underpaying a particular job. If, for example, a female secretary were to claim that her job was of equal value (in job evaluation terms) to a clerical role typically carried out by more highly paid men, it would not be an adequate defence to argue that this reflected the external market's valuation of the jobs in question.

The external market represents just one of the three factors that need to be taken into account in determining the appropriate level of reward.

■ SYSTEMS: PENSION SCHEMES

There are two obvious areas where equal opportunities affects pensions, both are concerned with ensuring equality between the sexes:

(1) retirement ages; and
(2) pro-rata'd treatment of part-timers.

All occupational pension schemes must provide for a 'common retirement age'. Many schemes now allow women to work on to 65 years of age. Others allow both men and women to retire at an earlier age – say, 62 or 60. There may come a time when organisations embrace a more radical approach and provide for a flexible decade of retirement between 60 and 70. Indeed, at Tesco, the normal retirement age is 65, but people can carry on, with accrued pension entitlement, until 70. This seems sensible – after all, some people at 60 are ready to retire and have given their all, others are quite happy to carry on working and contributing. As the population ages we will have to question some of our 'ageist' assumptions and we will no doubt discover a lot of potential that we are not currently tapping into.

Part-timers have typically been excluded from pension schemes. This can constitute indirect discrimination against women (who represent the vast majority of part-time workers). Accordingly, they need to be included in pension schemes, on a pro-rata'd basis and their continuity of service needs to be protected. For example, for anyone on a term-time contract, the typical pension scheme would have viewed the two-month period in the summer as a break in the employment contract.

There is another area, however, that ought to be examined. Many large organisations have favourable terms for 'early retirement' and these have been used, at times of recession, to reduce the size of the work force. In some organisations it is gradually being viewed as a 'right' to retire early, and employees actively look forward to it. For others, however, it is not seen so much as a 'right' as a threat. They wish to carry on working and are capable of doing so, but fear being 'counselled out' in order to make room for younger people. The ethics of this position can be debated, but the business logic is increasingly coming into question. Is it sensible to lose all this experience at once? Furthermore, it is a relatively expensive way of downsizing. Age is used as a short-hand when decisions are being made about redundancies. Perhaps sooner rather than later organisations will begin to treat redundancy just like any other selection decisions and apply some more rigorous, skill-based criteria.

■ ENVIRONMENT: BALANCING HOME AND WORK

As we saw in Chapter 3, employees are increasingly looking to balance home and work responsibilities.

Typically, this need to balance home and work has been a concern of women but increasingly it is shared by men. As the labour market swings in favour of employees (rather than employers) then organisations need to be able to respond flexibly to these employee aspirations.

Existing policies need to be reviewed in order to ensure that they are not at odds with the need to combine career and family responsibilities. The most obvious areas here are mobility clauses and relocation policies.

There are four sorts of policies that can be used specifically to help manage work and family demands:

(1) maternity leave;
(2) paternity leave;
(3) Career Break Schemes;
(4) childcare support; and
(5) flexible working arrangements.

Maternity leave

The worlds of home and work are brought forcibly together when female employees become pregnant.

Some organisations seem to regard attrition due to women leaving the organisation to raise children as an inevitability. They may lose up to 80 per cent of those who go on maternity leave.

Organisations that take this approach also tend to be those that conform to the minimum legal standards for maternity leave and maternity pay. In practice, the maternity leave policy can do much to influence the number of women who return, and the speed with which they return.

Eligibility for maternity leave
At first sight, it is only employees with two years' service who are eligible for maternity leave. In fact, this interpretation is increasingly

coming under question. If a man were to fall sick for six months after he had been employed for less than two years, how would he be treated? This is the logic that has led courts to question the requirement for two years' service. Many companies have reduced the service criterion for maternity leave to one year. In time, it would seem to be sensible to do away with the service criterion altogether. This would be in line with recent case law which has considered rejection of an applicant because she was pregnant as direct sex discrimination.

Maternity pay

This is the area where an organisation can use its flexibility most effectively. The statutory entitlement to maternity pay is : 9/10ths of weekly earnings for six weeks and 12 weeks of the government lower rate of State Maternity Pay. Many organisations have decided to be more generous than this.

At Esso UK, for example, there is an initial payment covering this 18 week period of two months' full pay plus 10 weeks at the government rate. This is then supplemented by a second lump sum of two months' pay if the woman returns to work within six months of commencing the leave. Within a six-month period a woman can receive four months of full pay and 10 weeks at the government rate. This means that she hardly suffers a significant drop in earnings. While this may appear generous, there is no doubt that the 'second lump sum' acts as an incentive and plays its part in enabling the company to attract back over 80 per cent of those who go on maternity leave.

Procedures

Maternity leave and maternity pay are complex areas and referring employees to the local DSS office for information is not overly helpful. Managers need to be able to help people calculate the date when maternity leave can begin, and to explain how benefits are affected by going on maternity leave. There needs to be a comprehensive guide that is available to both managers and employees.

Moreover, the procedures need to reflect the presumption that women will return rather than that they will not. They should not for instance, be immediately taken off the pay-roll. They should be included in any salary review that takes place while they are out on leave. They should be invited in for any important training events that are being run.

Arrangements for return

Some people will be very clear about their intentions – that they either do, or do not, wish to return to work – and they will carry them through. Others will change their minds. For this reason, people should probably be counselled not to resign at the point when they take leave. Managers, therefore, need to be in contact with women out on maternity leave in order to check out their intentions, and to ensure that their career plans still make sense.

An area of additional flexibility is enabling women to return from leave on a part-time basis. This may be a short-term arrangement, or it may be for the foreseeable future. This presents an alternative to what can otherwise seem to be a stark choice between family and work. An interesting point to note is that 'flexible return' has also proved a very successful, low-key way into flexible working. Many an 'experiment' has been prolonged because it is seen to meet the needs of all parties.

Paternity leave

Paternity leave is still in its infancy in the United Kingdom. Many companies use the discretion available to managers under 'exceptional leave of absence' policies to allow fathers two or three days paid absence at the time of birth. Some organisations have gone further and allowed up to two weeks' paid leave. Paternity leave, however, is still barely recognised and it will probably only be European influence that begins to change this.

For organisations that are prepared to lead, however, formalising paternity leave is a demonstrable way of illustrating a commitment to help employees manage both domestic and work responsibilities.

Career Break Schemes

Career Breaks enable men or women to take time out from their career to attend to family needs and then to return to the organisation at the same level they were on when they left.

The first Career Break was launched by National Westminster Bank in 1980. This followed interviews with 47 women who had recently left, or were about to leave, for domestic reasons. Since that date, many organisations have introduced Career Break Schemes. There is no 'ideal' scheme, the skill is in matching the needs of the organisation with the needs of employees and there are a variety of ways of doing this. The following are the issues that organisations need to address: eligibility, reason for break, length of break, keeping in contact during the break, employment and training during the break, terms for re-entry.

Eligibility

Some organisations have restricted schemes to women, and some to women only at management levels. Many have also included service criteria – after all, the rationale is that these policies enable organisations to retain skilled resources they might otherwise lose. There is also a rationale for putting in performance criteria – if someone has been turning in below average performances then maybe he or she should not be encouraged to return. The criteria for eligibility can be driven by the diagnostic work, which should have identified who leaves when and for what reasons. In our view, these criteria are best left open – open to men as well as women, open to staff at all levels. After all, if someone wants to take a break badly enough they will do so and if they are denied a Career Break they will simply leave. The evidence is that Career Break Schemes do not lead to extensive haemorrhaging.

Reason for the break

Again this can be phrased inclusively or exclusively. In some organisations, the break is confined to childcare. In other cases, the break can be for any domestic needs – for example, in order to care for an elderly relative. In still other cases, the principle of taking a break from a career has been widened to include people who want to 'see the world' and do some travelling. The best way to determine how widely to set these parameters is by asking employees.

Length of break

Typically, this varies between two and five years, although some schemes do allow for seven years out. The period needs to be long enough to meet the domestic need (say, the early years of raising children) yet also short enough to make the transition back to work effective.

Keeping in contact

There needs to be an identified person in the organisation who is charged with keeping in touch with someone out on a Career Break. Usually, this is the employee's manager. He or she needs to then ensure that there is a regular dialogue about how things are going and to discuss issues such as the likely timing of return.

Employment and training during the break
In order to help people out on a break keep in touch with developments at work, most schemes make a provision for a number of weeks work each year. Also, many organisations seek to encourage people to maintain their technical knowledge through open or 'distance' learning.

Terms for re-entry
Typically, the employment contract is not terminated; it is suspended. Obviously, it is unrealistic to hold a particular job open, but it is normal to guarantee re-employment at the same level. It is also usual to ensure that the two periods of service are added together for pension purposes and the Career Break does not constitute a break in the continuity of employment.

Childcare support

Government funded nurseries in the United Kingdom are few and far between. Not surprisingly, therefore, employees who have young children but wish to carry on working have begun to look to their employers for help.

If organisations choose to help with childcare, and in Chapter 7 we identified some very real business benefits for doing so, then there are three sorts of options they could pursue:

(1) setting up their own nursery;
(2) establishing a joint venture with other local organisations; and
(3) paying an allowance or providing childcare vouchers.

In each case, it must be stressed that the eligibility criteria should not discriminate, in any way, against men.

Whichever option is chosen, the decision should not be taken lightly. Apart from considerations of cost, it is absolutely vital to find out what employees want (instead of making assumptions about what they might want).

Own nursery
This is a costly option (as far as initial capital outlay is concerned anyway) but has its attractions. As we described in Chapter 7, The

London and Manchester Group, in Exeter, see their on-site nursery as a valuable aid to recruitment and retention. Bradford City Council have calculated that their nursery represents half the costs that would have been incurred if staff had to be replaced. An on-site nursery is only suitable in a centralised organisation and where it is feasible for staff to bring their children into work.

Joint venture

This is a way of reducing the cost to any one organisation. Midland Bank, for example, have joined together with the Royal Berkshire Hospital to open a crêche in Reading. Places in the nursery are distributed between the organisations involved in funding.

Childcare allowances or vouchers

In October 1989, the Luncheon Voucher Group launched their childcare vouchers. These, or paying allowances, are much more flexible ways of organisations providing assistance to employees with young children. This can be particularly suitable for a decentralised organisation where it does not make sense to provide a nursery in just one particular location.

There is no doubt that, as the 1990s proceed, more and more organisations will turn their attention to childcare. It may well become a popular, if not a standard, benefit. If organisations choose to move to providing cafeteria benefits, some employees may well choose childcare assistance ahead of a company car, for instance.

Flexible working arrangements

Career Break Schemes have their place, but there is no doubt that the message from the organisation is really: 'why don't you take some time off and come back to us when you are ready to devote yourself to us again?' This is not so much combining work and the family as keeping them at respectful distances. Flexible working is one way of genuinely helping people to combine both work and family responsibilities.

Organisations have been resistant to change. Even in the National Health Service, where women represent the majority of employees, they have been slow to move away from traditional work patterns.

In fact, once the key assumption is broken, and people are prepared to consider anything other than full-time working there are a variety of attractive alternatives. Moreover, the attraction is two-way. For employees it can provide the flexibility they need in order to manage their lives. For employers, there is the prospect of increased productivity (as well as more motivated, happier employees). As we describe in Chapter 12, at Rank Xerox's Customer Response Centre at Milton Keynes there are part-timers who answer the target number of calls set for full-timers.

The following are some variations to standard full-time office-based contracts.

Flex-time working
Under this arrangement, employees come in five days a week but may start late and/or leave early.

Part-time working
This may mean, for example, working two days or three days a week.

Job share
This is where part-timers share a job between them so that the job itself remains a full-time job.

Term-time working
This means what it says – a working contract which mirrors the school terms – obviously designed for parents who have school-age children.

Home working
This can be combined with any of the above. This can help people combine family and work responsibilities, particularly where there can be flexibility about when the work is done. F International is a case in point and the vast majority of its employees are women.

The principles to apply remain the same in each case. Compensation should be based on the ratio related to a full-time contract. So, someone who works two days a week, should receive 40 per cent of a full-time salary. This should also apply to all benefits – holidays, sickness schemes and, of course, pensions. Car allowances can be pro-rata'd but cars themselves cannot be – so some employers offer a lower priced vehicle instead. Where the car is a 'job' (rather than 'perk') car, there would be a case for keeping the same car as other colleagues.

Again, given the swing from employer to employee in the job market, and the increase in knowledge workers, we would argue that there will be an increase in these non-standard working contracts. Flexible working is not yet a 'right', but it can make good sense for both organisations and employees. Offering this sort of flexibility can today give employers an edge in the labour market, in the future it will probably be taken for granted.

■ ENVIRONMENT: PEOPLE WITH DISABILITIES

Despite the legislation, very few organisations meet the 3 per cent quota for disabled employees. Many do not bother to apply for the exemption certificate that enables them to carry on recruiting. Moreover, they do not have much time for their own employees who become disabled. In a recent survey , 85 per cent of people working with disabilities said that they had had to leave their previous jobs and 11 per cent had either been dismissed or felt that they had been pressured into leaving.

The apathy that surrounds most employers' attitudes to people with disabilities, displays a rather worrying lack of imagination.

People with disabilities have the same range of skills as the able-bodied community, it is just that we seem to become obsessed by their disabilities rather than their abilities. We get thrown by the symbol of the wheelchair, we get worried by access, and we think of all the potential problems rather than the opportunities. Imagine telling Professor Stephen Hawkin that he does not have a worthwhile contribution to make to society.

For this reason, we believe that organisations should develop a policy statement concerning people with disabilities. This can send a message to people both internally and externally and help to foster the sorts of local initiatives that will begin to make a difference. Forty-five major employers have created The Employers' Forum on Disability to share experience and support good practice, so that at least some organisations are beginning to take action.

People with disabilities are often covered obliquely in equal opportunities statements – tacked on the end as something of an afterthought. A specific policy would be designed to build on the principles of equality of opportunity and would constitute, in effect, a framework for positive action. As such, it is best developed after (or as a result of) the equal opportunities workshops described in Chapter 8. Such a policy would be designed to help organisations shift from the minimalist approach – applying for exemption certificates – to a more imaginative, proactive strategy.

This might take the form of an outreach campaign – deliberate efforts to attract applications from people with disabilities – or it could be a positive action training initiative. Certainly, it needs to cover both current employees who become disabled and also those who represent potential recruits. The key need is for employers to cease to see people with disabilities as a 'charity' issue – something for the Community Affairs Department – and to start seeing them as potential employees. A good starting point would be to carry out some targeted recruitment of people with disabilities for Youth Training of Employment Training Schemes.

There is government support available to employers who take a positive approach. There can be practical financial aid for special equipment needs or changes to office facilities. In 1990, the Department of Employment launched a disabled 'symbol' (for use in adverts and promotional literature) in order to provide employers, and potential recruits, with a way of distinguishing those who were serious about the topic. As yet it is unclear what people can expect from employers using the symbol.

Making better use of the talents and abilities of people with disabilities is a mainstream equal opportunities issue. It strikes at the heart of the topic which is about making judgements about individuals on the basis of skill, rather than any other extraneous factor. People with disabilities represent a significant proportion of the labour market – estimates vary between 10 per cent and 15 per cent – and on those grounds alone must merit serious attention. Yet, progress has been generally patchy. Like so much else in this area, it is the will to make it happen that is lacking. In our experience, once individuals have begun to 'buy in' to the concept of equality of opportunity – as described in Chapter 8 – then they will start to push for, and be active in, local initiatives targeted at people with disabilities. An overall policy can help to co-ordinate and 'steer' these activities.

■ ENVIRONMENT: SEXUAL AND RACIAL HARASSMENT

A survey conducted by the Alfred Marks Bureau in 1990 , suggested that sexual harassment for many women at work is 'part of daily life'. Of course there is a range of behaviour that is tied up in the word 'harassment'. It can be verbal or physical, offensive or threatening, but the key is that it is always unwanted by the recipient.

The European Council of Ministers adopted a Resolution in May 1990 which defined sexual harassment as

'unwanted conduct of a sexual nature, or other conduct based on sex, affecting the dignity of women and men at work.'

Asked about what jokes she would not tolerate at work, Diane McGarry, the Sales Director at Rank Xerox (UK), said:

'Anything that would make a member of the team feel uncomfortable.'

As we have discussed in previous chapters, we see an equal opportunities programme as a cultural change activity. Unless the culture changes – and the sorts of harassment discussed here are just the most obvious form of unwelcoming behaviour or intolerance of difference – then sustained progress cannot be achieved.

For these reasons we believe that there ought to be a firm policy statement about harassment at work. The workshop programme, as discussed in Chapter 8, will start to open people's minds to what harassment is. Often, people who are 'harassing' have no idea that that is how their behaviour is being construed. Others may begin to see that what they saw as jovial office banter, can actually be very discriminatory.

The policy needs to address two areas:

(1) the disciplinary procedure; and
(2) the grievance procedure.

This is not to expect policy changes, in themselves, to change the culture. These sorts of issues are best addressed well before they reach the formal procedural stage. The intent is rather to use this as an opportunity to send a message to people within the organisation which can signal the new standards of acceptable behaviour. The same Alfred Marks survey found that only 22 per cent of firms had a formal policy for dealing with sexual harassment.

As far as the disciplinary procedure is concerned, sexual and racial harassment need to feature as examples of misconduct. This, along with the behaviour of top management, will effectively redraw the line on what is considered acceptable.

As far as the grievance procedure is concerned, there needs to be a by-pass introduced which allows people to approach, say, a nominated person in the personnel department, in order to discuss complaints of harassment, particularly where the boss is doing the harassing. In this way, issues can be informally ironed out – or, if necessary, addressed through formal procedures.

■ CONCLUSION

Policy making is not the be-all and end-all of equal opportunities. There is no doubt, however, that good policies, developed with the commitment and understanding of those affected, have a vital role to play in any programme.

The key points are:

- Policies should be based on needs identified at the diagnostic stage and prioritised according to the aims set by the top management

- They should be developed with significant input from managers and employees who will be affected

- The human resources systems need to be up to the task of ensuring the best are recruited, developed and rewarded

- Policies need to be in place that help to create an environment that will support and embrace change.

Developing the policies is important, but as we shall see in the next chapter, there is still much to do to ensure that they are effectively implemented.

Chapter 10

TRAINING – MANAGING THE TRANSITION

Equal opportunities and training are often closely linked. 'Are you an equal opportunities employer?' 'Yes, we provide single sex training.' It's not quite a non-sequitur, but nor is it an axiom. Because the training is happening it indicates that someone is thinking about the issue, but it does not necessarily imply that all is well.

Clearly, training can play a significant role in an equal opportunities programme and when people refer to taking positive action for instance, they are typically thinking of running specialised training courses.

The link is made explicit in the EOC's Code of Practice:

'The Sex Discrimination Act does allow certain steps to redress the effects of previous unequal opportunities. Where there have been few or no members of one sex in particular work in their employment. . . the Act allows employers to give special encouragement to, and provide specific training for, the minority sex.'

In our view, however, training can play a wider role than just assisting minority groups to compete equally with the white male majority. In its broadest sense, training is about equipping people with the skills to face and manage change. The whole series of equal opportunities workshops, which we described in Chapter 8, could themselves be seen as a 'training' intervention. We have no doubt, therefore, that training has a vital role to play in preparing the whole organisation so that it can cope with (and take advantage of) an equal opportunities programme. We do, however, believe that it needs to be properly positioned within a programme and that it is definitely *not* the place to start.

Therefore, in this chapter we will cover:

- The significance of training to an equal opportunities programme
- The positioning of training within a strategic approach

- Training needs that are raised by an equal opportunities programme
- Illustrations of how these needs can be addressed.

■ THE SIGNIFICANCE OF TRAINING

In our view, training has a critical role to play in an equal opportunities programme.

At the diagnostic stage an organisation develops a clear understanding of the current state of equal opportunities – where the successes are, and where the difficulties lie. When, at the aims stage, the top managers cast their minds into the future they are trying to paint an updated picture of this diagnosis. They are describing the situation as they would like it to be: the desired state.

In Chapter 8 we described the process of gaining widespread ownership for the programme as a whole. Even if this has been extremely successful, the transition from the current state to the desired state will not just come about naturally. People need to behave differently in the future from the way they have behaved in the past. This is where training comes in. Training activities need to be designed which can help people to manage this transition from one way of doing things to another.

Without training there will be only limited behavioural change, and without behavioural change an equal opportunities programme will exist in name only.

Training can help in three complementary, but different, ways. Each relates, in turn, to the three aspects of the organisation explored at the diagnostic stage.

As we have mentioned above, there is *positive action* training. This is, as described in the Codes of Practice, training that is targeted at groups that are statistically in the minority. For instance, if an analysis of the employment profile suggested that there were very few female engineers, it would be possible for an organisation to run specific women-only engineering training courses. This links to the statistical work at the diagnostic stage – where significant statistical anomalies have been highlighted, positive action training could be considered as one option for closing the gap.

The purpose of this sort of training is to help prepare minorities to compete on equal terms with the majority for opportunities.

Then there are training courses which are developed to assist *policy implementation*. Naturally, these courses are targeted at those who have responsibility for policy implementation, and this will typically be managers. For example, there is no point changing the recruitment policy and deliberately seeking applications from women and minorities, if the managers responsible for selection are ill-equipped to be able to select genuinely on merit. This links to the work at the diagnostic stage of exploring the personnel policy framework. Where new policies are contemplated there will be (at the very least) a need to brief managers and (more frequently) a need to run some skill development courses.

The purpose of this training is to provide managers with the skills to implement personnel policies effectively.

The third area is related to broad-based *cultural change*. As organisations become more diverse – that is, employees have different, rather than common, backgrounds – so there is a need to capitalise on and exploit this diversity. This can be targeted towards managers, helping them manage diverse teams, or used more widely across whole teams.

This links to the issues that were explored in the employee discussions at the diagnostic stage. Quite frequently, the problems are based on assumptions, often stereotypical, that people hold about others. The programme of equal opportunities workshops, discussed in Chapter 8, is itself primarily directed at opening minds and helping individuals to review their own assumptions. Training activities in this area can then build directly on these workshops.

Before we examine each of these areas in turn, we need to address first the question of the positioning of training interventions within an equal opportunities programme.

■ POSITIONING OF TRAINING

Charged with 'doing something' about equal opportunities, people often immediately think about positive action training. After all, it is tangible, recommended by the Codes of Practice, and does not represent too much of a disturbance for the rest of the organisation. (The most obvious implication of positive action training is to suggest that 'the problem' lies with the minorities, and that they need a bit of help before they can join the throng and compete with the majority.)

The training becomes an end in itself rather than serving any overt business purpose.

As we have described above, we do believe that training has a unique contribution to make to the success of an equal opportunities programme. We are sure, however, that *training must support an equal opportunities programme, it cannot be that programme.*

There is a parallel here with customer care. In the 1980s many organisations ran what we would call 'smile courses'. Their analysis of the situation seemed to be that the problem was with the 'front of house' staff. If only they were a bit more pleasant to the customers, everything would be alright. They had no inkling that any more fundamental changes were required.

Staff came back, they 'smiled' a bit more, but it soon wore off. There had been no changes anywhere else in the organisation and they experienced exactly the same problems as before. They may have tried harder to pacify the customer, but they could not provide a better service.

In isolation, the training may have done a good job, but the rest of the organisation was not ready for it. This can be exactly the same with positive action training which is launched upon an unprepared organisation.

One example may serve to illustrate some of these points. In one company, with a high proportion of women in clerical functions but very few in management positions, they decided that they needed to run an assertiveness training course for women. The purposes for the course were not clear, and there was not much of an understanding among management – or employees – of how and why the company was tackling equal opportunities. Not surprisingly, this led to some problems. Delegates felt that they were being labelled ('awkward feminist type') and their male colleagues felt excluded, and suspicious. The outcome was that attendance for the course dropped, as women declined to go on the course, and neither the company nor employees gained much benefit from the courses that were run.

The key issue here was that no-one, neither the managers, the trainers or, therefore, the delegates seemed to know *why* the course was being run. Inevitably, this led to suspicion among the men that this represented a fast track through for the women. They were also able to make the assumption that this is what the 'pushy' women delegates were themselves looking for. It was a recipe for mistrust and suspicion.

Being clear about the reasons for running the training course is critical so that:

(1) the managers can effectively brief both the delegates and, if appropriate, their colleagues; and
(2) the managers can support their delegates on their return to work and help them apply the learning from the course.

Where we come across organisations that do not know why they are running a positive action training course, we find that this is usually a symptom of a wider problem: they do not know why they have an equal opportunities policy nor what it entails. Training aims must be driven by organisational aims. It should not be surprising that if there are not clear overall aims, then the training activities appear purposeless.

After all, a training programme cannot exist in isolation, if it is to be effective it must be part of a conscious and articulated strategy.

Training must be designed to: meet needs identified in the diagnosis, make progress towards the aims developed in a policy statement and support the introduction of any relevant new policies. Without these links, it is doubtful that the training will be the right sort of training and certain that any skills acquired cannot readily be transferred to the work environment. Neither delegates, nor their bosses will know why the course is being run and a high degree of mistrust all round is inevitable.

It is quite deliberate that this is the last chapter of our strategic approach. Training, if it is to be effective, must be integrated into an overall programme strategy. It must follow a diagnosis, upon which it relies to identify the different training needs, and there must be clear aims, which can explain how the training fits into the overall business.

■ POSITIVE ACTION TRAINING

First of all, we need to return to what we mean by 'positive action'. Essentially, it means taking steps to help minorities compete on an equal basis for opportunities – it is not guaranteeing them success, which would constitute 'positive discrimination'. Selection for any job must be on merit, positive action training is designed to overcome the problem: 'how can we recruit them, if they don't have the skills we need, or they don't apply?'

Positive action training can help people develop the relevant skills and give them the confidence to apply. It can help to break down the barriers: both those that exist within the organisation and also those that only exist in the mind. Such training programmes are not seeking to create a short-term change in the profile of the organisation, but over the longer term they should feed through into women and minorities taking up more positions within an organisation.

Positive action training is about widening the potential pool of applicants. It can be targeted to the outside world – to increase the numbers of external applicants – or it could be an internal course designed to increase the number of people who can progress within the organisation. In the examples below, therefore, we have grouped the positive action training into initiatives concerned with:

(1) external recruitment; or
(2) internal development.

External recruitment

Obviously, where the intent is to increase external applications, positive action training often goes hand-in-hand with 'outreach' programmes as described in Chapter 9. Sometimes, the training is itself the 'outreach'. Sometimes, the 'outreach' is provided by one party (the Government or a campaign group) and the training by another (an interested employer).

In this area, for once, there can be close co-operation between all those with an interest in increasing the 'pool' of recruits – Government, campaign groups, employers looking for similar skills. They all have the same aims in mind; to develop under-utilised talent. When contemplating positive action training, therefore, organisations can, and should, look to see how they can co-operate with others with similar interests. In this way, more can be obtained from the total resources invested. This trend is evident in the examples of positive action training that follow.

As we saw in Chapter 2, one of the most obvious sources of future recruits are women who want to return to work having taken time out to raise children. It was concern over the 'demographic dip' that led both the Government and the CBI to take a more positive attitude to women returners. 'Woman's Hour' running its 'Back To The Future' campaign was one of the more visible efforts of 'outreach'.

There have been a number of training courses aimed at helping the 'woman returner'. An interesting example of joint partnership is WIN (Women Into Industry) set up in 1989. It is estimated that there are 5,000 women science graduates who are not using their degree. WIN is a one-year masters degree, funded by the Training Agency, which links women who want to return to work with local employers. There is a mix between course work and time spent with employers, with a 'half-salary' being paid.

Another source of additional recruits is people from ethnic minority groups. Industry, in particular, has been very unsuccessful in attracting applications from minorities. Where 'blue chip' companies have carried out ethnic monitoring, they have found typically no greater than 2 per cent of their employees come from minorities. The excuse is often that 'they' do not apply or that 'they' do not have the skills.

The Windsor Fellowship was set up to address exactly these issues. The Fellowship brings together minority students and large companies in mutually beneficial partnerships. The students are sponsored through their tertiary education by individual companies, who also provide work experience through the vacations. This means the students get to see what it is like working in the company, and the company gets the chance to help the students develop the appropriate skills. Simply having a few more black faces around can help to break some stereotypical assumptions.

Internal development

The focus for internal positive action courses is to release the potential of existing employees who maybe do not have the appropriate skills or confidence to progress.

Given the typical profile of organisations – with the men in the management jobs and women performing clerical roles – it is not surprising that this training has been targeted overwhelmingly at women. To some (women as well as men) this smacks of 'reverse' discrimination. The rationale, however, is two-fold:

(1) that women are statistically in the minority as far as management positions are concerned (approximately 9%); and
(2) that women-only courses create a particularly supportive learning environment.

In our view, there is a place for women-only training, but it needs to be very clearly thought through. As we discussed above when we were explaining the significance and positioning of training within an equal opportunities programme, the most important factor is to be clear about the purpose of the training. If this is either not clear, or simply a cover for covert 'positive discrimination' in favour of women, then there will be an inevitable male backlash.

In addition, a case could be made for positive action training for ethnic minorities or, indeed, for any other disadvantaged minority. Ford UK, for example, found that minorities were not being promoted to supervisory positions and discovered that relatively poor communication skills were seen to be the main barrier. Accordingly, they offered suitable courses to help people improve these skills so that they could compete effectively for the supervisory jobs.

There is no doubt, however, that the majority of internally directed positive action training is for women. Indeed, it is probably the predominant form of positive action training and therefore we will explore it in some depth. It can take a number of forms. At one level, it could be concerned simply with imparting new skills – for example both the BBC and Thames Television have provided technical training for women who were interested in developing these skills (and earning more money). More often, however, it is focused on helping women progress up the hierarchy. There are two sorts of courses that we will look at here: management training and assertiveness training.

Management training

Essentially, the purpose of these courses is to equip women with the management skills so that they can put themselves forward for promotion opportunities.

Employers in the financial services organisations have led the way on management training. This is understandable given the profile of the typical company in this field, where women make up over 50 per cent of the staff but under 10 per cent of the management. Clearly there is a strong incentive: there must be hidden potential among this 50 per cent which is not being utilised.

Midland Bank have addressed this head on. In 1989 they launched their 'Campus' programme. It was targeted at helping clerical employees make the transition to management by enabling them to attend a year's full-time managerial diploma course in business and finance at Birmingham or Loughborough University. The course is open to men as well but is deliberately targeted at women who form 80 per cent of the students.

This is firmly targeted at helping women develop the technical management skills and requires an extensive commitment from both the employees and the organisation. The Peperell Unit of the Industrial Society, who have run development courses for women since 1985, take a slightly different approach. They run open courses which, over a number of days, help delegates both to develop management skills and also to review their own personal skills and career objectives.

One particular example of this work was the Esso Development Course For Women, which was run in 1986 and again in 1988. The course delegates included Esso staff but the majority of places were awarded by open competition nationally and included women from public, private and voluntary sector organisations.

The course, aimed at young high flyers, helped them both develop their skills at managing others and also ensured that they were clear about what they wanted from a career. As one delegate put it:

'We have set the goals for our lives, taking the whole and not the part'.

Or, as another explained:

'I found it opened my mind, helped me to identify my own goals and targets and showed me a possible way of achieving them.'

The degree of mutual support among the delegates was extremely high – and may have been related to the fact that these were women-only courses. For the delegates, one of the most valuable spin-offs from the courses was the creation of a number of informal support networks. One talked about the power of:

'33 motivated women supporting and forming new relationships with each other.'

Another revealed:

'I met some of the most interesting people and shared in their experiences. I know that if I had not been on the course, I would never have come into contact with them.'

In time, we would hope that the need for women-only management training will disappear. In an era, however, when women in management are still vastly in the minority, there must be some place for this training. It will not be for everyone – there will be some women who resent the idea of being treated differently from their male colleagues – but for some it will be just the boost they need in order to make their breakthrough.

Assertiveness training

Sometimes, the barrier to progress is actually the confidence to apply for the jobs in the first place. In this case, the emphasis here is not so much on developing technical skills as becoming aware of the skills that already exist. The purpose here is to build confidence so that delegates can make the best use of their skills.

Of course, this can be as relevant for men as it is for women. Some assertiveness training courses are mixed and some are open to women only. At Thames TV they run five courses a year – three are open to both sexes and two for women only.

There is no doubt, however, that women make up a significant proportion of those who attend such courses. So long as they form the majority of staff doing secretarial and clerical jobs, this will continue to be the case. These are the jobs that technology is either making redundant or altering out of all recognition. Many of the routine tasks are now becoming automated, many managers are beginning to do their own typing, therefore the challenge of the 'new' jobs demands a more open style of thinking. Anyone who has been used to tackling closed-down tasks, i.e. carrying out someone else's instructions, will need help in making this adjustment. The initial concern is: are my ideas good enough?

A carefully designed assertiveness training course can, therefore:

- Build individuals' confidence in themselves through increasing awareness of their own skills
- Develop delegates' skills at handling open situations by helping them to set their own aims for a piece of work
- Widen the range of communication styles that delegates are able to handle comfortably.

This all has the impact of encouraging self-development and enables delegates to set for themselves some realistic plans for their return to work.

Many of the clearing banks were pioneers in this field. It is now fairly commonplace for large companies to offer assertiveness type courses. Very sensibly, many have dropped the 'assertiveness' tag, made them open to men as well as women, and called them 'personal effectiveness' courses. This seems to us to be a very healthy trend.

Positive action training: conclusion

There is no doubt that, whether internally or externally focused, positive action training can provide powerful levers for change. In many cases, the results will take time to feed through the system, but in the long term they can increase the pool of qualified candidates for jobs and therefore help organisations to select from the very best.

■ POLICY IMPLEMENTATION TRAINING

At the diagnosis stage the need to adapt existing policies or to introduce new policies may well have been raised. In Chapter 9, we have provided examples of some of the best practice in this area. There would be no point, however, in developing these new policies unless some training is provided for those who are responsible for implementing these policies. At one level, they need to understand why the new policy has been adopted and, at a deeper level, how it affects the way they have traditionally worked. There are two obvious areas that organisations need to review:

Selection skills which covers the whole process of selection from the drafting of the job vacancy (or advert) through the interviewing of specific candidates.

Appraisal and coaching skills which covers both the application of the formal appraisal system and also the coaching that occurs on a regular basis.

Both of these are crucial areas and directly address the 'gate keepers' of the organisation – those responsible for making recruitment and promotion decisions. Without them 'on board', equal opportunities cannot make much headway.

One of the main aims of an equal opportunities policy is often to widen the pool of potential applicants, and considerable effort may have been invested in 'outreach' programmes as a result. It is essential that this is carried through all the way to the interview process otherwise traditional recruiting patterns will simply be maintained.

Nor, on the other hand, does it move us significantly forward if more women and minorities are recruited but then they fail to develop and be promoted. Obviously, selection skills are as applicable to making promotion decisions as recruitment decisions. It is not enough, however, to be making objective decisions at the point of selection. Ahead of that there needs to be effective management support and guidance. This is where the formal appraisal system and ongoing coaching come in.

We will tackle each of these areas in turn.

Selection skills

The first, and essential, point to make is that what is good for equal opportunities is good for 'normal' selection. There are not two separate needs and two separate courses. The overriding concern is to select the 'best' candidate, and what a selection skills course can do is ensure that this is what actually happens in practice. What a focus on equal opportunities can provide is an opportunity to look again at some of the 'short-cuts' and accepted practices that have been adopted over the years which may well be getting in the way of making the best selection decision.

For example, good interviewers do not ask relatively closed questions seeking to confirm judgements they have already made. These interviewers are likely to boast that they can sum up a candidate after the first five minutes of an interview. What they are actually doing, of course, is using the other 25 minutes (or however long) to confirm their initial 'gut feel'. If you look hard enough, it is always possible to find information that supports your initial snap judgement, but you may be ignoring a good deal of contrary information. This is bad interviewing and it is bad for equal opportunities. Operating in this way, interviewers are giving full reign to their prejudices which they never allow to be challenged.

Another habit that is bad for all concerned is the way that some interviewers believe that they have to put candidates under great pressure to see whether they will crack. This seems to be particularly true of women, who seemingly have to prove that they are tough enough to take it. Good interviewers know that they have an interest in the candidate being relaxed enough to be able to show what skills she/he actually has. They can make a judgement about how people cope with stress by asking candidates how they have handled stressful situations in the past.

Given all the bad interviewing habits that abound, perhaps we should not be surprised at the poor correlation between interview assessments and individuals' subsequent performance.

A course on selection skills, however, needs to address much more than just interviewing, and is as relevant for those involved in making internal promotion decisions as well as for those involved in recruitment. For instance, clarifying the skills which are required to do the job is the key to successful selection – whether for external recruitment or internal promotion. The course should:

- Help managers to review the *whole selection process* so that they are clear about the skills required
- Help managers to become aware of and thus avoid *stereotypical thinking*
- Provide some selection techniques, which aid objective decision making and experience of using these in practice.

The following are some indicators of the sorts of issues that get covered in each of these three areas.

Reviewing the whole selection process
The natural short-cut is to fill a vacancy by recruiting more of the same. After all, it's worked before, so it should work again. This spirit can imbue the whole recruitment process from start to finish – the vacancy notice or advert (which targets a narrow population and assumes the job should be done as it always has been done) the pre-screening of applications (looking for the same track record as the existing job holder) and the interview process (rejecting anyone who might not 'fit in'). The need is, of course, to re-focus on the actual skills required to do the job and forget about who currently does it.

Helping people become aware of stereotypical thinking
At one level stereotypical thinking can be as blatant as 'this is men's work' or 'blacks have got a chip on their shoulder'. More often, however, it is less conscious. One delegate on a course we were running exclaimed:

> *'Good grief, I've been discriminating against people from public schools all these years!'*

Often these subconscious attitudes come out in the questions that are asked at interview. Questions to women about family plans or 'what would your husband say?' reveal that the interviewer really thinks that women ought to give priority to their family life. Sometimes, the questions are simply patronising and show up the interviewer as somewhat old fashioned. In the early 1980s, interviewers could still ask female chemical engineers:

> '*Are you sure you want to join a refinery – it can be hazardous and dirty you know?*'

A final point in this area is to stress that stereotypical thinking can be as common in favour of particular groups of people as against them. All Asians are not good with figures, all women are not better at handling people sympathetically than men.

Selection techniques

As we discussed in Chapter 9, simple improvements to the paper work systems can prove very effective. If interviewers do not have the personal information on candidates they may not be so tempted to ask potentially illegal questions. At first, interviewers tend to feel somewhat naked, without their traditional props, which is why it is essential they get some practice, on a course, of trying out different ways of assessing application forms (or CVs) and new styles of interviewing. Given effective feed-back and coaching, they can establish their own ways of gathering the information they require which puts them in a position where they can then make judgements based on hard facts rather than subjective 'gut feel'.

In this way, those involved in the selection process will not only be meeting their legal obligations, they will also be increasing the likelihood that they genuinely select the best person for the job. For this reason, we believe that organisations should insist that everyone involved in the selection processes (both external recruitment and internal promotion) goes through such a course. To do otherwise, is not only to risk legal action, but also to undermine any attempts at consciously widening the recruitment net. An effective selection skills course is, in our view, an essential part (not a discretionary part) of an equal opportunities programme.

Appraisals and coaching

Clearly, there is no point recruiting a wider range of people if it is still the same old people who make it to the top. This is a challenge for a number of organisations, and professions, who have changed their recruitment profiles but are finding it rather more difficult to change the composition of those doing the senior jobs. For example, women now make up over 50 per cent of those entering the medical and legal professions. In time, we would hope that this is reflected in the numbers who make it through to become consultants or partners.

As discussed, at the diagnosis stage there can be a number of factors that influence who gets on in an organisation and by no means all of them are skill-based. Developing more objective selection processes (as described above) is vital. In addition, as we described in Chapter 9, there must be a fundamental role for good appraisal and career planning systems.

It goes further than this, however, because it is not enough to have the systems in place and for the candidates put forward for promotion to be chosen on merit. The way in which people are managed and 'developed' on an ongoing basis really determines who gets on and who does not. The paper work for appraisal and career planning systems may be there, but what is needed is the will and the skill to make them work.

Again, just as with selection skills, what is good for equal opportunities is also sound management practice. It cannot be healthy to have people who are written off, from the earliest years as 'no hopers'. Nor can it be sensible to have people who are labelled early on as 'stars' who then progress through the system almost regardless of their performance.

Similarly, it cannot be good for business if a small coterie of friends appoint each other to the 'plum' jobs to the exclusion of other equally qualified (or better qualified) candidates. Networking has its advantages, but needs to be managed.

The aims of appraisal and career planning systems are two-fold:

(1) to motivate employees to seek the highest levels of performance within their personal capacity; and
(2) to provide valid and reliable assessments of employees' current performance and promotability.

This means both employees and the company have the opportunity to make the most of their potential. To meet these two aims, the manager will have to play two complementary roles : as 'judge' and as 'coach'.

The aims of a training course, therefore, should be to:

• Gain managers' support for, and understanding of, the formal systems
• Help managers agree and review performance objectives with employees

- Increase managers' awareness of how stereotypical thinking influences assessments of 'potential' or 'promotability'
- Develop managers' appreciation of the positive role they have to play in supporting their staff
- Give managers the opportunity to develop their skills at giving factual, helpful feed-back.

In this way, the course should enable managers to function effectively as both judge and coach.

Manager as judge

At one level, there is an obvious need for managers to understand the paper work and to be able to see its importance (to themselves, their employees and to the organisation). There can be some deep-rooted concerns about these systems. For instance, some managers, anxious about their own career prospects, will not rate any of their own people very highly (after all, they represent the future competition). Of course, the thinking needs to be completely the reverse. Development of subordinates needs to be a key management objective and to have highly-rated subordinates to be seen as a sign of strength. Certainly, there will be concerns that need to be addressed, and it is only once these have been aired, and managers are able to see the benefits of the systems, that there is a sporting chance that the paper work might be completed.

It might mean we can move past the 'I've got a spare half hour, so I thought we could knock off your appraisal now.'

At a deeper level, the course also ought to help managers make objective assessments of performance – ideally by agreeing and reviewing measurable performance objectives with their employees. Frequently, managers and employees have markedly different ideas of what is expected from the job.

In addition, there will be a need, as with any selection process, to compare different employees in order to assess their potential for promotion. Despite the factual information gathered on a one-to-one basis, this is where subjective judgements abound. Managers resort to assertion: 'Of course, she's better than him!' and there is a distinct danger that it is the most articulate manager who determines the order of the listing rather than the skills of the subordinates concerned.

Again, as with selection, there is a need to help managers become aware of how their own 'value sets' are influencing their judgement.

People are typically keen to support the case of people who think and work as they do. Often, women do badly because they are deemed to be likely to take a break out to have children and are therefore 'unreliable'. The need, throughout this process, is to involve as wide a selection of managers as possible and to probe continually for the factual information behind the assertion. Sometimes it's there and sometimes it isn't.

Manager as coach

While the role of the manager as 'judge' may be highlighted at pre-ordained times in the year – for example, when annual appraisals are conducted or salaries are reviewed – it needs to be continually supported by the role of the manager as 'coach'. What is said at appraisal time should never come as a shock. It ought to be related to the feedback that has been exchanged continually as part of the evolving relationships between the manager and his or her staff. Issues should not be 'stored up' to be tackled at appraisal time.

There has been a great deal of research that indicates that 'coaching' or 'mentoring' can have a dramatic impact on an individual's progress – particularly in the early years. People need to know how the 'informal' as well as the 'formal' systems work. They need to have someone that they can talk to in confidence about their career aspirations, and from whom they can gain some guidance. 'Which are the jobs that I am best placed to go for?' The manager needs high quality observation and listening skills, which need to be supported by an ability to give honest, factual feed back. Above all, managers need to be prepared to dedicate time to this activity.

There is a difficulty here, in particular, for women. Most managers are men and, as we know, there are difficulties in cross-sex 'mentoring'. While it might be perfectly acceptable for an older man to develop a 'mentoring' relationship with a younger man, it is more difficult to do this with a younger woman. As the pair are seen going off to lunch together, different motivations may be assumed. However, as some of our job stereotypes break down and mixed teams become increasingly common, this ought to be less of a problem.

Managers need help, therefore, in thinking through their 'coaching' responsibilities and in developing the skills of giving accurate helpful feed back and support – to all their employees.

In our view, a training course in appraisal and coaching skills is as essential as the selection skills course. Without this sort of practical help, managers will continue to behave as they have always behaved

193

and development and promotion will be a mostly 'hit and miss' affair.

Policy implementation training

Managers determine who joins and then progresses within an organisation. They are the 'gate keepers'. They need help to develop the skills that will ensure that it is the best people who are recruited, developed and promoted.

At a more pragmatic level, it is also essential that equal opportunities is integrated into any induction training and that those involved in specific policies – such as home working or harassment procedures – are given specific training.

■ TRAINING FOR CULTURAL CHANGE

As we saw when we were looking at the diagnosis stage, it may well be that an organisation's culture represents one of the most powerful barriers to change. What is more, unless this culture shifts, it can effectively block the beneficial impact of changes made in policy or recruiting patterns. Unless the prevailing culture is supportive, new policies will not be implemented, and women or minorities recruited will leave. Already, at every stage of our strategic approach we have begun to address these cultural issues.

At the stage of carrying out the diagnosis, the review of the existing training courses should have begun to identify how equal opportunities themes can be integrated into these courses and therefore become part of the 'way we work here'.

At the stage of setting aims, where the top managers are describing their 'vision' they should have seized upon the role of each employee in creating the appropriate environment for the success of an equal opportunities programme.

Of course, the whole of the stage of gaining ownership constitutes a 'cultural intervention'. The purpose of the equal opportunities workshops is to help people think again about the way they behave and the culture this creates.

At the policy development stage, the development of disciplinary and grievance procedures are one way of indicating the sort of culture that the organisation is seeking to create.

Within the training stage, which we are discussing here, the positive action training and policy implementation training are attempts to change behaviour and therefore to change culture.

We believe, however, that more is required. There needs to be a training activity that brings all these strands together. We call this 'managing diversity'. Linked to our redefinition of equal opportunities in Chapter 4 as being primarily about valuing and utilising diversity, we see this as being rather different from what is known as 'awareness training'.

Awareness training

In the equal opportunities world, there has been a tradition of awareness training. Frequently (but not exclusively) this training is aimed at the majority group to increase their understanding of minorities.

There is a case for this sort of training. At the most obvious level, police officers need to understand about the customs and practices of the ethnic minority communities they are supposed to be policing. Similarly, however, managers need to know how different cultural values can have an impact at work. To offer just one example, some cultures place a higher value on age than is now normal within the Anglo-Saxon world. Therefore, a young person from such a culture, would be profoundly uncomfortable if asked to manage an older person. There is clearly a need for managers to increase their sensitivity to these issues.

Certainly, there is case for disability awareness training. Although approximately 10 per cent of the working age population has a disability, the non-disabled do seem to have many fears and preconceptions about disability. The barriers are so strong here that it can lead to an unspoken apartheid: people with disabilities are alright for these sorts of jobs but not for those.

There is the problem, however, with 'awareness training' that unless it is carefully handled, the overriding message that comes across is that 'the problem' with equal opportunities lies with the majority. This is the reverse of the implications of positive action training (where 'the problem' is deemed to lie with the minority) and can have as many drawbacks. In this situation, the 'majority' may well feel threatened or lectured at, and therefore simply switch off. Accordingly, they block out much of what is being said and their 'awareness' remains at precisely the level it was before the course.

Well targeted 'awareness training', where it is directly related to the jobs people do, can be successful. In our view, it is probably best

195

integrated into the policy implementation courses we have described above. One of the specific aims of these courses is to open managers' minds to the sorts of people who might have the skills they are looking for, and this sits very neatly with some of the aspects of 'awareness training'.

In itself, however, this is still insufficient. We need to move beyond training focused on the 'majority' in order to enlighten them about particular 'minorities'. In the final analysis, we are all in a minority of one – we are all individuals influenced by our own backgrounds – and we need to help managers see these individual differences as a source of strength rather than as a problem that has to be managed. This is what we mean by 'managing diversity'.

Managing diversity

Training to help people 'manage diversity' has some of its aims in common with awareness training – the idea is to increase sensitivity to different cultures (including 'male' and 'female' as different cultures) – however, the way in which this is done differs significantly. The need is to be sensitive to, but not mesmerised by, differences.

This is no longer a programme for the minority group to understand the culture of the majority group so that they can compete effectively (which is positive action training). Nor is it a programme aimed at the majority so that it can accommodate the needs of the minority group (which is awareness training). The attendees for a 'managing diversity' course should not be targeted as a majority or a minority, but as mixed a group as possible. There is no longer an implication that this is someone else's problem, indeed, it is not a 'problem' at all. There is a shared 'opportunity' to make the most of the talents of the people involved. For this reason, it is ideal if there is a problem solving focus and the mixed group tackle a real work issue together.

The emphasis here is not so much on tolerating cultural differences as on actively seeking them out and exploiting them. Difference becomes a source of strength rather than something that needs to be accommodated.

After all, the one thing we do know about the future of organisations is that their employees will be increasingly 'diverse'. The old polarities are going. There will no longer be ghettoes of 'male' or 'female' employment. People from ethnic minorities will be making up increasing proportions of recruits. As the impact of opening up the Single Market becomes increasingly evident, there will be more continental Europeans working in the United Kingdom and more managers from the United Kingdom will be abroad in Europe securing orders. In effect, we will all be working cross-culturally.

The purpose of the training is, therefore, to take the increasing diversity of organisations as a 'given fact' and to help ensure that multicultural teams achieve synergy (better output than could be achieved by each working in isolation). This is how the business benefits associated with 'managing change' (as described in Chapter 7) can be realised.

Therefore, the aims of a 'managing diversity' training course should be to:

- Identify and describe 'cultural diversity' within the organisation
- Increase awareness of how our own cultural values affect us
- Share perceptions about our own, and others' cultures
- Look at how people can manage successfully across cultures

The following are the sorts of issues that can be addressed under each of these aims.

Identifying cultural diversity

The first need is to anchor what may seem to be a fairly esoteric subject to organisational reality. People need to know why the issue is important to the organisation and why therefore it is a topic of concern to managers. This needs to be done by defining cultural diversity and providing information about the employee (and customer) profiles. This can be related to particular 'changes' that the organisation is facing.

Increasing awareness of our own cultural values

The starting point for most people is that there is simply one way of doing things that is 'right' and everything else is 'wrong'. People do not see that this may well only look 'right' from their particular cultural perspective. As mentioned above, we see men and women working together as a cross-cultural issue. At work, usually it is the 'male' way that has become enshrined as the 'norm' and women are seen to deviate from the 'norm'. The women, therefore, have a choice – either fit in and behave like a man, or do not expect to get promoted.

Beginning to see the way in which one's own cultural background shapes one's values and hence one's perception of the world, is the starting point for becoming more open to other ways of doing things.

Sharing perceptions

At this point, it can be worthwhile to share perceptions about different cultures. Within the North American culture, there is a great desire to be seen to be getting on with the 'action'. To this culture, making the decision is the important thing and any decision is better than no decision. Conversely, Scandinavian culture places a great emphasis upon the need to involve people in the decision-making process. These two approaches can be effectively contrasted as 'Ready, Fire, Aim' (American) and 'Ready, Aim, Aim, Aim, Fire' (Scandinavian). The point is not that one is right and the other is wrong. The skill is to match the style to the appropriate circumstances and therefore ensure that the organisation can genuinely get the 'best of all worlds'.

Sharing and contrasting perceptions opens minds. Judgements that seemed 'fair' may actually be seen to be culturally conditioned. Behaviour that was dismissed as 'inexplicable' becomes understandable. For men at work doing things together seems to be the way of building closer relationships, for example, playing golf or squash. For women the need seems to be to share personal confidences. People need to be sensitive to each other's needs so that they can respond to them.

Successfully managing across cultures

This has some profound implications for management. The need becomes not so much to impose a standard way of doing things as to make the most of the different approaches that people will bring. The criteria for progression, for example, may need reviewing. Do they express real requirements or are they actually just an expression of the way white men have typically tackled the job? Are there other means to achieving the same ends?

The need to ensure that a multicultural team makes the most of its combined talents becomes one of the critical management tasks. Being aware of cultural values means that this cultural diversity can be managed and effectively harnessed to the achievement of organisational objectives.

Training for cultural change: conclusion

In order to realise the full range of business benefits that an equal opportunities programme can provide, there must be a culture that not only tolerates but also positively embraces 'diversity'. This is not a 'problem' associated with either a majority or a minority group. It represents a joint opportunity to make the most of whatever it is that each individual can contribute.

■ CONCLUSION

In this chapter we have explored the significance and the positioning of training within an equal opportunities programme and the positive role it can play in helping to develop the skills needed to bring about change. In our view training:

- Enables people to manage the transition from one way of doing things to another
- Must be integrated into an overall strategy and support previously identified needs and aims
- Can help minorities compete on an equal basis – positive action training
- Can help managers apply selection and development policies effectively
- Can equip people with the skills to manage diversity.

It therefore represents the final piece in the jigsaw of our strategic approach. Without training, an equal opportunities programme will remain a concept rather than a reality. Behaviour – the way we work now – must change and this cannot happen unless people are given help in managing the transition. Training provides that help.

Chapter 11

MANAGING THE PROGRAMME TO SUSTAIN MOMENTUM

In our strategic approach to equal opportunities we believe we have identified the five areas that need to be addressed in order for organisations to make sustained progress. While we have discussed each element separately in turn, there is, of course, a complex set of interactions between the five elements and these interactions need to be managed.

In this chapter, therefore, we hope to bring together all the themes outlined in Part Two of this book and show how they can be marshalled into a coherent whole. This chapter is about managing and monitoring an equal opportunities programme.

It is one thing to construct a compelling equal opportunities 'vision' and to run a series of equal opportunities workshops to communicate this vision to the rest of the organisation, it is quite another to achieve a sustained shift in organisational culture. Unfortunately, this shift will not occur of its own accord simply because the groundwork has been successfully completed.

Of course, the policy and training initiatives outlined in the preceding chapters represent follow-up actions, which are ways of helping the organisation, and its employees, make the transition from the 'current state' to the 'desired state'.

Again, however, it is not quite as straightforward as it may appear – these initiatives need to be co-ordinated and managed. Decisions need to be made about which issues to address when. As we have argued, introducing a policy or training initiative before the organisation has been properly prepared is to guarantee rejection. Moreover, it would be quite impractical to try to change everything overnight. Organisations have a lot of change to cope with, and equal opportunities – while we would argue that it can facilitate the change process – represents in itself a significant challenge to the way things have traditionally been conducted.

Decisions, therefore, need to be made about which are the priority issues and a programme of actions evolved that is: led by business needs, coherent, and practical.

In this chapter, therefore, we are concerned with how these decisions are made and we will cover:

- Resourcing an equal opportunities programme
- Harnessing ownership: the process of developing initiatives
- Measuring achievement of business benefits
- Measuring overall progress: another diagnosis
- A strategic approach to sustaining momentum
- Communicating success.

■ RESOURCING AN EQUAL OPPORTUNITIES PROGRAMME

Managing the programme

Managing an equal opportunities programme takes time and effort and needs to be properly resourced. This issue needs to be addressed by senior management and should be incorporated into their thinking at the stage when they are setting aims for the programme.

As will be readily apparent from everything that we have argued to date, we believe that an equal opportunities programme should be viewed as an integral part of an organisation's business strategy. Hence, we believe that setting up separate, highly visible equal opportunities units is probably counter-productive. It provides the necessary resource to 'kick-start' a programme but, by its very existence, it undermines the principle of line-management responsibility. If there is an equal opportunities manager then equal opportunities must be his or her responsibility.

All of which is not to deny that an equal opportunities programme will need someone to 'champion' it and 'steer' it. This is probably best achieved by appointing a manager, maybe from the human resources function, to take responsibility for managing the programme, while still retaining other responsibilities.

The main advantage of this route is that it avoids the label of an 'equal opportunities manager'. It also avoids a potential pitfall – that of people at the centre clinging on to 'their' programme and resisting spreading the ownership for it. If equal opportunities is the be-all and end-all of their jobs, it should not be surprising if they resist giving any of it up. They will look to justify their existence, they will seek to 'control', when they should be looking to 'enable'. The reverse tends to be the case with a manager who has wider responsibilities – he or she is usually only too glad for the extra support. In addition, by selecting the appropriate manager, organisations can give added credibility to the programme. By choosing someone with a good track record, who is able to take an overall business perspective, the organisation avoids equal opportunities drifting off into a little world of its own, and is saying that it sees the topic as a mainstream issue.

Appointing, in effect, a part-time programme manager may seem to be setting that person a very 'tall order', and indeed it is. The point, however, is to be clear about what is required from the manager. He or she is not going to be expected to do everything. The role is similar to that of a project manager – taking responsibility for delivering the end product on time, on cost, but working with a multi-disciplined team to achieve the results. This is one of the reasons why it is so important to spend time setting credible programme aims, and spreading the ownership for the programme within the organisation. These are vital tools which enable the programme manager to draw on support, and resources, from the rest of the organisation. His or her role is not so much to force initiatives upon a reluctant organisation, as to co-ordinate and 'steer' the initiatives that are being generated locally.

In our view, equal opportunities programmes are best managed by someone who:

- Is a part-time programme manager
- Is responsible for helping to achieve the business benefits
- Works with senior management in order to ensure the programme is integrated into the overall business objectives
- Establishes a coherent programme action plan based on clearly defined aims
- Steers and co-ordinates local initiatives within the context of this plan.

Senior management involvement

To date, the key role for senior management has been to establish the equal opportunities 'vision' and draft the initial programme aims. They would also have probably decided whether to appoint a programme manager and selected the appropriate person.

Their role, with a programme manager in place, does not end there. The 'over to you and let me know how you're getting on in six months' approach will be seen to be the act of 'passing the buck' that it is. As we described in Chapter 7, senior managers have an important part to play as role models, so they must behave personally in a way that supports equal opportunities. They also have a wider organisational role to play. Just as they would 'steward' any other business activity – for example, reviewing whether the prospective benefits of an investment are being realised – so they need to review the progress of the equal opportunities programme.

There are essentially two ways of doing this, either as part of regular board reviews, or by setting up a separate equal opportunities review. At Littlewoods, for example, the Chairman, John Moores, set up an equal opportunities committee in 1986, so that he could personally show his commitment and review progress quarterly.

In addition, senior management can ensure that equal opportunities is a matter of concern for each of the managers who report to them. It might be counter-productive to set them equal opportunities objectives, but they can certainly encourage the managers to set some objectives for themselves. In one company, the directors let it become known that, on a quarterly basis, they wanted to review the number of women in each department who were considered to possess 'high potential'. This was a way of raising the profile of the issue and ensuring that it was regularly reviewed.

To sum up, it is essential that senior managers not only put equal opportunities on the business agenda, but that they also keep it there.

Human resources department involvement

The human resources or personnel function obviously has an important role to play in an equal opportunities programme. As we have suggested, the programme manager may well be chosen from such a department.

Human resources departments are responsible for ensuring that their policies and systems support the overall business strategy. Clearly, equal opportunities must represent one element of a human resources strategy. On a more pragmatic basis, human resources staff can have a significant bearing on the success of an equal opportunities programme. They are the organisation's initial 'gate keepers'. If they choose not to send on applications from women and minorities it does not matter how 'enlightened' the line management might be, they still will not be able to select minority candidates.

For these reasons, we argued in Chapter 8 that it would be worthwhile running specially designed equal opportunities workshops for human resources staff.

For the programme manager, the human resources staff must be considered as 'allies' who can help in three separate ways. They can:

(1) stimulate departmental initiatives;
(2) help draft policies; and
(3) provide statistical data.

Stimulating departmental initiatives

For larger organisations it will be particularly important that there are people in each department who can advise line management and, if necessary, challenge their thinking. It is not only impractical to expect one programme manager to be able to fulfil this function for six or seven departments, it also carries a different message if the advice comes from someone closely involved with the department. In this way, equal opportunities can be more closely allied to departmental needs and the initiatives actively sponsored by the people in human resources who will often have to 'make them happen'.

Drafting policies

We shall explore the policy development process in more depth later, but there must be a central role for the HR specialists. Very often, organisations will have nominated heads of recruitment, training and compensation. If the equal opportunities programme manager, or anyone else for that matter, seeks to develop policies without involving these specialists, they not only miss out on the expertise they would have provided, they also put these influential 'noses' out of joint. It will subsequently be difficult to gain their whole-hearted support for the implementation of any new policies and this may, in itself, be sufficient to kill the initiative.

Providing data

The equal opportunities programme manager is unlikely to be the person responsible for the personnel database, although (as we shall see during the course of this chapter) he or she will need to have access to its files. How many women, minorities and people with disabilities are in management positions? Without access to the computerised database it would take a long time to come up with an answer. Similarly, there will be further relevant information which is not stored on computer. How successful was the last advertising campaign? How many applications were received? What proportion came from women, minorities and people with disabilities?

All of which can represent a significant additional workload for the human resources department. For the programme manager, the key, of course, is to help the human resources staff to see equal opportunities as a means to their ends. Equal opportunities should not be seen as 'additional' work, it should be seen as part of their role – providing valuable tools to help them help the organisation manage its people more effectively.

Trade union involvement

Where there are formally recognised trade unions, there needs to be a role for them in the equal opportunities programme. In some organisations they will be actively looking for change and using the negotiating process to bring it about. In recent years the TUC has been taking an increasing interest in equal opportunities (partly because they see that women and minorities will represent an increasing proportion of the future work force and hence of their potential membership).

Where unions are taking a positive approach, the programme manager can look to involve them as 'change agents'. At Esso's refinery at Fawley, the senior stewards were the first to fill in their ethnic origin forms, because they wanted to set a standard for the work force to follow. Indeed, unions can be used as a sounding board for proposals and representatives can be invited into groups to review equal opportunities progress. Their involvement ought to ensure that all practicalities are covered.

There will be some instances, however, where the unions will be formally supportive (in line with official policy) but informally resistant. This may be because they view equal opportunities as being at odds with the interests of their membership, or it may be because the representatives themselves are uneasy with the topic. Whatever formal union policy says, this should not be surprising, shop stewards are often the defenders of 'custom and practice' and the 'status quo'. The approach here will need to be exactly the same as for managers who are practising 'passive resistance' – people need to be able to see how equal opportunities can help them.

Effective resourcing of an equal opportunities programme therefore can be facilitated by gaining the ownership and commitment from certain key groups:

- Senior management to 'steward' progress
- Human resources staff to stimulate departmental initiatives, draft policies and provide data
- Trade unions (where appropriate) to review proposals and negotiate change.

All this has an implication for leadership style. As we see the role of an equal opportunities programme manager, it will be important for this person to be able to use the whole range of styles. The temptation, just as with the senior managers, is for the manager to adopt 'tell' and 'sell' styles. A certain amount of change can be achieved in this way, but it will be highly dependent upon the drive and energy of one person. Perhaps this explains the finding in a recent survey that equal opportunities managers were among the most stressed at work!

It is the 'consult' and 'share' styles of leadership that the programme manager will need to be employing most frequently. This is the way to spread 'ownership' and so get the necessary resources to do the job. The following, therefore, are some factors that might be borne in mind when choosing a programme manager:

- Interested in the topic, but an enthusiast rather than a zealot
- Well respected by colleagues and senior managers
- Experienced in introducing change into the work place
- Able to use a range of leadership styles
- Willing and able to perform the role for at least two years.

These might be demanding requirements, but they are typical for the sorts of roles that are going to be critical in our evolving organisations, where managing change is *the* priority. The equal opportunity programme manager might be a part-time appointment, but he or she should aim to have the whole organisation working on the project. There should not be a dearth of resource, the skill should be in channelling the resource effectively, as we shall now look at further.

■ HARNESSING OWNERSHIP: THE PROCESS OF DEVELOPING INITIATIVES

At the launch of the programme, the senior managers may well have identified some particular initiatives for the organisation to concentrate on right away. These might be areas, for example, where the organisation is in danger of breaking the law, and hence there is an urgency about putting things right. Alternatively, the diagnosis might have identified areas where considerable savings could be made, which would thus deserve immediate attention.

Senior management, however, are not omnipotent. Even with the best management information systems imaginable, there is still a role for people lower down the organisation in deciding what actions need to be taken. Moreover, it is essential that this is the case. It is precisely this process of deciding which initiatives to pursue and then implementing them that carries the precious gift of widespread 'ownership'. Immediately, this is no longer 'their' programme, it is 'our' programme.

To some this no doubt seems to be a recipe for chaos. Unless 'the management' control the programme and decide the actions that need to be taken, the programme will get out of hand, eyes will be taken off the 'real' work and there will be an orgy of self-indulgent policy making. The answer, of course, is that there are other ways of 'controlling' the programme than by simply telling people what to do.

Letting go yet remaining in control

It is the programme manager who has to exercise this controlling influence and harness the energy that the launch of the programme releases. There are effectively two key tools at his or her disposal:

(1) the overall programme aims; and
(2) the process of review.

At this point we will explore how clear aims can act, in effect, as a 'control tool'. They do so by specifying the direction and conveying an attractive vision, thus preventing any need to coerce people or bring them into line. Subsequently, we will explore how the review process acts as a vehicle for ensuring the programme is 'on track' when we look at 'measuring achievement of business benefits' and 'measuring overall progress'.

The leadership of aims

The reason why it is so important for senior management to agree some clear equal opportunities aims is that they become, in effect, a way of 'steering' the activity without telling people what to do. The 'vision' becomes the 'touchstone' and the specific programme aims – its purposes, and criteria – can be used to check the validity of any particular initiative.

For example, one of the purposes of the programme might be: to reduce attrition caused by domestic circumstances. Some criteria associated with that purpose might be:

(1) at least 85 per cent of those who go on maternity leave return on either a part-time or full-time basis within six months; and
(2) no-one resigns from employment due to domestic circumstances other than maternity leave.

With these particular aims clearly communicated, then managers should feel free to develop local solutions to particular issues. They may be able to do this within the umbrella of an existing policy – and the more these are phrased in an enabling way, then the likelier this is – or they may need to break new ground. In which case, providing the proposal meets legal requirements and it has the full support of both the employee concerned and his or her line management, why not go ahead? Employers should be actively looking for innovative solutions rather than trying to keep the lid on them. 'Setting a precedent' seems to hold a horror for many personnel departments, but this is precisely what equal opportunities will require. So long as each case is taken on its merits, and the same principles applied, then this should be a source of strength rather than weakness.

Organisations that can offer this sort of flexibility will be the organisations that prosper in the future.

Of course, there will be some proposals that will require organisational investment, and some decisions that need to be made corporately. It would be inappropriate for one department, for example, to support its employees with childcare facilities before the other departments have thought through their positions. Well set aims will be able to 'flag' these areas. For instance, the criteria might include financial limits, or include the proviso that proposals with implications for the whole organisation are worked through an inter-departmental group. What should not happen is that departments are deprived of the power to initiate discussion on these cross-organisational issues. This is precisely what the equal opportunities programme manager should be looking to encourage.

Using the equal opportunities workshops

When we discussed the equal opportunities workshops in Chapter 8, we suggested that one of their purposes might be to: begin to get some input to the policy development process.

This is an opportunity which the equal opportunities programme manager needs to grab. It is so much more effective for managers and their staff to be saying that there should be a comprehensive policy covering people with disabilities, than for this to be a remote initiative pushed from the centre. Similarly, the programme manager is probably not the best person to propose a support network for women in the organisation, but if the workshops identify this need, then he or she can start the initial co-ordination and help get the network off the ground.

Of course, this sort of invitation to input to policy development needs to be positioned appropriately. Again, the programme aims will be essential in providing direction and acknowledging any pre-existing constraints. There cannot be a blank cheque book and falsely high expectations should not be raised. The activity needs to be presented for what it is – a unique opportunity to get some grass-roots input so that this can be taken into account in the policy development process. As we suggest below, there will need to be a deliberate follow-up process and this needs to be explained so that people know what will be happening to their ideas.

The workshops, therefore, can be used quite deliberately as a way of trying out and developing ideas. There may be a particular area that senior managers have identified as a priority and they need some ideas for what can, or should, be done in practice. For example, the directors at Rank Xerox (UK) knew they wanted to include measures of the contribution of each manager to the effectiveness of the programme, and they knew what some of the measurement tools might be, but they were not sure of the best way of going about it. The managers themselves were obviously the best people to provide the ideas. Alternatively, there may well be issues that the senior management team are unaware of that need to be sorted out. The workshops can both identify the issues and start the process of thinking about the solutions.

Managing the output from the workshops

As a result of running the workshops, the programme manager ought to have a number of proposals that are at the 'good idea' stage.

That is to say, the proposals would seem to have some benefits and there is a measure of support for them, but there has been no detailed planning about how to implement them.

This is where the programme manager needs to exercise a powerful co-ordinating role. In our view, it is essential that these proposals are fed back into the normal decision-making processes.

For cross-organisational issues, this will mean reviewing the proposals with the senior management team. This team need to consider the ideas and, in the context of the overall programme aims that they have set, choose some of the proposals to incorporate into an action plan. Obviously, everything cannot happen at once and this plan may have a fair amount of detail for the first year, but do no more than indicate the issues that will be tackled, and their sequence, for future years. Therefore, although all the ideas that have come from the workshops will not find their way into the organisation's action plan, there should be some issues that people will be able to identify as 'theirs'. In this way, the action plan belongs to the organisation, not just to the senior management team and the programme manager.

Moreover, some of the ideas will be for department initiatives – for example, about how to attract more applications for engineering vacancies. These sorts of proposals are departmentally specific; they may have an effect on another department to the extent that they represent an example of good practice, but they do not require corporate sanction.

All these ideas need to be reviewed by the top management team in the department, who can then, in the light of their own specific needs and the overall programme aims, generate their own action plan. Obviously, key actors in all this would be the head of the department and his or her human resources manager.

Not all the ideas will be picked up, and only a few will be implemented in the short term, but the process will have begun. With regular communication within the department, and using ad hoc groups involving staff to develop the ideas to implementation, a real shift in 'ownership' from the centre to the departments will have been achieved.

Therefore, under the overall umbrella of the programme aims it should be possible to develop both an organisational action plan and a set of departmental action plans, which are consistent and channel energy into the appropriate initiatives. The programme manager may need to 'champion' the organisational action plan and take

211

responsibility for pulling together the appropriate resources in order to get the proposals implemented. As far as the departmental action plans are concerned, however, these need to be the responsibility of the departments themselves. The overall programme manager may be a provider of advice and will certainly be interested in the outcomes of initiatives, but he or she is not responsible for making them happen.

■ MEASURING THE ACHIEVEMENT OF BUSINESS BENEFITS

While discussing how the programme manager could 'let go yet remain in control' we identified two tools that he or she could use. As we have seen, the first is concerned with the clarity of the programme aims in terms of setting direction. The second is the use of a review process in order to ensure progress is on track.

As we argued above, it is essential that the senior management team do not simply wash their hands of equal opportunities once they have 'done their bit', gone through their workshop, and set some aims. They need to be involved in reviewing progress. After all, they ought to want to know whether they are achieving their aims. Perhaps more importantly in our ever-changing world, it will be essential to review the aims themselves to see whether they are still appropriate or whether they need to be re-drafted in order to accommodate new developments.

The review process for most equal opportunities programmes has focused on analysing the statistical profile of the organisation. Monitoring has been seen to be the be-all and end-all of the review process. This is particularly the case where organisations have set themselves 'goals' or 'targets' for the proportion of women, or minorities or people with disabilities at the different organisational levels.

As we argued in Chapter 6, this is to make these criteria (measures of progress towards the desired end result) into purposes (the reasons for having an equal opportunities programme). Of course, organisational goals are useful, but they should not be an end in themselves and we prefer to put the initial emphasis of measurement elsewhere.

If an equal opportunities programme is a way of realising particular organisational benefits, then the fundamental review question must be : 'Have we achieved these benefits?' After all, if little progress has been made in a particular area then this might indicate the need to amend the current action plans and give some priority to this issue.

In Chapter 7 we identified the following areas as potential benefits: managing change, supporting Total Quality Management, improving the interface with customers, choosing the best, keeping the best, improving productivity, and improving profitability. In each of these areas it will be important to be able to measure progress, and while some of the measures will have to be more qualitative than quantitative, they are still important. We will discuss each of these areas in turn.

Managing change

This is one of the longer-term areas and one where it will be impossible to pick out precisely the contribution that equal opportunities has made (as opposed to any other initiatives). Some measures might be: the emergence of any new products or services, the effectiveness of any joint ventures with European partners, or the handling of any new issues that have been 'sprung' on the organisation. The sorts of things to look for would be examples of where mixed problem-solving groups have been instrumental in developing new ideas.

Supporting total quality

There will be many measures that an organisation will be using to gauge the effectiveness of its approach to total quality. Equal opportunities will have its part to play in ensuring that round pegs are in round holes. Evidence for this might come from departmental transfers and promotions. It may also be having an impact in helping cross-departmental co-operation. Here, the best examples may be found where traditionally male and traditionally female departments are working effectively together.

Improving the interface with customers

Many organisations monitor levels of customer satisfaction and there may be an influence on these figures due to higher levels of staff motivation and productivity. There may also be an increase in customers that is directly attributable to equal opportunities. For example, it may help to tip the balance in gaining an order from a local authority. Or, by introducing a wider range of people into the sales force new areas may be opened up. As one manager explained, when they had an all-white sales force, Bradford was a 'lost' territory, they knew that they would not get any orders there.

Choosing the best

In the short term, this should be reflected in an increase in the number of applicants and feed back from the recruiters confirming that they have been able to raise standards. In the longer term, productivity should also go up (because the best person has been appointed) and attrition should reduce (because no recent recruit, for instance, should be dismissed for poor performance). Where there are appraisal schemes with performance grades, then new recruits should feature strongly in the higher grades.

Keeping the best

The overall turnover rate should reduce. Specifically, there should be a reduction in the numbers who leave for 'domestic reasons'. Changes in the percentages of those who return from maternity leave can easily be monitored. The number of people who choose to take up a Career Break would also represent people who would otherwise have left the organisation.

Increasing productivity

At an organisational level, if people are more productive it should be possible to do more work with the same number of people or the same amount of work with less. There will obviously be a number of factors at work here. More specifically, it should be possible to measure an increase in productivity related to the introduction of more part-time and flexible working arrangements.

Increasing profitability

Savings made due to reduced attrition can be calculated. Recruitment costs should also show a reduction – due to increased success in filling vacancies and reduction in the time taken to fill them. Over-time working, filling in while the recruitment campaign is underway, should also fall.

In this way, an organisation ought to be able to see whether it is realising the business benefits that equal opportunities can bring. Moreover, while this sort of overall check can be done on an annual basis, each initiative should be consciously seeking to bring about particular benefits and these can therefore be assessed on a case by case basis. Is the nursery paying for itself? Has the positive action advertising campaign for ethnic minorities increased the number of quality applicants?

It will be the responsibility of the programme manager to ensure questions like these are answered. Sometimes, he or she will have to 'ferret out' the information. More often, we hope, he or she will be able to ensure that those involved in undertaking the initiatives set for themselves measures which will indicate their success or otherwise. In this way, they will 'own' the assessment process and be committed to ensuring that their particular project achieves its organisational aims.

■ MEASURING OVERALL PROGRESS: ANOTHER DIAGNOSIS

Reviewing the extent to which the business purposes have been achieved is one way of assessing the impact of an equal opportunities programme. In itself, however, it is probably not enough. There is a need to return to the broad overview, to return to the vision of the organisation, and see what progress has been made. There will be some changes that will not necessarily translate directly into business benefits. Also, there is a need to take a look again at the organisational profile that was envisaged and see what progress has been made towards it.

Moreover, it is not enough to look internally, there needs to be an external perspective too. There may well be changes in society's values, legislation, competitive practice or in the labour market that need to be reflected in organisational thinking.

For these reasons, the review process should also include – at a strategic point in the overall programme – a repeat diagnosis. This will enable the programme manager, and hence the senior managers and the rest of the organisation, to gain a comprehensive picture of the revised state of equal opportunities. Again, there will be a need to use the original diagnostic framework and review progress in three areas: statistics, personnel policies, and culture. Once this review is complete, the senior management team can revisit and reset the equal opportunities programme aims. These will, in turn, drive the succeeding action plans and ensure that there remains a balance in progress in the three areas (statistical profile, personnel policies, and culture).

Statistics

These are the traditional 'monitoring' tools of the equal opportunities world. Statistical analysis has its place – it can indicate whether an organisation is getting its fair share of the 'best'. Both national labour market statistics, and employment profiles of other organisations, can provide useful 'benchmarks'. On the basis of this information, organisations may choose to set themselves particular goals. The

BBC, for example, has said that it wants to increase the proportion of women among its management and the Bar Council is keen to set a target for the percentage of barristers who will come from ethnic minorities.

It would be a mistake, however, to identify the success of an equal opportunities programme with the achievement of numerical goals. Any particular goal may have been set on the high, or the low, side. It is the trend that is important; all that goals represent is the stage that is expected to be reached at a particular moment along the journey. Moreover, it is always possible to manipulate statistics. People are used to being managed by criteria and therefore will provide their superiors with the information they want to hear. This may not always be a good thing for genuine equality of opportunity.

Nevertheless, it would be folly to ignore the statistics. They offer the facts by showing what the trends really are. They can reveal whether the proportion of women, minorities and people with disabilities in the various grades is increasing.

Other measures of progress might include reviewing recruitment campaign and promotion appointments. Success rates for different groups can be calculated and might be helpful in identifying the need for further positive action initiatives. In addition, the age profiles of those recruited or promoted might show whether traditional thinking has been successfully challenged in this area.

One of the main concerns will be to look at how the career planning process is working out in practice. Who is being promoted into the key jobs? What percentage of women, minorities and people with disabilities have been assessed as having high potential?

Personnel policies

Any of the areas covered in the original diagnosis might require updating in the light of legal developments or improvements in competitive practice. It is more likely, however, that the task here will be to review the policies that have been introduced and to assess their impact. It should place the organisation ahead of the law, and there may be examples where it is at the forefront of competition.

In the light of experience, this review may, of course, also highlight the need to adapt policies or to take fresh initiatives. Moreover, the extent to which these new policies have been taken up will be a powerful indicator of the state of the prevailing culture. If there is a flexible working policy, but nobody is actually working on this basis, then there would appear to be much still to do.

Prevailing culture

Here, it will be possible to look beyond the formal policies and return to what actually happens in practice. This will capture some of the subtler transitions, some of the by-products of the programme, as well as some of the more overt changes.

As we have suggested, one measure of the change in culture would be the spread of new policies. There are also other statistical measures of cultural change. At IBM and Rank Xerox, where they conduct regular employee attitude surveys, the questionnaires include questions about equal opportunities. Changes in the results from these questions will obviously provide valuable material. Sustained change in the profile of a department would also be evidence of a changing culture. It is relatively easy to recruit in women, minorities, and people with disabilities, but if they are also prospering and getting on, then the *culture* must be receptive and helping them to progress.

Looking at the trend in complaints of harassment can also provide feed back on changes in the culture. At first, the trend may actually seem to go the 'wrong' way. As the environment becomes more open, and people feel more able to tackle the issues, there may be an increase in the number of complaints. All that has happened here is that the previous culture masked the true situation, and an increase in the number of complaints can actually be taken as a success. Thereafter, however, the trend should be downwards.

We believe that there is also a place for a more subjective impression of what the working culture is actually like. Just as with the original diagnosis, this could be achieved by holding discussions with a cross-section of managers and staff. Alternatively, if there appears to be a need to concentrate on particular areas, interested parties could be brought together to provide their views. For example, if there are few women in the sales function, then it might well be worth asking those who do work in sales why they think this might be – as well as asking some likely candidates why they have not looked to make the transfer into that department.

There may also be some quite deliberate changes to record as indicators of progress in the culture. A 'salesman' might have become a 'salesperson'. The embarrassing jokes might have disappeared from the conference platform. Somebody in a wheelchair might have a chance of gaining access to the office. They may be small, but it is actually these sorts of signs that really herald progress. They mean that equal opportunities is becoming part of the culture.

Measuring progress: conclusion

Conducting a second diagnosis enables the equal opportunities programme manager to gauge progress, and perhaps more significantly, to adjust the strategy for the future. It may suggest that there needs to be more energy directed at increasing the representation of women, minorities and people with disabilities at management level (statistical representation). It may highlight the need to review the career planning policy and to train those involved in the process (personnel policy). It may suggest that the expectation that managers will work 50-hour weeks needs to be re-examined (cultural change). It may suggest that the three issues are all interlinked, that the latter two cause the first, and that they therefore must all be addressed in order to make sustained progress.

Whatever the diagnosis actually comes up with, it should provide a sound basis, along with the review of the business benefits, for the programme manager to go back to the senior management and reset their equal opportunities aims. The overall 'vision' should remain the same, but the particular emphases, and their relationship with the current business issues, may well be different.

With the aims in place, the proposed action plans – both organisational and departmental – can be reviewed and adjusted. Once again, we should then be in a position where there are a sequence of initiatives which actually support the declared equal opportunities aims.

■ A STRATEGIC APPROACH TO SUSTAINING MOMENTUM

To sum up, our strategic approach is, of course, cyclical. Once the first cycle has been completed, then it is time to revisit the diagnosis and the aims. Only then can sensible policy and training initiatives be undertaken once more. The process of 'spreading ownership' however, is a continual task – from the moment of the 'launch' of the programme – and the development of the policy and training initiatives becomes the vehicle for sustaining and spreading this sense of 'ownership'.

One of the skills that the programme manager will need to develop is being able to decide when it is time to launch a new 'cycle'. A factor that may help make this decision is the information coming from the regular reviews of the business benefits. If progress seems slow, another cycle may help to re-focus effort. Alternatively, the number of initiatives in place, and their phasing over a number of years, may suggest a natural pause when a diagnosis could be undertaken. Or, sometimes there might be such a significant external change – either in the organisation's business climate, or in society as a whole – that this will provoke the need for an immediate review.

■ COMMUNICATING SUCCESS

There is one other aspect of the role of the programme manager that we have not yet explicitly covered. In addition to all the reviewing and planning activities that we have described above, it is vital that the whole organisation is kept up-to-date with progress. Since this is no longer 'the management's' activity, because it actually belongs to the whole organisation, then the styles and methods of communication need to reflect this.

There are four main purposes for communicating:

To give people a sense of progress
Equal opportunities is a long journey, and without regular signposts along the way people may give up hope of ever getting there. Regular updates of organisational or departmental initiatives show that progress is being made and generate a sense of momentum. Communication can also ensure that expectations are kept in line with reality. If the introduction of a nursery is not a short-term prospect, then there needs to be a clear communication stating this and giving the reasons why earlier implementation is not practical.

To spread successes
It is quite possible that a successful initiative in one area will go unnoticed outside that department unless it is picked up and passed on by the programme manager. The achievements of one group might open the minds of others to a similar approach. Even departmental rivalry can be harnessed effectively as a spur to new thinking.

To recognise people's contribution
Change will only occur if people stir themselves and do something differently. Those who are prepared to do this deserve recognition. It is easy for the 'glory' to be attributed at too high a level in the

219

organisation. The head of department may be an 'enabler', but those who have really made things happen will be staff in the lower levels of the organisation. Acknowledging their contribution publicly may act as an incentive for them to carry on coming up with new initiatives, it may also stimulate others to break the 'do' barrier, and propose an initiative of their own.

To practise the value of openness

It would be somewhat inconsistent to look to the equal opportunities programme to increase 'openness' and trust within an organisation, but then to refuse to share any information about its progress. People will have been actively involved in the programme and they will expect to be kept up-to-date with developments. Some of the information may be considered sensitive – such as the profile of women, minorities and people with disabilities within the organisation – but our experience suggests that there are more risks in not sharing the information than in openly publishing it. After all, there is a natural tendency to doubt someone's motives if they are not prepared to share the full information. An equal opportunities programme can arouse so many potential sensitivities that organisations cannot afford to be seen to be less than open in their communication.

All this, of course, cannot be achieved by chance. The programme manager needs to seek out and use all the available channels of communication – both internally and externally. Again, the priority would be to integrate equal opportunities into existing communication mechanisms. For example, it could be a regular feature in the in-house magazine, or a regular item at team meetings and joint consultative committees. A degree of external publicity can also be helpful. It would, of course, help to support any current (or future) outreach activities, but it can also add a degree of credibility internally. So long as the message is consistent with the approach that is being taken internally (and is not simply a 'gloss' put out for PR purposes) it reinforces the fact that the organisation is prepared to take a public stand on the issue.

■ CONCLUSION

In our view, managing an equal opportunities programme effectively is not about setting up a separate unit to conduct in-depth monitoring activities and to 'police' recalcitrant line management.

The skill is actually to continue the process of spreading 'ownership' by integrating equal opportunities into the existing management mechanisms rather than setting up new and separate systems. The senior management have business aims and they need to consider equal opportunities as part of these aims. Departments will have departmental aims, they need to include equal opportunities initiatives among these. The responsibility for achieving these aims lies, as with any other issue, with the line management.

That is not to say that there is not a role for an equal opportunities programme manager. We have argued, throughout this chapter, that his or her task is not to keep, but to spread 'ownership'. For this reason, we believe the position is best established as a part–time post. In effect, he or she should be looking to do away with the job.

In the meantime, the programme manager has a number of key roles to perform. He or she needs to:

- Review progress with senior management and agree organisation-wide action plans with them
- Manage the implementation of this organisation action plan
- Co-ordinate and stimulate departmental initiatives
- Assist and advise departments in drawing up their own action plans, working with local HR professionals
- Regularly review against the business benefits that the programme is seeking to realise
- After an appropriate period, conduct a second diagnosis of the state of equal opportunities within the organisation
- Review the original programme aims and action plans with senior management in the light of the information from the diagnosis
- Ensure regular, open communication of progress to the whole organisation.

Working in this way, while the programme manager may be part-time, he or she will have the whole organisation working for the success of the programme. And, as we know from events in Eastern Europe, if enough people want something to happen badly enough, ultimately there is nothing that is going to stop them.

Part 3

DIVERSITY AT WORK

Chapter 12

A VISION OF THE FUTURE – DIVERSITY AT WORK

We recognise that it is all very well to theorise about equal opportunities and to pull particular examples from organisations in order to illustrate a particular point, but the question remains: what does it all add up to? What will an equal opportunities organisation of the future look like? Just as we suggest that organisations need to make their 'vision' of the future tangible, so do we. Therefore, what we have sought to do here is to identify an organisation which epitomises what we mean by equal opportunities.

■ **CASE STUDY**

We have chosen what might seem a surprising example. Equal opportunities has often been associated with improving the lot of women at work. At Rank Xerox's Customer Response Centre, in contrast, they have increased the number of men who work in a traditionally female environment. This fits, however, with our interpretation of what equal opportunities is actually about. It is not about favouring one group at the expense of another. The Customer Response Centre offers an altogether healthier model which should encourage any organisation to move away from the all male – or all female – ghettoes and to discover the real benefits of embracing 'diversity' at work.

To suggest that Rank Xerox's Customer Response Centre (or CRC as it is known) comes the closest of all the organisations we are familiar with to our 'vision' of what an equal opportunities organisation should be like, is not to suggest that it is an 'ideal' model which should be replicated elsewhere. The CRC did not set out to become as 'diverse' an organisation as possible. Indeed, in an environment that might be considered particularly suitable for people with disabilities, it is perhaps surprising that there are none among the CRC's staff. The management team at the CRC has simply been focusing on achieving their particular business goals. Similarly, every other organisation will be responding to its own unique situation and will therefore find different solutions to its problems. We believe, however, that both in the sort of organisation it has become, and the way that it has achieved this, it does offer some lessons for other organisations.

We will explore these themes in the following way:

- We will start by briefly giving some background information on Rank Xerox (UK) and describing the role of the CRC within the company
- We will then examine the employee profile of the CRC which, in its diversity, illustrates the sort of equal opportunities organisation we have in mind
- At this point, we will consider how successful the organisation is
- We will then discuss the causes of this success and go on to examine the role that equal opportunities has had to play
- At the end of this chapter, we will highlight key lessons for other organisations.

RANK XEROX (UK) LTD

Rank Xerox (UK) employ about 4,500 people in this country. They are best known as suppliers of Document Management Technology.

The UK company, with the support and encouragement of its US parent, has long had an equal opportunities policy. In practice, however, like many other organisations it found in the late 1980s that it had policies in place but that the employee profile remained static – predominantly young, white and male. Viki Ford had responsibility for the equal opportunity policy, as well as for other personnel initiatives, and she was determined to bring about some change.

We began working with them as consultants in the autumn of 1989. The initiative came from Shaun Pantling, the Director of the Customer Services Division, who believed that the Division needed to be more open-minded in its recruitment practices. Together with Viki Ford, we ran a series of workshops for the CSD management team.

■ THE CUSTOMER RESPONSE CENTRE (CRC)

The CRC is one of the departments within the Customer Services Division. The number one company goal is 'customer satisfaction' and the CRC is at the 'sharp end' of this particular objective. Its aim is to provide a single point of contact for Rank Xerox's UK customers to deal with any queries that arise 'after sale'. As Jenny Ivy, the Manager of the CRC puts it:

'We own the problem, we should never ask a customer to phone another number.'

On average, they take 4,500 calls a day.

This means that they deal with a wide range of issues: anything from handling requests for a visit from a service engineer, to processing requests for toner supplies, or handling a query about an invoice. They also have responsibility for ensuring that there is a databank which keeps customers' records up-to-date.

Having a national CRC is a recent innovation for Rank Xerox. Previously, requests were handled through a number of different units spread across the United Kingdom. The idea for a national centre came from the customers themselves who, in a survey, indicated that they wanted to be able to call a single number in order to handle all their queries.

There has been a progressive handover from the regions to the CRC and, at the moment, customers in the North are still partly served locally. Accordingly, the organisation and structure at the CRC has been able to evolve steadily over the last two-and-a-half years. When it first opened, there were just nine staff. Currently there are 59.

■ **THE CRC ORGANISATION: DIVERSITY AT WORK**

Not surprisingly, the vast majority (51 out of 59) of the employees at the CRC are controllers, who are responsible for taking customer calls, processing the paper work and keeping the database up-to-date. They sit at desks with headphones waiting for calls. If they need to attend to some paper work, then they can make themselves 'unavailable' to the 'phone system, but this time is obviously monitored in order to ensure it does not get out of hand. Each controller has a minimum target of handling 120 calls a day.

The controllers are organised into five teams, each with a team leader, who is responsible for ensuring that the teams meet their targets. They monitor the performance of people in their team and are responsible for identifying training needs which may emerge if someone is not meeting their targets. They hold regular team meetings and are encouraged to keep close to their controllers, so that they know how people are feeling about the job as well as how they are actually performing. There are two other members of the management team: a supervisor and the CRC manager.

The typical 'work control' unit, the predecessors to the CRC, was staffed by eight or nine young women aged between 25 and 35 working full-time. The job itself did not demand skills or experience which would exclude men, but somehow 'work control' had come to typify the 'pink collar': fairly routine jobs that had become, in effect, a female 'ghetto'.

■ EMPLOYEE PROFILE

The profile of the staff at the CRC is rather different. There is a wide *age profile, men* as well as women, a proportion of people from *ethnic minority* backgrounds, and a number on *flexible working* contracts. The team leaders themselves reflect this diversity: there are two men and three women, the youngest is 19 and the oldest 53. As one of the controllers put it:

'We have a wide range of people, with different views and backgrounds, and we pull each other along.'

Age profile

The most frequent age range is still 25 to 35 (46% of controllers and team leaders) but there is a healthier distribution than in the old work control units, with representation in all the other ranges, including 9 per cent who are over 45 years old. This includes recruiting one controller who was aged 61 and had been out of work for three years previously.

Age range	Number	Percentage
less than 24 years old	15	27
25 years to 34 years	26	46
35 years to 44 years	10	18
over 45 years old	5	9

Gender profile

There are 17 men (29%), of whom 14 are at controller level (27%) and three are part of the management team (42%). While men make up a high proportion of the management team, because the total numbers are so low there is a high sensitivity to small changes. One fewer man would bring their representation among the management team to 29 per cent.

Ethnic origin profile

There are six employees (10%) from ethnic minority backgrounds. The catchment area for the CRC is within five to 10 miles of Milton Keynes, and it is estimated that for the Buckinghamshire and North-amptonshire areas, about 3.6 per cent of the total population are ethnic minorities. All the ethnic minority staff, are in controller positions.

Flexible working contracts

In total, there are 11 people on flexible working contracts. This represents 22 per cent of the controllers. Over the two-and-a-half years people have changed their employment contracts as their domestic circumstances have changed – some have moved from full-time to part-time and some from part-time back to full-time.

This is a review of some of the more obvious 'categories' of employees. It is not as 'diverse' a group as it is possible to be, with strict proportions of each category represented at each level – but that is not what it set out to achieve. The CRC was set up to achieve its business goals, not to act as a model equal opportunities organisation. As we shall see, the equal opportunities aspect of its development grew out of a simple desire to recruit and develop the best people.

■ MEASURING SUCCESS AT THE CRC

Choosing to recruit 'different' people into an organisation is sometimes seen to be something of a risk. It seems to be much safer to recruit 'more of the same'. Why bother having part-timers when you can recruit full-timers? The CRC offers a wonderful challenge to this pedestrian thinking. For them, diversity has been a source of strength, not a potential weakness.

In order to grow, the CRC has had to be successful. It had to show that it could handle work previously being done regionally and as it has done so, then it has been able to expand and take on more work. In this way, it has moved from an organisation of nine people to one employing 59. There can be no denying that it has been a success.

There are two aspects to the success of the CRC:

(1) performance against departmental goals; and
(2) the high level of motivation which lies behind the achievement of these goals.

We will examine each of these areas in turn.

Achievement of departmental goals

The work being done at the CRC lends itself to performance measurement. The telephone system that they have installed enables them to monitor the number of calls coming in and the time each caller has had to wait before being answered. On the basis of this information, they have then been able to set some realistic targets. Each controller has a minimum target of 120 calls a day. Calls are expected to be answered on average within 20 seconds, with 80 per cent of calls being answered within 30 seconds.

The CRC is meeting or exceeding these targets. Controllers are meeting their minimum number of calls and some reach up to 160 in a day. One part-timer handles 100 calls in her four-hour day (which would equate to 188 calls in a full day). Moreover, 90 per cent of calls are answered within 20 seconds, which exceeds the target they set for calls being answered within 30 seconds. They are now setting targets for the percentage of calls they will answer within 10 seconds.

These figures suggest that they are handling the quantity of business, but they do not necessarily indicate that when a call is answered the customer gets handled satisfactorily. The telephone system, as well as monitoring the number of calls also provides information on the duration of the call. The average length is 90 seconds, which suggests that customers' queries are being addressed swiftly. There is another way of measuring the quality of the service and this is through what they call 'silent monitoring'. This allows a team leader to listen in on calls in order to check that the controller is providing the sort of service that is expected.

All this may seem to smack a little of 'Big Brother' where the organisation has far too much information about people and their performance. The management team, however, are alive to this problem and handle it sensitively. As one of the controllers said:

'It's in the nature of the job that calls have to be monitored.'

This says a great deal about the way in which the CRC management team have ensured that the company goal of customer satisfaction has been taken 'on board'. As another explained:

'The figures are used in a low key way. It's not a drama. We're helped, not shouted at!'

In order to be able to handle the number of calls that they do, controllers need to keep up-to-date with a great deal of information, and some of the performance measures may simply indicate a training need.

High level of motivation

There is more to the success of the CRC, however, than just this performance against departmental goals. There are other indicators which would also suggest that they have got a winning formula. Morale appears to be high and people can sense this atmosphere. A customer on a visit to the CRC remarked:

'It's a super environment, and it even sounds like it when you ring up'.

It comes as no surprise to hear that many of the staff, and their families, choose to socialise together out of hours.

There is some compelling evidence for this high morale and it marks a sharp contrast with the record at previous work control units. The most obvious change is in turnover. In what the controllers themselves recognise can be a fairly boring job, turnover has traditionally been very high, often running at 40 per cent. At the CRC, this has dropped to 10 per cent − and of the six people who have left, two transferred to other parts of the company and two emigrated to Italy. This represents a considerable reduction in costs and also leads to an improved service to customers which comes from this increase in continuity. Another indicator of the high morale in the CRC is the relatively low level of sickness absence. In the past, this would typically have been running above 10 per cent, and is now at 5 per cent.

There is a sense that everyone at the CRC is pulling together as a member of the team. Controllers see all the performance information and congratulate each other when they see particularly high call rates. Two controllers who had had relatively low levels of calls, decided to have a competition to see who could answer the most number of calls and kept within one call of each other all day. At the end of the day, one ended up with 156, the other 157 – both comfortably exceeding the minimum target of 120.

They can therefore help to spur each other on, but they can also support each other in other ways. No one controller can know everything there is to know about the company's range of products. Some will be strong on one product, others on another. They consciously use each other to test out ideas. As one of the controllers put it:

'That way, we know we've always got an answer.'

This is real synergy at work and, of course, the more diverse the team, the greater the potential there is for being able to add different, helpful perspectives.

Another indicator of the high morale is the willingness of the part-timers to attend the unpaid quarterly departmental meeting. This takes place after the end of business at 5:30 p.m. and lasts a couple of hours. For full-timers this simply means staying on at work; for the part-timers, many of whom have young children, this means coming back into work having left at lunch-time. Perhaps this finally quashes the assumption that part-timers are simply working for 'pin-money' and do not really bother about the work they do.

The environment is one of tolerance and mutual respect.

'We've all got something we like about each other.'

People are taken for what they are. One young female controller contrasted the CRC with a previous company, where the male manager had invited her into his office to ask: 'Aren't you going to wear any make-up today?' 'Here', she said 'I can come to work as me.' A male homosexual controller, who had previously been employed in a local authority, was particularly impressed.

'Here, they practise what they preach. There, equal opportunities was on the letterhead, but the managers did nothing to stop harassment.'

All of which is reflected in the fact that the manager has a fat file of application forms from people who want to come and work at the

CRC. They have heard about the work there from their friends or relatives. One applicant is the mother of one of the controllers. This is a nice position for the manager to be in. This can supplement, and reduce the costs of, recruitment campaigns – and because her existing employees are such a diverse group, so are the potential recruits – and it also represents a strong vote of confidence from the existing employees.

In our view, the CRC are in a 'virtuous circle' (as opposed to a vicious one). This does not mean that they are, or could afford to be, complacent. It does mean that they have established some successful patterns, and found ways to cope with and manage change. The question for us, therefore, is to find out what is causing this success and to see what part the diversity of the people who make up the CRC plays in these causes.

■ CAUSES OF SUCCESS AT THE CRC

Obviously, this success is not directly caused by equal opportunities, and it would be surprising if it were. As we will discuss below, however, we believe that the way in which equal opportunities principles have been integrated by the management team into the way they manage, has had a very powerful and positive impact. Once the technology was in place – a highly effective telephone system which enables 'automatic call distribution' – the rest (as in so many other businesses) was down to the people. Selecting the right people and managing them appropriately was therefore absolutely critical.

The following are what appear to us to be the key causes of this success at the CRC.

Clear communication of the business goals

People at the CRC know what their objectives are and how they relate to the overall company goals. Team meetings are held on a monthly basis and the whole department gets together quarterly. These are opportunities to review performance and communicate goals. There is a demonstrable commitment to 'customer satisfaction'. For example, the CRC used to open at 9:00 a.m., but they found that people were trying to make calls in the preceding hour, so they moved the start time to 8:00 a.m. The logic of the change was so clear that it provoked no resistance.

Developing clear performance measures

All the controllers know how they are doing. There are objective measures of performance which have nothing to do with whether you happen to get on with the boss or not. Moreover, this information is not kept secret. It is openly shared and people are encouraged to take an interest in it.

Treating employees on the basis of merit

As a consequence of having clear performance measures, it is possible then to reward people according to their contribution. Accordingly, the salary budget is allocated on merit – a reflection of performance and commitment (one sign of which would be an individual's attendance record).

This applies to promotion decisions also. The team leaders, a very diverse group, were promoted from controller positions because they were assessed as having the appropriate skills for the job. Today, the five team leaders join the supervisor and manager in assessing the potential of the existing controllers. Every quarter, the management team get together to assess who is demonstrating signs of potential and then consider what opportunities they need to provide in order to help those people develop further.

Choosing recruits on the basis of merit

The diversity of the current controllers itself suggests that the selection process focuses on whether applicants can do the job, rather than looking for applicants with particular track records. The management team broke the cultural barrier that said that this sort of job should be done by young women. The 61 year old turned up to the interview saying that he did not expect to get the job. When he was appointed, it was also something of a shock for the rest of the company. Apparently, there were a few sharp intakes of breath when he joined the company induction course.

Specifically, the CRC went out of their way to ensure that they attracted men into jobs that had traditionally been filled by women. They ran a positive action recruitment advert and ended up recruiting five women and four men to fill their nine vacancies.

Coaching role of team leaders

When they are assessing potential or making decisions about salary awards, the team leaders are exercising their managerial role as 'judge'. Complementing this, however, is the equally important role of manager as 'coach'. For example, performance figures are an opportunity to discuss training needs with controllers. Moreover, the team leaders are encouraged to keep close to their staff and keep alive to any concerns. In this way, any issues are brought out into the open and resolved.

Moreover, because the team leaders are close to the individuals in their teams, it means that they are able to respond to their individual needs. If one of the controllers wants to change to or from a part-time contract, then this is something they can discuss together and resolve.

Because the manager of the CRC recognises the importance of the coaching role played by the team leaders, she is also keen to keep the size of each team at a realistic level. Currently, the typical team has about 10 controllers.

Creating a supportive team environment

When new recruits first arrive, the supervisor, Bob Ballantyne, drums into them:

'If you don't know, ask!'

This encourages controllers to see each other as colleagues rather than competitors. As one of the controllers points out:

'No one is unapproachable. It helps to be on first name terms with the bosses.'

This extends to any agency 'temps' who are employed. They join in the departmental meetings and social events just like everyone else. When the manager found out that they were receiving only 50 per cent of what she was paying the agency, she had their pay increased and this came out of the agency's cut.

To sum up, the success at the CRC has been based on some standard, sound management principles. What interests us is that this provides an example where sound principles have been translated into sound practices. This is not always such an easy transition.

■ THE ROLE OF EQUAL OPPORTUNITIES IN THIS SUCCESS

For the management team, equal opportunities cannot be separated out as a unique issue, it is an integral part of their overall management style. Quite simply, they have taken off the blinkers – they will recruit or promote the best person for the job whatever their background. This is reflected in some of the causes of success that we have identified above. It goes further than this, however, because they are not passively waiting for the 'best' to come to them. They are prepared to do new and different things in order to ensure that they are getting the best talent available. There are two specific areas that are worth highlighting:

(1) 'positive action' recruitment; and
(2) providing flexible working arrangements.

Positive action recruitment

In late 1989, the company ran an advert in the Milton Keynes press with the title : 'Why are good men so difficult to find?' The intention was not to recruit just men, but Jenny Ivy, the Manager of the CRC, felt it was important that the new organisation did not become – as the old work control units had been – the sole province of women.

Running a positive action advert for men, however, was not just different, it was actually unheard of at that time. Where the relevant clause of the Sex Discrimination Act had been invoked before, 'positive action' had been about encouraging women to apply for jobs traditionally done by men. The initial reaction from the company's advertising agency was to reject the idea out of hand. It took a long conversation with Viki Ford, the Programme Manager for equal opportunities in Rank Xerox, before the agency were persuaded that it was legal and agreed to go ahead with the advert.

The results of this positive action advert speak for themselves. Traditional adverts had brought in 60 or 70 applications. This time there were over 100 applications, of which 40 per cent were from men. They were able to fill all nine vacancies from the one advert, and they ended up recruiting five women and four men.

In any terms, it was a successful advert. A point that a number of organisations have found when using positive action adverts to encourage applications from a minority is that this does not put off the majority – as many, if not more, continue to apply. Indeed, it is an essential legal requirement that the vacancies are open to both

236

sexes. The accompanying photograph to the advert showed a man and a woman working side-by-side and the text of the advert included the message:

'We're still as keen as ever to hear from equally qualified women'.

The overriding impression is of an organisation that is determined to recruit the best person for the job, but is also sure that the relevant skills are not just to be found in the traditional labour pool. The management team know that by thinking 'outside the square' they will be able to get the best.

Flexible working arrangements

The spread of flexible working practices is another sign of the CRC shedding traditional thought patterns and challenging existing norms. This might seem an obvious development for the type of work that is required at the CRC – and, indeed, the telephone system could easily identify 'peak periods' when it would be useful to have additional staff – but it represented a significant challenge to the company's culture. Commitment was traditionally measured not so much by output as input – the number of hours that individuals put in being seemingly more important than what they were able to achieve during that time. In that culture, part-time working was little short of heresy.

Six of the part-timers were actually taken on as part of the same recruitment exercise and the decision was taken, at that time, to create a team of part-timers so that they could support each other most effectively. They were subsequently asked whether they wanted to join other teams, but they preferred to remain as they were.

There are now 11 controllers on flexible working contracts. All of them want to work on this basis because they have pressing commitments outside work. Some of these part-time employees are mothers with young children, and others working part-time through job sharing include two people who, as Jehovah's Witnesses, have obligations outside work which they want to fulfil. None of these controllers would be able to continue to work for the company if they were not able to work on a part-time basis.

As we have seen, the level of commitment from these part-timers is high. They voluntarily come in for the quarterly departmental meetings and their general attendance record at work is described by the manager as 'superb'. All the part-timers hit their target number of calls and one has consistently high call rates (100 calls in four hours). As far as the manager is concerned, there are no disadvantages in having part-timers and there are certainly some advantages.

By helping employees to meet both their personal and work needs, the CRC seem to have devised a 'win/win' situation. Employees get what they want – flexibility to combine work with other commitments – and in return the company gets their whole-hearted commitment for the hours that they have contracted (and a bit more). Again, by being prepared to do something a bit different, the CRC management team have very properly reaped the rewards.

These are two examples of initiatives that the CRC management team have taken in order to ensure that they are able to recruit and retain the best people. By embracing this refreshing approach to the labour market, they have ended up with a very diverse organisation: an organisation that is comfortable with change and justifiably proud of its achievements.

■ LESSONS FOR OTHER ORGANISATIONS

Of course, there are special factors that may have made it easier for the CRC to have embraced equal opportunities principles in such a progressive way. They were in the fortunate position of having a new start – there were no legacies from earlier times, and all the controllers were newly recruited. Above all, there *were opportunities*: the CRC has been growing steadily over the last two-and-a-half years. In addition, the work of the CRC lends itself readily to objective assessment of performance and is ideally suited to part-time work. Also, because it does not require a lengthy apprenticeship, it can make sense to take on an employee within five years of statutory retirement.

Nevertheless, there are plenty of similar organisations in the tele-sales world, for example, who have not 'grasped the nettle' and remain staffed by young women. Their managements seem happy to settle for relatively low productivity and high turnover. Therefore, all credit to the CRC, for having the foresight and making the most of their opportunity.

More than this, however, we believe that there are some fundamental lessons that come out of the CRC experience, which are general in their application regardless of the type of organisation.

There is no reason why other organisations should not similarly challenge stereotypical thinking and, in their own way, seek to emulate the six causes of success that we identified earlier:

- Clearly communicating business goals
- Developing clear performance measures
- Treating employees on merit
- Choosing recruits on merit
- Encouraging team leaders to play a coaching role
- Creating a supportive environment.

Most importantly, there is a message for the way in which organisations go about tackling equal opportunities. For Jenny Ivy, equal opportunities was never an end in itself. She saw the benefits of having a diverse organisation, and took steps to ensure that she made it possible to attract and retain a wide range of people. Her focus was on creating the most appropriate organisation to meet her departmental goals. Equal opportunities was simply a means towards that end.

■ CONCLUSION

In this case study, we hope we have been able to show that the 'diverse organisation' is not a theoretical construct, but a real possibility, for which it is worth striving.

In Chapter 4, we described the principles to which organisations would need to aspire, to shift equal opportunities from being externally imposed, to being internally driven, to shift the emphasis from 'equality' to 'diversity'.

For us, the 'diverse organisation' is the organisation of the future and diversity will be part of the formula for success for Britain in the 1990s and beyond. Equal opportunities is a means of achieving diversity, and not an end in itself. Eventually it will become part of organisational values, and be seen as part of normal good management practice.

As the businesswoman Steve Shirley, of FI International, put it:

> *'All sorts of skills are required in any team, and different ages, cultures and genders are needed to create a balanced, long-term view.'*

Once this approach is the norm, we will see an end to equal opportunities: the need to describe it as something special will no longer exist.

Index